Nicholas Patrick Wiseman, Thomas Edward Bridgett

Characteristics from the Writings of Nicholas Cardinal Wiseman

Nicholas Patrick Wiseman, Thomas Edward Bridgett

Characteristics from the Writings of Nicholas Cardinal Wiseman

ISBN/EAN: 9783744653145

Printed in Europe, USA, Canada, Australia, Japan

Cover: Foto ©Thomas Meinert / pixelio.de

More available books at **www.hansebooks.com**

CHARACTERISTICS

FROM THE WRITINGS OF

CARDINAL WISEMAN

CHARACTERISTICS

FROM THE WRITINGS OF

NICHOLAS CARDINAL WISEMAN

ARCHBISHOP OF WESTMINSTER

SELECTED BY

REV. T. E. BRIDGETT, C.SS.R.

LONDON: BURNS & OATES, Limited
NEW YORK, CINCINNATI, CHICAGO: BENZIGER BROTHERS
1898

PREFACE

THE published works of Nicholas [Patrick Stephen [1]] Wiseman, Cardinal-Priest of the title of St. Pudentiana, and first Archbishop of Westminster, were both numerous and miscellaneous, and published in many places. No attempt was made to form a complete and uniform edition during his lifetime, nor has any such been as yet undertaken since his death. The following selection from his writings may, it is hoped, promote a more general demand for a reprint of books now not easily procurable, and in danger of being forgotten, to the great loss both of literature and of Catholic interests.

Even the library of the British Museum lacks many of his sermons and lectures. The following list has been gathered from many catalogues, yet is probably incomplete, and some few publications may be twice mentioned under different titles. The Editor trusts that the selections he has made will be found varied and characteristic; but they by no means exhaust the beauties of Wiseman.

NOT IN ENGLISH

Horæ Syriacæ (*Latin*). Rome. *Bourlié.* (1828.)
Paper on Science and Religion (*Latin*). Presented to Pope Pius VIII. (1836.)

---

[1] So called in the British Museum Library Catalogue; but Patrick and Stephen were his confirmation names.

Preface to Dr. Newsham's Edition of Blosius (*Latin*).
16 pp. *Richardson*. (1859.)

Hymnus in Honorem S. Edmundi. London. (1860.)

Elogium Card. Weld. (Latin translation of funeral sermon.)
London. (1837.)

Four Papers (in *Italian*) read before Roman Academia, On
the Barrenness of Protestant Missions (1830); On
Oxford Movement (1837); On St. Gregory VII.; On
Boniface VIII. (1840).[1]

Various Memoranda to Roman Congregations. (See Life,
by Wilfrid Ward.)

Discourse (in *French*) at Translation of Relics of St. Theodosia.
Amiens. (1854.)

Address (in *French*) to Congress of Malines. (1863.)

IN ENGLISH

Papers in *Catholic Magazine*, on 1 John v. 7 (1832–33);
Reprinted with Additions (Rome), 1835. Reprinted in
Essays, i. 3.

Remarks on Lady Morgan's Statements regarding St. Peter's
Chair. Rome. (1833.) Reprinted in Essays, iii. 297.

Moorfields' Lectures on the Principal Doctrines and Practices
of the Catholic Church. (1836.) *Dolman*. 2 vols
Often reprinted.

Letters to John Poynder on his Work, "Popery in Alliance
with Heathenism." *Booker*. (1836.) Reprinted in
Essays, i. 245.

Lectures on the Real Presence. *Booker*. (1836.) Only
one volume printed.

Lectures on the Connection between Science and Revealed
Religion. *Booker*. (1836.) 2 vols. Often reprinted.

A Reply to Dr. Turton, &c. *Dolman*. (1839.)

---

[1] See Preface to "Inaugural Lecture to Academia," p. 29.

Preface vii

Four Lectures on the Offices and Ceremonies of Holy Week. *Dolman.* (1839.)
Memorandum to Lord Palmerston. (1847.) First printed in Life of Card. Wiseman, by W. Ward, Appendix to vol. i.
Essays from *Dublin Review*, &c. 3 vols. *Dolman.* (1853.)
Various Essays in *Dublin Review*. Thirty-five republished, twenty-four not republished, ten or more written subsequently to 1853.[1]
Lectures on the Last Four Popes. *Hurst & Co.* (1858.)
Tour in Ireland. *Hall.* (1858.)
Fabiola. *Burns & Oates.* (1855.) Often reprinted.
The Hidden Gem. *Burns & Oates.* (1859.)
Lamp of Sanctuary.
Witch of Rosenberg. *Richardson.*
A Few Flowers from Roman Campagna. *Philp.* (1861.)
Two Mysteries or Sacred Dramas—Shepherdesses of Bethlehem and St. Ursula. *Philp.* (1863.)
In Verse. Translation of St. Casimir's Hymn. Hymn for Pope, &c.
In Verse. A Retrospect of Many Years. (1864.)
Papers in *Rambler*. (Uncertain.)
Papers in *Month*. Vol. i.: Ancient Saints—French Officer's Story.
Preface to Seager's Edition of St. Ignatius's Exercises. 15 pp. *Dolman.* (1847.)
Preface to New Glories of the Catholic Church. 11 pp. *Richardson.* (1859.)
Preface to Spiritual Conferences of St. Francis de Sales. 44 pp. *Richardson.* (1862.)
Preface to Lewis's Translation of St. John of Cross. 29 pp. *Longmans.* (1864.)

---

[1] Compare list in Essays, and that in *Dublin Review*, April 1896.

LETTERS, SERMONS, LECTURES, Etc.

Letter to Rev. J. H. Newman. *Dolman*. (1841.)
Remarks on Letter of Rev. W. Palmer. *Dolman*. (1841.)
Letter to Earl of Shrewsbury on Catholic Unity. *Dolman*. (1841.)
Letter on Conversion. *Rockliffe's* Catalogue. (1862.)
Letter on Catholic Institutes. (Do.)
Rome and the Catholic Episcopate. Reply to Clergy. (5th August 1852.)
Words of Peace and Justice to Clergy and Laity on Diplomatic Relations with Holy See. (April 1848.) *Dolman*.
Letter (for private circulation) in Answer to Canon Tierney, on Dr. Baines and Dr. Lingard.
Correspondence with Dr. Cumming.
Remarks on Catholic Doctrine. *Rivington*.
Manner in which Catholics use the Bible. Reprint of an Article on Maynooth in *Dublin Review* (Sept. 1852). *Richardson*. (1853.)
Two Sermons in Rome. London. (1831.)
Funeral Oration of Cardinal Weld. Rome. (1837.) Reprinted by *Duffy*. (1889.)
Funeral Discourse on the Begum Sumoo. (Jan. 1838.) Reprinted in Essays, iii. 323.
Sermon on Development, at Opening of Church. Derby. (Oct. 1839.) *Richardson*.
Sermon at Consecration of Bishop Wilson of Hobart's Town. London. (1842.) Reprinted by *Duffy*, 1889.
Sermon for Aged Poor Society, 12th Dec. 1847. London (1848.)
Six Sermons (unrevised) reported in *Catholic Pulpit*. Vol. i. (1849.)
Sermon on Social and Intellectual State of England, compared with its Moral Condition. *Richardson*. (1850.)

Two Sermons on 11th August 1850. *Richardson.*
Sermon on Final Appeal in Matters of Faith (Gorham Case), in St. George's, Southwark (17th March 1850). *Richardson.*
Three Sermons on the Gorham Case. (1850.) Manchester. *Stutter.*
Three Lectures on the Hierarchy. (1850.)
Appeal to the English People on the Hierarchy. (1850.) *Richardson.*
Sermon on St. Thomas of Canterbury in English College, Rome (21st Dec. 1853). *Richardson.* (1854.)
Four Lectures on Austrian Concordat. (1855.) *Burns and Oates.*
Panegyric of St. Philip. (1856.) *Richardson.*
The Perpetuity of the Church, at Opening of Church at Romford. *Richardson.* (1856.)
Sermon on Stewardship of the English Nation. *Stutter.* Manchester. (1857.)
Sermons in Ireland in 1858. In Tour in Ireland. *Hall.*
Sermons at Bath, on Convents. (1863.)
Sermons at Southampton. (1863.)
Lecture at Malines, on the Religious and Social Position of Catholics in England. (Translation from *French.*) *Duffy.* (1864.)
Compromises of Truth. *Rockliffe's* Catalogue. (1862.)
Sermons and Lectures on Various Subjects. *Richardson.* (1860.)
I. Sermons on Our Lord and His Blessed Mother. *Duffy.* (1864.)
II. Sermons on Moral Subjects. *Duffy.* (1864.)
III. Sermons on Various Subjects. *Duffy.* (1889.)
Daily Meditations. *Duffy.* (1868.) Only one volume published.
Meditations on the Passion. *Burns & Oates.* (1898.)
Pastorals, several; some reprinted in Sermons. *Duffy.* Vol. i.

Two Lectures on Home Education of Poor. St. Martin's Hall. (August 1854.)
The Future Historian of the Present (Crimean) War. London. (1855.)
Lecture on Recent Excavations on Aventine Hill. In *Transactions of Royal Society of Literature*. (1856.)
Lecture on Perception of Natural Beauty in Ancient and Modern Times. (1856.)
Lecture on the Influence of Words on Thought and on Civilisation, at Marylebone Institution. (1856.)
Lecture on the Nature of an Inaugural Discourse, to St. James's Young Men's Society. (1856.) *Richardson*.
Two Lectures on the Best Mode of Collecting and Arranging a National Gallery of Paintings, at Marylebone Institute. (May and June 1857.)
Lecture on Ornamental Glass found in the Catacombs, at Rotunda. Dublin. (1858.) Printed in Irish Tour.
Lecture on Scientific Progress, at Music Hall, Dublin. (1858.) Irish Tour.
Lecture on Difficulties of Historical and Literary Forgeries (1859.)[1]
Lecture on Important Results from Observation of Slight Facts. (1859.)[1]
Lecture on Impressions of a Recent Visit to Ireland, at Hanover Square Rooms (Nov. 1858). In Irish Tour.
Lecture on the Highways of Peaceful Commerce.
Inaugural Discourse at Academia, 29th June 1861. *Burns and Co.* Also in Essays on Religion and Literature.
Lecture on the Truth of Supposed Legends, to Academia. (Ibid.)
Lecture on Points of Contact between Science and Art, to Royal Institution, Jan. 1863. *Hurst & Blackett*.

---

[1] Mentioned in a letter by the Cardinal, printed in *Irish Monthly*, vol. xxi. p. 261; but perhaps not delivered or printed.

Preface

Lecture on Prospects of Good Architecture in London. (1864.) *Murray.*

Lecture on William Shakespeare. (Not completed.) (1865.) *Hurst & Blackett.*

The Lives of St. Alphonsus, St. Francis Girolamo, St. John Joseph, St. Pacificus, and St. Veronica, canonised on 26th May 1839, are in some catalogues attributed to Dr. Wiseman, but with no apparent authority or probability.

Many Letters given in the Life of Wiseman by Wilfrid Ward.

TABLE OF CONTENTS

PART I

POLEMICAL

	PAGE
INDIFFERENCE	3
THEORY OF CORRUPTION	8
THE CHURCH'S LOVE OF SCRIPTURE	10
MISUNDERSTANDINGS	13
EARNEST INQUIRY	14
VARIETY OF EVIDENCE	18
MYSTERY	22
DEVELOPMENT	27
THE HOLY SEE	31
UNITY	34
OUR OWN TIMES	43
LOVE OF OUR FAITH	44

PART II

DOCTRINAL

GOD IMMENSE AND ETERNAL	49
THE EYE OF GOD	51
PRESENCE OF GOD	57
GOD'S POWER AND WISDOM	59
INCARNATION	61
DIVINE ABASEMENT	63
POVERTY OF OUR LORD'S BIRTH	67

	PAGE
OUR LORD, THE TYPE	68
OUR LORD'S CHARACTER	71
OUR LORD'S TEACHING	75
OUR LORD'S MEEKNESS	77
THE SACRED HEART	78
OUR LORD AND THE CHILDREN	81
TRANSFIGURATION	85
THABOR AND OLIVET	89
THE PRECIOUS BLOOD	90
OUR LORD'S AGONY	93
THE REDEMPTION	97
THE HOLY NAME OF JESUS	102
SWEETNESS OF THE NAME OF JESUS	104
VISION OF JESUS	106
OUR LADY, A WITNESS	110
THE ANNUNCIATION	114
MARY, ALL-MOTHER	118
OUR LADY AT THE CROSS	120
DEVOTION TO THE BLESSED VIRGIN	123
OUR LADY'S DOWRY	126
HONOUR DUE TO SAINTS	127
OUR GOOD ANGEL	129

PART III
MORAL

SIN AGAINST THE JUDGE	133
WHAT THE SINNER RENOUNCES	136
STATE OF HABITUAL SINNER	140
SOUL MURDER	142
DEATH	146
DELIRIOUS DEATH	149
DEATH UNHEEDED	151

Contents

	PAGE
SALVATION	155
CHRISTIAN ATHLETE	157
FICKLENESS	160
PERSEVERANCE	166
SPECIAL PROVIDENCE	169
PRESUMPTION	170
FASTING	174
NON-FASTERS	176
CHARITY DINNERS	177
TRIBULATION	181

PART IV
DEVOTIONAL

HOUSE OF PRAYER	187
ADORATION	189
FORTY HOURS' ADORATION	190
VISITS TO THE BLESSED SACRAMENT	199
THE BANQUET HALL	201
INSTITUTION OF THE COMMUNION	203
BALANCE OF DANGER	205
CARELESS COMMUNION	207
COMMUNION OF JUDAS	208
FERVENT COMMUNION	215
PROGRESS BY COMMUNIONS	216
MONUMENTAL WORSHIP	218
DRAMATIC WORSHIP	221
PRAYERS AGAINST EVIL SPIRITS	223
DIABOLICAL SUGGESTIONS	226
THE ROSARY	229
"IMAGE-WORSHIP"	237
MEDITATION	238
CONTEMPLATION	240

PART V

MISCELLANEOUS

	PAGE
DEVELOPMENT OF THE BIBLE CANON	249
CHURCH AND WORLD	255
CYCLES	261
LANGUAGES	263
GEOLOGY AND POETRY	267
ALLIANCE OF CHURCH AND EMPIRE	269
VILLAGE WORSHIP IN ITALY	272
IRISH CHARACTER	277
THE IRISH FAMINE	279
ENGLISH MISSIONARY PRIESTS	282
ISOLATION OF THE ANGLICAN CHURCH	285
ANGLICAN WORSHIP	288
WORK OF THE LAITY	292
HOPEFULNESS	297

PART I
POLEMICAL

INDIFFERENCE

THE first thing on which all must make a salutary decision, and for which God will bring us to judgment, is correctness of faith and religious principle. There can be no doubt that, besides the grand work of our redemption, the Son of God came amongst us to manifest to the world religious truths of which till then it had been ignorant. It has been a favourite theory that this communication regarded chiefly the moral law; that the principles of belief were not meant to be so strictly defined; that it will be expected of all that their *lives* be virtuous, but that as to their *creeds*, every latitude is to be allowed; for, as God looks only to the good intentions and dispositions of the heart, and well knows that the understanding is a weak and erring faculty, which frequently wanders in its best-intentioned search after truth, it seems inconsistent with His amiable and loving goodness, that He should exact exactness of belief on every point from so fallacious a guide, or precise justice of decision in so unenlightened a tribunal. It would be, contrary to His own principles, expecting to gather grapes from thorns, and figs from thistles.

Yet, if Christ did communicate any truths addressed purely to our belief, it must have been with the intention that all men should accept them. The idea that

He should have manifested them to the world without an earnest desire to have them universally adopted, is self-repugnant. But then the truth which came from Him *can* be only one; whatever is at variance with this must be false; and falsehood cannot possibly be pleasing to Him. The Jews, when He came among them, were in possession of a code of doctrines delivered by the Almighty: to these they clung with sincerity, and were justified in doing so. But when Christ preached His additional articles to them, did He treat their rejection of these as an affair of no consequence? Did He ever say, "As to belief, act as you please; it is a matter of comparative indifference. Only attend to My moral law—practise its precepts, lead good, virtuous lives; and whether you attach yourselves to one society or to another, God, who only looks at the heart, will be perfectly satisfied by your moral conduct, and you shall be saved"? Oh no; instead of this gentle, comfortable doctrine, He tells them, that to the heaven where He was going they could not follow Him; not because they neglected the moral law, but because they did not believe His doctrines. "I go My way, and you shall die in your sins; whither I go, you cannot come. For if you believe not that I am He, you shall die in your sins."

Did He say to His apostles: "Go proclaim My religion through the world. With regard to articles of belief, leave every one to choose for himself. Only insist upon My moral code; for, those alone who neglect this shall incur My indignation." In place of this lax and consoling commission, how differently does He send them forth! In terms which we almost fear to use, He thus gives them His last injunctions: "Go ye into the whole world, and preach the Gospel to every creature. He that believeth and is baptized, shall be saved; but he that believeth not, shall be condemned." After these clear denunciations from the mouth of Jesus Christ Himself, can any one, for a moment, entertain a suspicion that He was indifferent as to what is believed, so long as men's actions are moral?

The doctrine of the Master is no less that of the disciples. Why is Paul so anxious that the Ephesians should not be moved by every wind of doctrine, if it mattered not what doctrines they believed? Why does he, in writing to the Galatians, pronounce an anathema against any one who should preach a doctrine different from his own, even should he be an angel from heaven? Why does he so earnestly exhort Timothy to be zealous for preserving the doctrines which he had received, and even careful to transmit them in the very form of sound words in which they had been given to him; or inculcate on Titus that one of the principal qualities of a bishop is his "embracing that faithful word which is according to doctrine, that he may be able to exhort in sound doctrine," when he should rather have left all doctrines to their own choice? With what right, in fine, did St. Peter assert, that many wrested the Epistles of St. Paul to their own ruin, by interpreting them according to their private opinion, if every one is justified in following what interpretation he pleases, and all, in doing so, are equally acceptable in the sight of God? The apostles should, one would think, have confined themselves to the teaching of the moral law, if this alone was to be valued in the dread judgments of the Almighty. But, in fact, as the code of belief and that of morals come equally from the same Lawgiver, is it not an equal offence against Him whichever we violate?

Why should the weakness of the understanding be made a plea for this liberty of creed? Might not the libertine as much complain, that God should expect him to preserve virtue in a mind which His own Scriptures acknowledge is prone to evil from its youth?—that He should exact unbroken perfection in vessels which His apostle owns to be frail and easily shattered?—that He should, in fine, demand immunity from sin and all offence, in a world wherein He Himself has declared it *necessary* that scandals should come? The heart is no less weak than the mind; their tendency is to evil and error, in consequence of our original transgression; both are bound, therefore, to strive after what is right. When every effort has been made for this purpose, God will certainly be satisfied. He will not impute to us the wanderings of either when acting under the influence of sincere, conscientious principles. But as a systematic rule, He cannot love truth equally with error, any more than He can love equally virtue and vice; and therefore every one must be fully and conscientiously convinced of the correctness of his belief, to escape the just judgment of God.

The remark which I have just made at once clears this doctrine of all harshness and uncharitableness. With those who in all simplicity of heart have sought out the truth and are convinced that they have found it, who would be ready to embrace any doctrine, however repugnant to their ideas or feelings, which they might discover to come from God, and who, with the sincerity of the distressed father in the Gospel, cry out in their hearts, "Lord, I believe, do Thou help my unbelief,"—with such as these the Almighty must be fully pleased. But with those who neglect to search after the truth, from malice, from interest, or from prejudice, or having found it do not embrace it,—with these certainly it is not harsh to say, that the God of truth cannot be satisfied. Far be it from any one to "judge another man's servant; to his own master he must stand or fall." The inward motives and dispositions on which all depends, can be ascertained and valued by Him alone who searches the reins and hearts. Hence it is that we presume not to condemn any person, whatever his spoken creed may be. Nay, we hope, in God and His charity, that he follows it in singleness and sincerity of heart; and that even those who so unrelentingly charge us with the worst crimes in religion, with superstition and idolatry, do so from the best of mistaken motives, and think, as Christ told His disciples their enemies would, that in doing so they are rendering a service to God. ("Sermons," ii. 403.)

THEORY OF CORRUPTION

LEAVING aside, therefore, that class of applications, let us simply take and try the position, that a general defection from the truth is foretold in the New Testament, and that this prediction is even to be reckoned among the evidences of Christianity. Good God! and is it possible that any believer in the divinity of our Lord can assert so monstrous a proposition as that He could have ever given such a proof as this of His heavenly mission and authority? I will present the case familiarly to you in the form of a parable. A certain king lived at a great distance from his children, whom he tenderly loved. They dwelt in a tabernacle frail and perishable, which he had long and often promised should be replaced by a solid and magnificent abode, worthy of his greatness and of his affection towards them. And after many days there came unto them one who said he was sent by him to raise this goodly building. And they asked him, "What evidence or proof dost thou give us that the king our father hath sent you, as fully qualified and able to build us such a house as shall worthily replace the other, and be our future dwelling?" And he answered and said, "I will raise a costly building, spacious and beautiful; its walls shall be of marble, and its roofs of cedar, and its ornaments of gold and precious stones; and I will labour and toil to make it worthy of him that sent me, and of me its architect, even so that my very life shall be laid out on the good work. And this shall be an evidence of my mission to the work, and of my approved fitness for undertaking it : that scarcely shall it be completed but the lustre of its precious stones shall be dimmed and the brightness of its gold shall tarnish, and its ornaments shall be defiled with foul spots, and then its walls shall be rent with many cracks and crannies in every part, and then it shall crumble and fall, and a few generations shall see the whole in ruins and overspread with howling desolation!" And what would they reply unto him? "Go to," they would say, " for a fool, or one who taketh us for such. Are these the proofs thou givest us of thy fitness to build a house for our abode?"

And if so, my brethren, must we not call it almost impious and blasphemous to suppose that our Saviour can have given as evidence of His divine commission to establish a religion and a church, that His work should not stand, but after a few years become disfigured with error and crime, and in a few centuries perish, or, what is worse, relapse into idolatry and corruption?[1] For let those who say that the whole Church fell away into idolatry remember that it was to overcome this foul usurpation of the devil that Jesus Christ taught and preached, and suffered and died.

[1] "So that clergy and laity, learned and unlearned, all ages, sects, and degrees of men, women, and children, *of whole Christendom* (an horrible and dreadful thing to think), *have been at once drowned in abominable idolatry*, of all other vices most detested of God, and most damnable to man, and that by the space of 800 years and more—*to the destruction and subversion of all good religion universally.*"—" Book of Homilies" (Hom. viii. p. 261, ed. of Society for Propagating Christian Knowledge), pronounced in the 35th of the 39 Articles " to contain godly and wholesome doctrine, and necessary for these times."

And shall we dare to say that He conquered not? Shall we presume to assert that after having wrestled with the monster, even unto the shedding of His priceless blood, and having crushed its head and left it apparently lifeless, yet it did too soon revive, to assail and lay waste His inheritance, and tear up the vineyard which His hands had planted? Why, the weak and material prototype of His truth and law had more power of old! For when the Ark of His Covenant was placed, even by the hands of His enemies, in the temple of Dagon, it not only overthrew the idol, but it broke off its feet, so that it might no more be replaced upon its pedestal. Even the false prophet of the East shall have proved more successful! For so powerful is the dogma of God's Unity, that wherever the doctrines of Islamism have been proclaimed, idolatry has been banished, so as never more to have returned. And shall Christianity have proved feebler than they? Shall it alone have been compelled to yield to the power of Satan? Shall Jesus Christ alone have been baffled by His enemy, and unable to establish what He came to teach? Away from us such impious and ungodly thoughts! ("Moorfields' Lectures," IV.)

THE CHURCH'S LOVE OF SCRIPTURE

WE are told that the Catholic loves not the Scriptures; that his Church esteems not the Word of God; that it wishes to suppress it, to put the light of God under a bushel, and so extinguish it. The Catholic Church not love and esteem the Word of God! Is there any other Church that places a heavier stake on the authority of the Scriptures than the Catholic? Is there any other Church that pretends to base so much of rule over men on the words of that book? Is there any one, consequently, that has a greater interest in maintaining, preserving, and exhibiting that Word? For those who have been educated in that religion know that when the Church claims authority it is on the Holy Scriptures that she grounds it; and is not this giving it a weighty importance, beyond what any other Church will attempt? And not only has she ever loved and cherished it, but she has been jealous of its honour and preservation, so as no other religion can pretend to boast. Will you say that a mother hath not loved her child, who has warmed and nursed it in her bosom for years, when nothing else would have saved it from perishing; who has spent her blood and her strength in defending and rescuing it from the attempts of foes and rivals on its life; who has doted on it till scoffed at by others, lavished treasures on its embellishment, and done whatever her means would allow, to make it seem beautiful and lovely and estimable in the eyes of men? For if you would say this, then may you also say that the Church hath not cherished and esteemed the Word of God.

For first she caught up its different fragments and portions as they proceeded from the inspired writers, and united them together. To those who pretend that the Catholic Church extended not so far back, I will say that it was the Catholic principle of unity which alone could have enabled churches to communicate to one another the respective books and letters addressed to them by the apostles, and it was only on the communication of the authority which their testimony gave that the canon of Scripture was framed. Did she not afterwards keep men by hundreds and thousands employed in nothing else than in transcribing the Holy Word of God—ay, in letters of gold, and upon parchment of purple—to show her respect and veneration for it? Has she not commanded it to be studied in every religious house, in every university, in every ecclesiastical college, and to be expounded to the faithful in every place and at all times? Has she not produced, in every age, learned and holy men who have dedicated themselves to its illustration, by erudite commentaries and popular expositions? Were there not, in what are called the darkest ages, men like Alcuin and Lanfranc, who devoted much of their lives to the detection of such errors as had crept into it by accident? And is it not to all this fostering care that we are indebted that the Word of God now exists? And while we have copies of it so splendid as to attest the immense labour devoted to their production, we have others in the cheapest and most portable form that could be procured from the pen, to show that they were in the hands of all who could possibly, under such circumstances, be able to obtain them. But every copy was the work of the penman, and could not be so easily produced nor so widely circulated. ("Moorfields' Lectures," II.)

MISUNDERSTANDINGS

THIS repeated wish that Rome may be different from what she is, may be satisfied in various ways; and though expressed in one sense, may find an answer in another. For instance, blots may be removed from an object by being wiped away from the medium through which it was viewed, and which transferred its own defects to the object; and, in like manner, Rome may soon appear and be very different to sincere eyes that look at her now through distorted representations, or descriptions highly coloured in some parts, or even through slighter misunderstandings. Again, a part of a picture may seem dark and unpleasant, not because its colours are so, but because sufficient light is not cast upon it; and so many things appear cheerless and painful to others, not because truly so, but because they want proper light to be cast upon them by reasonable explanation. Or the defect may arise from the very position of the spectator. A pious and intelligent person observed to me the other day, that our devotions to the saints might be compared to their representations on our beautiful old church windows: when seen from without, they present but dark surfaces and ill-shaped outlines; when from within the church, they seem to glow with the rich and varied light of heaven in pure and majestic forms. Thus I am by no means terrified or dejected when I find this condition for unity strongly and repeatedly expressed, because I know how much of it depends upon the manner of looking at things more than on the things themselves. And your Lordship and myself have known sufficient instances of persons whose prejudices had been most violent against Rome, but were overcome in Rome, and by Rome itself. ("Letter to Earl of Shrewsbury," p. 28; 1841.)

EARNEST INQUIRY

AND from His Holy Word we may easily learn the dispositions and feelings wherewith you should come unto Him.

Come not, as did the Sadducees, determined to doubt and to dispute everything, even to the first foundations whereon faith may be built; nor as the Herodians, putting to the test of captious and irrelevant consequences, and of political considerations, the pure dogmas of religion.

Come not, as did the Pharisees, to catch Him in His words, by merely laying hold of expressions rather than things, and taking offence and scandal at words, without attending to the spirit which directs them and the meaning they enclose.

Come not, as did the doctor of the law, and many others, tempting Him. By which expression two different things are meant in Holy Writ. First, demanding of God some definite and specific line of evidence, or laying down some self-willed terms of conviction, upon which alone we will yield to what is proposed to us as His truth; in which sense Achaz said, "I will not ask (a sign), and I will not tempt the Lord" (Is. vii. 12), and Judith reproached the rulers of Bethulia, saying, "Who are ye that this day have tempted the Lord" (Jud. viii. 11) by fixing a day for His deliverance? And St. Luke tells of some who, "tempting Jesus, asked of Him a sign from heaven" (Luc. xi. 16). And again, by the same phrase is signified the constant recurrence and repetition of the same difficulties and dissatisfaction, the returning to them once answered and removed; in which sense the Jews are said repeatedly in Scripture to have tempted or provoked God, or rather His Word in the wilderness, by ever murmuring anew, and refusing to be content with what He had done for their satisfaction, rejecting ever the proofs of divine mission given to His servant Moses. And in either of these ways, beware ye tempt not Jesus.

Come not as did the young man, eagerly asking what he should do to be saved, and upon finding that the terms of salvation touched him in his worldly goods, and must bring with it their loss, went away again sorrowful.

Come not, in fine, as did the Jewish multitude, following Him even into the wilderness to hear His word, and then when His doctrines shocked their prejudices and attacked their national religion, took up stones to insult and injure Him; nor like those disciples who first eagerly cleaved unto Him, and followed Him over all the land, but as soon as they heard a proposition which wounded reason's pride, exclaimed, "This is a hard saying, who can hear it? and went back and walked no more with Him."

But rather come unto Him as did the father of him possessed, " crying out with tears: I do believe; Lord, help Thou my unbelief."

Come like Nicodemus, who, not content with the general instruction he might receive by standing in the Temple's porch or attending Jesus in the crowd, sought to have private speech of Him, to propose his own particular doubts, and consult in the silence of night the interests of his own salvation, receiving with meekness the severe reproof given him for his ill-timed objection, and becoming one of those few steadfast followers who feared not to own Him as a master immediately after the ignominy of His cross.

Come to Him as Peter and the eleven, who, after they had heard, on His sufficient authority, doctrines incomprehensible to their reason, and repugnant to their senses, surrendered their belief into His hands without reserve, exclaiming, "Unto whom shall we go? Thou hast the words of eternal life."

Come to Him like Mary Magdalen, leaving to Martha, or those of your household, the cares and anxiety of domestic and worldly concerns, and heedless of their reproof, cast yourself at His feet, sit there in lowly and respectful attitude, in teachable and humble mood, looking upwards into a countenance whose calm majesty stamps truth on all He teaches, and whose winning smile can engage any one to embrace and practise it.

Or rather aim at still nobler feelings; and if the solemn rite which I have interrupted form, as it generally does, the great stumbling-block of your unsettled faith, come with John the beloved unto Him, when instituting the mysteries of unspeakable and unimaginable charity at His last supper, and lean in childlike love and abandonment upon the bosom that conceives it. Hear well its throbs and sighs after your redemption, the throes and pangs of this your birth-hour unto life; take well the measurements of this deep and full cistern of mercy and graciousness, that "ye may be able to comprehend, with all the saints, what is the breadth, and length, and height, and depth of the charity of Christ, which surpasseth all knowledge;" consider the majesty of divine almightiness, the ineffable energies of creative wisdom, and the boundless efficacy of redeeming love, which dwelt therein together as in a holy temple, now joined in solemn counsel how to leave some last Godlike legacy to man worthy of them all; feel that bosom, as you repose thereon, swelling and heaving with this great and majestical birth, this crowning work of love; and then assuredly will your doubts change into confidence, your hesitations into assurance, your perplexity into peace, and nothing will appear too bold, too mighty, too divine, for such love to have given at such an hour, or for a soul like yours to believe in such an attitude. There, there at length in that belief, you will have opened the full fountains of life; there you may slake your burning thirst, and feel in Jesus refreshment after the weariness of anxious doubt. ("Sermons," i. 129.)

VARIETY OF EVIDENCE

THAT the grounds upon which men may be brought to the true religion of Christ are various, is evident, both from the conduct of those whom the Word of God has proposed to us as examples, and from what we have witnessed in all ages, even unto our own. For there can be no doubt that in the preaching of the apostles, Christianity was not proposed upon one inflexible, unvarying system; but the announcers of God's word drew their evidences from any just grounds which they knew must make the greatest impression upon those whom they addressed. It is, in fact, the beauty and the perfection of truth, that it should stand the action of the most varied tests. That is only an impure ore which, while it perhaps resists the action of one or two reagents, will in the end yield before the energy of a third; for the pure metal will defy the action of every successive test. Truth may be compared to a gem without a flaw, which may be viewed in different lights, which, though held up to the eye on any side, and without artificial assistance, shall always present the same beauty and purity. But it is the characteristic of error, that it may, by the assistance of an artful setting, and by a certain play of light thrown upon it, produce the appearance of being without fault; but if it be slightly turned, or shown under another angle, it instantly discovers its imperfections. It was evidently with this feeling that the apostles acted, and thus by them was Christianity preached. It was considered by them as a system, intended to meet the wants of all mankind; so that its true evidence resided in the mind of every individual, as well as in the general feelings and cravings of the entire human race. They felt that, whatever characteristic of truth their hearers might have adopted—whether the counterpart of a previous revelation, or the certain conclusions of profound philosophy; whether drawn from the yearnings of human nature after perfection, or from individual consciousness of misery and ignorance; whether consisting in the harmonious beauty of all the parts of a system, or in strong evidence in favour of special propositions—any would equally lead to the verification of Christianity. Thus, consequently, when they preached to the Jews—who possessed the volume of the old law, and in it types, prophecies, and other foreshadowings of the dispensation that was to come—the task was simply to assume what these already believed, and show them its counterpart and fulfilment in the truths of Christianity and in the character of our Saviour; and thus they generally won their way to conviction through principles already held. When Philip met the eunuch of the queen of Ethiopia on the highway, he found him reading a certain passage in the prophet Isaiah; and, from that passage alone, he convinced him of the truth of Christianity, and admitted him to baptism. He was searching for something that would correspond to the description there given. Philip merely proposes to him what a simple comparison led him to see must be the counterpart to what he had read; and he instantly yielded himself a captive to faith, and adopted all the scheme of Christianity implied in the baptismal rite. But when St. Paul goes among the Gentiles, and stands before the learned Athenians, he does not appeal to prophecies wherein they believed not and which they knew not; for he does not consider it necessary that they must, in a manner, first become Jews before they be brought to Christianity. He has recourse to a totally different character of evidence: he preaches to them—men of a philosophical and studious mind—a sublimer morality than they had been accustomed to hear; he presents to them the striking doctrine of the resurrection; he shows them the futility and absurdity of their idolatry; he quotes to them the words of their own poets, to prove how necessary a purer belief in God, such as he preached, was to the human soul; he intimates that already among them was discernible a dissatisfaction with their present religion, and a certain longing after a better faith, from their having erected an altar "to the unknown God." He lays hold of those threads which he found already prepared in the minds of his hearers, he attaches to them the evidences of Christianity, and thus ensures the introduction of its doctrines within their breasts.

When we come down to a later period we find the same practice in the Church—for in the first century, and in the second and in the third, we see totally different classes of motives whereupon religion was preached and received by men. We find, for instance, that in the first century it was the courage of the martyrs, the seeing how flesh and blood could endure tortures and death in support of a religion, which brought the greater portion of converts to the truth. In the following centuries a new system of evidences was introduced. The study of philosophy, which, under the patronage of the Antonines in the West, and through the impulse of the great Platonist schools in the East, was become very prevalent, led to the examination of Christianity in connection with the philosophical systems of ancient Greece. It was soon seen that in all these there were problems innumerable regarding the nature of God, the human soul, the origin and end of man, which all the acuteness and meditation of sages had not been able to solve, and whose solution, however interesting and necessary, they even acknowledge to be out of reason's power. But when Christianity was examined, it was discovered to present a full and consistent answer to every query, a satisfactory solution of every doubt, and a perfect code of ethics and mental philosophy. And this was considered by the Justins, the Clements, the Origens, and other philosophical minds, a sufficient evidence of its truth. For as we should not require other proof that a key was made for a certain lock, than finding that it at once insinuates itself through all its complicated wards, and fits in them, and moves among them without grating or resistance, and easily turns the bolts which they kept drawn; so did the true religion then, and so does it now, require no better demonstration of its being truly made for the mind and soul of man, and of its having come from the same all-wise Artist's hands as created them, than the simple discovery of how admirably it winds into all their recesses, and fits into all their intricate mazes, turning at will the bars, and opening the entrance, of all the secret mysteries of self-knowledge. ("Moorfields' Lectures," I.)

MYSTERY

GOD would have seemed to wound when He meant to heal, had He enlightened our ignorance at the expense of our humility. He had been offended in the very first instance by the ambition of man to be like to God, with his eyes open to the knowledge of good and evil. This overweening desire of unwholesome and unfitting knowledge led to man's fall; and ignorance, one of its principal consequences, was the offspring of pride. In repairing the mischiefs of this fall, and once more revealing to man eternal truths, God took care that no room should be left for the exercise of our pride; but so communicated them, that in themselves we should find the confusion and the remedy of this baneful inclination. Hence, even in those points wherein He cleared up the dark errors of a corrupt religion, this knowledge which He imparted was a mystery so deep, that in believing it the mind must no less own its incapacity to fathom or to comprehend it.

Thus, the idea of God, in the natural condition of man, was one of perplexity and doubt, from the conflicting and degrading notions entertained of Him, from the corruption in His worship, and from the incapability of man ever properly to rise from the forms of heathenish idolatry to a pure, or even a clear, idea of His spiritual nature. All this error and darkness was dissipated at once by the revelation of God as a pure spirit, one, eternal, and infinite. But the grandeur of this simple idea was, at the same time, overpowering. It removed man to a distance from God, whereof he had entertained no previous thought, at the same time that it taught him to see His power, and wisdom, and providential care in every part of creation and every incident of his own life. It thus at once placed him in contact with Him, though infinitely removed from Him; it set the grandeur of God's attributes beyond the sphere of his contemplation, while he was ever moving and living within the sphere of their action; it made the very tabernacle of brightness, wherein God seemed enveloped, an impenetrable veil to his dazzled sight; and when he thus knew God reflected completely, yet darkly, in the glass of faith, his frame could not but fall prostrate before Him; he covered his face, as the prophet in the cavern of Horeb, and adored Him throughout the depths of his spirit. The busy inquisitiveness of his mind was bound up by the cords of salutary fear, and the brightness of truth seemed to flash from a brandished flame, that forbade access to a nearer view. It was holy ground, and the shoes needed to be loosed from the feet of all that approached.

Every other doctrine of Christianity, the sweetest

manifestations of love, equally with the most terrible revelations of justice, are involved in mystery that defies our penetration, and forbids too close a search. Is there less darkness in the wonders of redemption than in the awful prospect of resurrection and judgment? Who shall fathom the depths of a love that devised the scheme of our salvation, and that accomplished it? Who shall understand but most remotely the motives that suggested that marvellous accord between justice and mercy, that compact between unyielding rigour and infinite power of propitiation, which, on the one side, demanded a God-victim, and, on the other, gave it? Whose eyes can gaze upon the cross, if tears will let them, without being overpowered by the magnitude of the mysteries which it displays, the sufferings of Him it bears, and their mystical effects upon heaven and earth, on man and God? And if so, should not the heart and soul of every one who embraces Christianity be despoiled of every proud inclination to pry into what God has taught, beyond the terms of His teaching, so as to be without a power to doubt the resources, without a desire to search into the ways, of His omnipotence?

Nay, I will go further, and ask, Should he not be surprised, and begin to hesitate, when he hears its doctrines so proposed to him as to seem brought down to the level of his understanding, and fear that it cannot be what God has taught, the moment it has lost all mysterious sublimity, and presents no more than a higher order of human wisdom? At least, in the nobler and more spiritual institutions of Christian practice, should he not be prepared for something more akin to the infinite grandeur of all God's revelation? When, for instance, he reads the inauguration of the eucharistic feast, knowing it to be the last and solemnest of his Saviour's actions while master of Himself; knowing it to have been meant for a permanent ordinance as a fountain of grace to the end of time; knowing it intended for an enduring memorial of love to all that loved Him; knowing it to be the last legacy which He bequeathed to His friends; knowing it, in fine, to be the great and principal instrument for applying to our souls the infinite benefits of His death and passion—shall a Christian feel anxious to discover in it nothing mysterious and sublime beyond the possible devices of man, nothing save a commemorative rite, devoid of efficacy and all saving power? Shall he think it necessary to depart from the clear and most obvious meaning of his Redeemer's words, because they would otherwise lead him to acknowledge a mystery of love which his reason cannot comprehend? No; in the name of God and of His redemption, let him bow as low into the depths of his humble gratitude as he knows the height of God's wisdom to be above his conception. Let him throw away the fathom-line with which he was tempted to sound the abyss, and commit himself, with fearless confidence, to its bosom. For know, that if God hath loved to triumph over the resistance of the world and its interests, to the acceptance of His holy faith, there is another triumph dearer to Him still, over the heart of man. In both, the wisdom and the pride and the strength of man must be broken down and confounded, and led as captive to His conquering wisdom. To the eye of flesh the one seemed most glorious, while the other can hardly be observed. But, believe me, small as the conquest seems, and narrow as its field, to Jesus, that passionate lover of souls, it is a source of sincerest joy. His victory over the tyrants that opposed the triumphant progress of His faith, and over the public resistance of great and national errors, was a triumph of vengeance, a treading under foot of a people in the wine-press of His wrath, and reddening of His garments with their blood. His victory over the heart of man, the subduing of his pride and weakness, is a triumph of love, wherein He wins those whom He subjects, and leads them, not as captives, but as friends, not in chains, but with palm-branches, to the glory of His Father.

Let us, then, approach with gladness, but in due humility, to the light of God; let us in it seek guidance and protection during this our wearisome pilgrimage; and let it be our fervent prayer, that if any there be among us to whom as yet the dark and cloudy side of His pillar be turned, they may speedily be brought into the congregation of the faithful, wherein they may enjoy the comforts of its light, faintly, indeed, now, but in its fulness hereafter. Amen. ("Sermons," ii. 292.)

DEVELOPMENT (1)

BUT there is a higher thought to which these our poor inquiries have led us; and we trust it will not be deemed presumptuous. Our blessed Lord speaks His parables off-hand, if we may reverently use the word; with reference often to passing demands on His instruction. Even they who have impiously pretended that the whole Gospel was an after-thought, and the composition of disciples in early ages, must admit at least that the record of these parables is far anterior to the age when Catholicity (according to them) took its present development. How then account for the coincidence of the two in every part? Let us observe that the marvellous structure of Christianity was from its foundations without a formal plan: its laws were embodied in no stiff code; its government was not defined in one formal decree; its doctrines were not compressed into a symbol; and its precepts and maxims were not extended into a treatise. Nor were men chosen to raise the edifice, who, from scattered materials, were likely to compile a beautiful and perfect whole. Yet this was the result. Stone joined itself to stone, as if by instinct or mutual attraction: the whole building stood, as if by magic, weather-tight, massive, solid, yet regular, rich, and magnificent. Government, law, faith, morals, discipline, all were found to have been provided for; and as it grew, and extended on every side, ample provision appeared to have been made for its increase, in regard both of plan and of materials. And so it expanded still, until some thought that it had outgrown its measure and original design. In all this, who does not see proof of a Divine Wisdom that designed and superintended the work? But let us suppose, even, that our Lord left, as some would say, the details of the system to natural causes and the working of time; that He merely put together the main lines, and allowed them to be filled up; or that even, upon a Protestant theory, the corruptions and superstitions of ages have shaped the Catholic Church as it now is—still, in every hypothesis, the fact is the same, and will go far to overthrow the erroneous supposition. Whatever led to the Church's present organisation and development, it is plain that Christ's parables, that have reference to it, or His workings, fit exactly to it as it is. Call confession an abuse, a mistake, or what you like, there is nothing else on earth that will make the close of the prodigal's history look like a lesson or a home-truth. Then our Saviour foresaw all this, and provided for it its rules and principles; and He who could cast into the world but the rudimental forms of a religion, and yet throw out, in a mysterious form, what would describe its state, and regulate its institutions, after a thousand years and more of vicissitudes, could be only what He claimed to be, the Lawgiver Himself, the supreme Author of the New Law, the Incarnate Word of God. And that system with which His prophetic teaching so approvingly accords, can be no delusion, or corruption of men. ("Essays," i. 146.)

DEVELOPMENT (2)

IF, from the very day of the Holy Ghost's descent, the Church, like a grain of mustard-seed, commenced its system of outward growth, so did its increase no less begin in the order of interior development. Everything was gradual. At first the Jewish worship was attended, and many of its ceremonial rites observed, with scrupulous precision. The interior resources of the Christian system for a majestic and most noble worship were not at once called upon; but this was left gradually to unfold itself by time and experience. The hierarchy was not planted by our Saviour, nor by the apostles themselves, in a systematic form; but the episcopal body, if I may so speak, evolved from itself, in due season, the priestly order; and when the expediency of circumstances called for it, the third degree, till then reserved, was constituted in the nomination of the deacons. The very doctrines of Christianity were communicated with a similar proportion: there was a milk of doctrine, to use the figure of Scripture, and a more solid food, that formed a gradation of spiritual nourishment, suited to the powers of different converts. Time soon gave perfection to the happy beginning made.

There are seasons when the husbandman that really desires his crop to flourish, on looking up to heaven, will desire not so much a continuation of its serenity, as its clouds and storms of rain. And so did the heavenly Husbandman, with whom to wish is to do, act in regard to His new-sown field. He sent it its first rain in the rage of the persecutor, and its latter rain in the assaults of heresy; and both came in due season, to advance and ripen His harvest. Not only were those virtues which had formed the solid foundation of the Church from the beginning, such as constancy, charity, and piety, still further consolidated by these trials; but new feelings were brought into play which otherwise would have continued to lie dormant. It is almost impossible to enumerate the modifications which the Christians' worship underwent from their admiration and love of their martyrs. The form and the number of their churches and oratories, the celebration of their festivals, the observance of feasts, the very liturgy itself, both in substance and structure, received such strong impressions, as yet to remain marked, more or less, upon every form of Christianity, in proportion as it has more or less preserved of early usages. It is not improbable that, had not persecution assailed the Church in its infancy, there would have been no opportunity of developing to such an extent that feeling of admiration, love, and reverence to the friends and champions of Christ which so soon came forth. And yet it would not have been less true, that its principle had existed in the Christian religion from the beginning, even if several centuries of peace, instead of a few years, had intervened between its establishment and the opportunity to display that principle.

In like manner, no sooner was peace restored than

error took its turn to attack the Church of Christ, and thus gave occasion to her to unfold and display all the rich stores of traditional learning which for three centuries had lain buried in her bosom, and which might have been delayed in its production, but for the early occurrence of such a cause. When once unlocked, the tide of eloquence, vigour of reasoning, and variety of learning, went swelling on from year to year, till it formed the golden period of ecclesiastical literature. And during these two periods all the visible beauty of religion had been gradually growing to perfection; its forms of prayer, through the piety and genius of successive Pontiffs, improved in dignity and feeling, without the unity of thought being in the least impaired; the times and rules of penitential observances in various parts had imperceptibly arranged themselves into a system; the offices of the hierarchy and the limits of respective jurisdictions had been settled without contest or noise; so that the internal power of development, inherent in the Church, acted unceasingly, till it produced that grand, harmonious whole, which, while it grew up without effort, so far from exhausting, only recruited its original vigour. ("Sermons," iii. 219.)

THE HOLY SEE

MY brethren, a system for so many centuries thus closely interwoven with Christianity, and regulating its very existence, cannot be a mere accidental modification: it must be either an integrant part of its scheme, or it must have existed thus long in its despite. It is either an important organ, necessary to its vital functions, and vigorously acting to the farthest extremities of the frame, yea, its very core and heart; or it is a monstrous concretion, which hath become deeply seated, and, as it were, inrooted, and it exerts an unnatural and morbid influence through the body. Do you wish to consider it in the latter sense? Then see what difficulties you incur.

First, you break in pieces, yea, utterly crush to dust, all the most beautiful wonders of Christianity. The submission of the heart and of the will to the teaching of faith, the anchorage which hope giveth in another world, the bonds of religious charity and affection between persons of the most various dispositions, the attachment under every extremity to the great maxims of religion, all the learning of doctors, all the constancy of martyrs, all the self-devotion of pastors, all that makes Christianity something holier, nobler, diviner, than what earth or man had before produced — all these existed nowhere for ages, save in communion with this usurped authority, as you suppose it, and gloried in paying it deference and supporting it, and bearing testimony to it. You then proclaim that they may be testimonies to monstrous falsehood and deceit; you deprive them consequently of all efficacy in proof; and you must therefore seek elsewhere for the most touching and most beautiful evidences of Christianity.

Secondly, you must account for the regular, unbroken support which it received from the providence of God.

The Holy See

For the fate of human institutions is to grow, to flourish, and to wither: to be raised with labour, to stand for a while, then crumble for ever. Never was dynasty, never was kingdom prolonged for half its duration, never was the most favoured design of God carried triumphantly through such varied vicissitudes. Nay, its lot seemed that of the just—tribulation appeared sent to try and chasten, and not to overthrow. Yet are we to suppose that this extraordinary exertion of Providence was all in favour of an antichristian usurpation which was misleading men and ruining the cause of God?

Lastly, you must account how the Almighty uniformly made use of this dreadful apostasy as the only means in His hand to preserve and disseminate His religion. As the only means to preserve it; for, during the lapse of so many centuries, not a single heresy—I speak of such as Protestants themselves must call by that name—was condemned, crushed, and eradicated, except by its means, and through its decrees: Arians, Macedonians, Eutychians, Nestorians, Pelagians, and a thousand more, were anathematised by the Popes; and thus alone the doctrine of the Church was kept pure, and its faith unimpaired by their errors. Councils were called, canons framed only under their names and authority; and thus the morals of the faithful were improved and preserved. As the only means to disseminate it; for all portions of the earth which have been converted to Christianity since the days of the apostles, owe the benefit to the Holy See. Scotland,

Ireland, England, Germany, Denmark, Hungary, Poland, and Livonia were converted, from the fifth to the tenth centuries, by missionaries sent from Rome. The East and West Indies are under the same obligation: they may be said to know nothing of Christianity, except as the faith of the Roman Church, to which they bow with submission. And I will say, without fear of contradiction, that while there is hardly a country on the globe where the sovereign Pontiff has not *many* subjects, no other Church, as I have before shown, can boast of the power of conversion to any extent or with any durability. Now, at the very time that you must suppose this antichristian system to have been employed by God as His only instrument in preserving and disseminating Christianity, observe that it publicly boasted and referred to those very circumstances as a proof that it was the rock whereon Christianity was founded—the representative of the only authority whereon it was to be received as coming from God. And would He not have been countenancing to the utmost so horrible an untruth and deceit, if you admit this hypothesis? ("Moorfields' Lectures," VIII.)

UNITY (1)

WHEN from this centre of our religion I cast my view in any direction, I behold an unbounded prospect, independent of any natural or political horizon. Under every climate, under every form of government, I discover myriads who daily recite the same act of faith and perform the same worship as myself; who look at the same objects and institutions with reverence, and acknowledge the same supreme power, under whose more immediate authority I now address you. I see in every part the missionaries of religion advancing each day farther into unconquered territories, treading the dark forests of the Western Hemisphere, or disguising themselves in the populous cities of the ends of the East—in both directions daily adding new subjects to the kingdom of the Lord. I see this vast and extended, yet compact and coherent society everywhere a conspicuous and distinguished body, the boast of many powerful monarchs, the pride of learned and eminent persons, and, even where existing in a more humble and depressed state, still the object of universal attention and curiosity, from the splendour of its worship, the uniformity of its doctrines, and the constant increase of its numbers.

But if, instead of directing my looks abroad for these characterising marks, I cast an eye upon the ground on which I tread, I find still more speaking evidence of their existence here. When I trace back through every age the ecclesiastical monuments which surround me, and find them carry me back to the earliest period of Christian history; when I see myself kneeling before the very altars which a Sylvester anointed, and where a Constantine adored ; above all, when, standing in the proudest temple which the hands or imaginations of man ever raised to the Divinity, I behold myself placed between the tomb of the Prince of the Apostles and the throne of his present successor in a direct lineal descent, and can trace almost every link which unites these two extremes, through the ashes that repose in the tombs, or beneath the altars that surround me—oh! will any one ask why I cling with a feeling of pride and of affection to that body which carries me back to the foundation of the Church, and unites in unbroken connection, through ages of fulfilment and of prophecy, the creed which I profess, with the inspired visions of earlier dispensations! . . .

But there are characteristics and qualities attributed to God's kingdom on earth which can be felt rather than described, and which are intended more to attach "the children of the kingdom" than to attract the stranger to it. For while the signal grandeur, extent, and durability of the Church, as clearly foretold in prophecy, form powerful and really incontestable evidence to those without, the fulfilment of those predictions which promise to it abundance of peace, unity, internal tranquillity, and security, can only be recognised, or rather felt, by those who live within, as in their own house.

These alone can enjoy the peace of conviction, through the consistency, firmness, and unchangeableness of their grounds of faith, qualities communicated to every doctrine they profess: the peace of unanimity, for all who bear the name of Catholic believe the same truths without dissension or doubt, especially in the bosom of the family; a peace of direction, from the feeling of confidence in the divine guidance granted by the Holy

Spirit to the Church and to its ministers, and through them to the individual conscience; a peace of reconciliation, after transgressions and amidst frailties, from the thorough assurance that God has lodged in the hands of His priesthood the power to forgive sins and to restore to grace; a peace of assured confidence, arising from the abundance of cherished graces in so many sacraments and other helps to salvation, in the power of holy indulgences, in the community of merits throughout the Church, in the intercession of angels and saints in heaven, and the sublime patronage of Mary ever pure, in life and death, and in the suffrages of the living after our departure; finally, a peace of sweetest charity, affection, and closest union with God, in that unspeakable mystery of grace and love in which Jesus Christ gives us Himself. ("Sermons," i. 285.)

UNITY (2)

AND now, my brethren, I exhort and entreat you in the bowels of the Lord Jesus, and by the price you set upon His redemption, that ye all and severally resolve, above all things, to exert yourselves, wherever Providence gives you influence, for the removal of this reproach from amongst us, and the bringing of men's minds to the uniform and unvarying possession of religious belief. "Be instant in season and out of season; reprove, entreat, rebuke in all patience and doctrine;" urge on all sides the importance of this great investigation and of settling such important claims. Oh! do not say that such an object is beyond hope, and that religious party has run too high for all to be again brought back to unity of religion. Tempt not the jealous God, by surmising that His arm is shortened, or that there is a sore He cannot cure. That which once has been, may be again, through the might of His hand. Think, then, rather of the days of old, when we were an united people, linked in brotherhood with every other nation, and closely knitted together among ourselves in the profession of a common faith; when, instead of several mean and puny conventicles springing up suddenly in every town, those majestic monuments of ancient unity, our matchless minsters, rose majestically from the earth. . . .

Oh! had our forefathers judged as our generation, or thought it possible that a few years would have torn the nation into morsels, each creeping to its peculiar worship in some hidden nook, they would have plucked down their own noble work, rather than see it shamed by the desertion of their descendants and the desolation of their sanctuaries. Have not three centuries of experience proved, that when the unity of faith was once violated, the grandeur of religion, and its power over the soul to command great sacrifices, disappeared from amongst us?

But let us not brood over the past and its judgments; let us rather turn to the future and its hopes. So long as we remain a people of conflicting creeds, it is impossible that the vital functions of our social being can be properly discharged. For, believe me, a nation, being a body fitted together for magnificent purposes, hath well need of great and healthy organs for its life. It shall have its hands in the strong grasp wherewith it holds together its large possessions and gathers up its riches; it shall have its arms in the strength wherewith it beats and holds off an assailant; its mouth, in the wisdom of its laws and the justice of its decisions; its sense and intelligence, in the prudence of its policy. But its heart must be its religion. Through this it must love both God and man; and woe to that nation wherein this necessary action is long suspended. If, then, our heart be divided, shall we not perish? not, perhaps, in the material grandeur of this world, but in moral greatness, in nobleness of character, in loftiness of mind. Already has religious acrimony engendered civil hate; nor will human policy or the statesman's art find the plant to sweeten this Mara, this bitter fountain, at which all now drink, save that which the Son of man came to raise, when He cast His seed forth upon the earth. Let us be again, as the first Christians were, firmly united in one faith; and we shall soon be as they, possessed of one heart.

Who will refuse his co-operation for the attainment of so noble, so beautiful a purpose? Who will decline, in his own sphere, however humble, to arouse attention to this great lesson of our gospel, that amidst the various plants that overgrow our country, one only can have sprung from the seed which Jesus cast? And, O blessed Saviour, if ever it be lawful for us to depart from Thy injunctions, let it be in this: that we may exert ourselves, not as the imprudent servants would have done, by violence and strong hand, but by gentle arts and persevering diligence, to pluck up the tares which have sprung up in this crop, that when the harvest shall come, Thou mayest find nothing but wheat to be gathered into Thine eternal granary. ("Sermons," i. 313.)

UNITY (3)

O MY brethren! if there be any doctrine upon earth that has been more sadly misunderstood and misrepresented in Catholic teaching, it is this, that salvation belongs to only one system of doctrine or to only one Church. I mean when represented, for so it constantly is, as a narrow and uncharitable view. For, my brethren, that doctrine is the very mainspring of the most magnificent charity of the whole earth. No apostle would have gone forth to teach nations, and have faced prison, racks, and death, if he had not believed in his soul that it was necessary that men should believe as he did, that they might be saved. For what motive less than this could induce one to trample upon all that human nature takes delight in, and this for the sake of others? Can any one for a moment imagine that we, or any others who act upon this Catholic principle, being ready even to die, if necessary, that all might be like ourselves except our bonds; is it credible that we would do all this for a foolish, vain, stupid, and unsatisfactory motive, which some think sufficient to account for it, a desire to domineer over the minds of men, or bring them into a captivity similar to our own ? Whatever has been accomplished in the Church from the time of the apostles until now, in the conversion of nations, one and all have had that conversion undertaken and accomplished solely as the result of this great conviction, that the true faith was the greatest of God's blessings unto man—that that faith it · was of paramount importance, and even necessity, that all, if possible, should have it brought to them, that all who once had learned it should embrace it, and that all who had embraced it should preserve it.

This, and this alone, has led the Catholic Church to the accomplishment of the last great development of this lesson of our blessed Redeemer, that the neighbour whom we have to love, whom we have to love not merely with a barely speculative inward love, but whom we have to love with active, with zealous, and generous love, may be a stranger and a foreigner, and one living even on the most distant islands of ocean.

Then how much more are they neighbours, in every sense of the word, who, though at our side in the body, though living in the midst of us, as we in the midst of them, being one people, yet look upon us as aliens, on account of our creed, of that which should form our strongest bond of union ; and consider us as not belonging to themselves, as almost out of race, because we hold doctrines which we deem far more precious than our very lives.

Yes, truly, my brethren, this will be reason enough, not merely now, but for ever, for the Church in this country to continue her untiring efforts; not satisfied, whatever may oppose her course, till she sees, if God reserves such a blessing for us, the whole of our native land bound together in one tie of charity and faith. For, see you not, that love men as we may, there is no bond so strait, so tight, and at the same time so tender, as that bond of charity which is intertwined likewise with community of faith; which unites not only hearts, but intellects also, in a common belief; which makes men partakers of the same spiritual consolations, breathers of the same divine life that is in the Church, closely knitted together, as parts of the same plant, or of the same body, to one root, or one head, our Lord Jesus Christ? . . .

Therefore I own that were I desired to name the blessing which of all others I would wish to this country, it would not be greater political influence and dominion; it would not be an increase of its already exuberant wealth; it would not be the advancement of science and of literature, already so vastly developed; it would not be a still greater display and expansion of its innate forces, which astonish the world, in the creation of works requiring almost unbounded enterprise united with unlimited wealth. No; it would be none of these. I speak it boldly and without disguise, it would be that the Catholic faith should be the religion of this land.

For I see here all the elements of human grandeur,

wanting only the spiritual life added to them, which, quickening them with the divine principle, would make them truly magnificent, not only for this our earth, but infinitely more for the rewards of another and a better world. If, commensurately with this grace, there were also an exercise of that intense and truly sincere energy in matters of religion that is shown in all other pursuits; and if men's minds were as active about the other world as they are about this earth, and, turning themselves to the study of spiritual things, were to be brought, as of consequence they must infallibly be, to earnestness of thought on the truths of salvation: then, indeed, we should see an example of what the world never before has contemplated, an example of what would be so great and so divine a work, and there would be nothing equal left for earth afterwards to attempt—a combination of all that is magnificent, and glorious, and noble upon earth, with all that is sacred, all that is honoured, all that is divine in heaven. ("Sermons," i. 349.)

OUR OWN TIMES

FUTURE ages will know how to characterise this by its proper marks, even as we do those that have preceded it. That from the annealing furnace wherein no inconsiderable portions of His Church are being cleansed from their dross, they will come forth again, as did John from the seething cauldron, fresher and more vigorous, we cannot doubt. Whether it will be to conquer with might, or to win by beauty, or to invite by dignity; whether it will be a great and sudden display of new virtue, breaking on the world as the light when first created, or a slow and gradual unfolding of excellence, like the morning dawn spreading over the heavens; of this we may be sure, that it will be suited to *our* wants, and appear most admirable to them that follow.

And if it be lawful to pray to the "sower of chaste counsels" for one development rather than another of the various energies yet reserved in His holy religion, methinks it should be for some splendid exhibition of its power to heal the long and slowly inflicted wounds of error and schism. It has been seen to crush heresy at its birth by its simple anathema, it has gradually uprooted it when spread amidst the flock; but a mighty example is yet wanted of entire nations, once separated from the unity of faith, again returning to its pale. Yes, let our prayer be for such a manifestation in our age, that, in the words of the prophet, "the places that have been desolate for ages may be built up in us, that we may raise up the foundation of generation and generation," and that our age may be hereafter called, "the repairer of fences, turning the paths into rest" (Isa. lviii. 12). ("Sermons," iii. 236.)

LOVE OF OUR FAITH

MOREOVER, if we truly appreciated the great blessing of God's revelations, they would be a constant subject of our study and contemplation. We should ever be pondering on the mighty truths they contain, studying how to defend them when impiously attacked, and how to illustrate them when misunderstood, and how to enforce them when neglected. But what is still more important, our faith should not be a cold assent of the understanding, but a fervent and deep-seated consent and love of its truth. We should be penetrated with a feeling of the benefit we possess in it, of the love of God in giving it us; we should lay up every particle of it as a treasure of supreme value, as a pearl, small in appearance, but of immense price; we should feel grieved and shocked when even the most secondary parts (as they seem) of God's revelations are attacked or lightly treated. This was the faith of the martyrs, who truly understood the greatness of this virtue, and were ready to die rather than sacrifice to the prejudices of man the least portion of the sacred deposit. This was the faith of the Jeromes and Augustines, who beat down with energetic writings every attempt of heretics to wound the integrity of faith, in matters even of lesser interest. If once our faith be such as this, how differently from the generality of men shall we feel in regard to the maintenance and propagation of truth. She will become to us dear as a spouse or a sister, of whose honour we should ever feel most jealous, of whom we should never allow any one to speak in our presence save with respect. We should declare ourselves her champion, and proclaim her glories before all the world. We should fervently desire and enthusiastically strive to make her beauty and perfectness known to all men, and valued by them as by ourselves. Our faith would be a fuel to charity, and an incentive to zeal. It would be not only a light, but a torch, which would spread its rays without as within us, and set on fire the hearts of many. ("Meditations," p. 86.)

PART II
DOCTRINAL

GOD IMMENSE AND ETERNAL

REFLECT how the attributes most exclusively essential to God, and those that most powerfully overcome the mind of man, are such as consist rather in the absence of limit than in actual qualities, which have some faint images upon earth. Power and wisdom and goodness are in small degrees possessed by men, and one of the children of men, the incarnate Son of God, has exhibited them for us in excellent splendour. But even He never displayed upon this earth the immensity of God; for, without entangling the mind with the idea of shape and form, who can imagine a being filling, occupying, and pervading all things, yet uncircumscribed and unmodified by them? "He is higher than heaven, and what wilt thou do? He is deeper than hell, and how wilt thou know? The measure of Him is longer than the earth and broader than the sea" (Job xi. 8, 9). The farthest of the stars, whose twinkling light hardly reaches our earth, is as far removed from the outskirts of His immensity as this sun, which, when we look up to heaven, seems to us placed upon His bosom; and that star, again, in the energetic figure of Scripture, calls out to its fellows placed as far again from it as it is from us, and they answer that they are in the very centre and fulness of

God's infinity. And so multiplying systems of creation beyond these, and then as much farther, all will be floating, and moving, and having their being in the same unchangeable abyss of power and glory. Who shall comprehend this God? Who shall fathom His depths, or stretch the measure of his understanding to His height? And as in space He is so interminable, so He is no less in duration; for He is eternal. Not by time is this attribute to be measured any more than by space the other. If we should group together the duration of many worlds and call it a minute, and multiply it into hours and days and years and ages, yet when we shall have applied the scale in any extent to the duration of God's existence, it will be as though we had tried by grains of sand to measure the earth's entire surface. His eternity is as indivisible as a moment, as inseparable into beginning and end, as complete, and yet it defies the revolving course of ages to reach its term. They may go back to the beginning of their chain, and its first link will be found in the very midst of this ocean, buoyed upon its bosom; they may stretch it to the farthest extreme that their course will bear them, and it will never have reached across. But what a calm, what an endless repose in this Being in whom extension and duration are absorbed, in this undisturbed abyss of infinity! What a sublime idea of the Godhead does it not give us, to imagine it thus, not as a waste and passive expanse, undisturbed yet inert, but in this immensity including all perfection of beauty, of power, of holiness, of happiness, of glory, each commensurate with His immensity in greatness, and with His eternity in duration! As in this expanse of heaven which we see, the light and the heat which fill it occupy the whole space, so that in every part each is, and both equally occupy the entire distance in length and breadth between us and heaven, even so is each attribute of itself God's immensity and God's eternity, and excludes not the infinity of every other. Such, then, is the Almighty God. ("Meditations," p. 7.)

THE EYE OF GOD

"SYRA, put that stupid book down. Here is something, I am told, very amusing, and only just come out. It will be new to both of us."

The handmaid did as she was told, looked at the title of the proposed volume, and blushed. She glanced over the few first lines, and her fears were confirmed. She saw that it was one of those trashy works which were freely allowed to circulate, as St. Justin complained, though grossly immoral, and making light of all virtue; while every Christian writing was suppressed, or as much as possible discountenanced. She put down the book with a calm resolution, and said—

"Do not, my good mistress, ask me to read to you from that book. It is fit neither for me to recite nor for you to hear."

Fabiola was astonished. She had never heard, or even thought, of such a thing as restraint put upon her studies. What in our days would be looked upon as unfit for common perusal formed part of current and fashionable literature. From Horace to Ausonius, all classical writers demonstrate this. And what rule of virtue could have made that reading seem indelicate, which only described by the pen a system of morals which the pencil and the chisel made hourly familiar to every eye? Fabiola had no higher standard of right and wrong than the system under which she had been educated could give her.

"What possible harm can it do either of us?" she asked, smiling. "I have no doubt there are plenty of foul crimes and wicked actions described in the book, but it will not induce us to commit them; and, in the meantime, it is amusing to read them of others."

"Would you yourself, for any consideration, do them?"

"Not for the world."

"Yet, as you hear them read, their image must occupy your mind; as they amuse you, your thoughts must dwell upon them with pleasure."

"Certainly. What then?"

"That image is foulness, that thought is wickedness."

"How is that possible? Does not wickedness require an action to have any existence?"

"True, my mistress; and what is the action of the mind, or as I call it the soul, but thought? A passion which *wishes* death is the action of this invisible power, like it, unseen; the blow which inflicts it is but the mechanical action of the body, discernible, like its origin. But which power commands, and which obeys? In which resides the responsibility of the final effect?"

"I understand you," said Fabiola, after a pause of some little mortification. "But one difficulty remains. There is responsibility, you maintain, for the inward as well as the outward act. To whom? If the second follow, there is joint responsibility for both, to society, to the laws, to principles of justice, to self; for painful results will ensue. But if only the inward action exist, to whom can there be responsibility? Who sees it? Who can presume to judge it? Who to control it?

"God," answered Syra, with simple earnestness.

Fabiola was disappointed. She expected some new theory, some striking principle, to come out. Instead, they had sunk down into what she feared was mere superstition, though not so much as she once had deemed it. "What, Syra, do you, then, really believe in Jupiter and Juno, or perhaps Minerva, who is about the most respectable of the Olympian family? Do you think they have anything to do with our affairs?"

"Far indeed from it. I loathe their very names, and I detest the wickedness which their histories or fables symbolise on earth. No, I spoke not of gods and goddesses, but of one only God."

"And what do you call him, Syra, in your system?"

"He has no name but God; and that only men have given Him, that they may speak of Him. It describes not His nature, His origin, His attributes."

"And what are these?" asked the mistress, with awakened curiosity.

"Simple as light is His nature, one and the same everywhere, indivisible, undefilable, penetrating yet diffusive, ubiquitous and unlimited. He existed before there was any beginning; He will exist after all ending has ceased. Power, wisdom, goodness, love, justice too, and unerring judgment belong to Him by His nature, and are as unlimited and unrestrained as it. He alone can create, He alone preserve, and He alone destroy."

Fabiola had often read of the inspired looks which animated a sibyl, or the priestess of an oracle; but she had never witnessed them till now. The slave's countenance glowed, her eyes shone with a calm brilliancy, her frame was immovable, the words flowed from her lips as if these were but the opening of a musical reed made vocal by another's breath. Her expression and manner forcibly reminded Fabiola of that abstracted and mysterious look which she had so often noticed in Agnes; and though in the child it was more tender and graceful, in the maid it seemed more earnest and oracular. "How enthusiastic and excitable an Eastern temperament is, to be sure!" thought Fabiola, as she gazed upon her slave. "No wonder the East should be thought the land of poetry and inspiration." When she saw Syra relaxed from the evident tension of her mind, she said, in as light a tone as she could assume, "But, Syra, can you think that a Being such as you have described, far beyond all the conception of ancient fable, can occupy Himself with constantly watching the actions, still more the paltry thoughts, of millions of creatures?"

"It is no occupation, lady; it is not even choice. I called Him light. Is it occupation or labour to the sun to send his rays through the crystal of this fountain to the very pebbles in its bed? See how of themselves they disclose not only the beautiful, but the foul that harbours there; not only the sparkles that the falling drops strike from its rough sides; not only the pearly bubbles that merely rise, glisten for a moment, then break against the surface; not only the golden fish that bask in their light, but black and loathsome creeping things, which seek to hide and bury themselves in dark nooks below, and cannot, for the light pursues them. Is there toil or occupation in all this to the sun that thus visits them? Far more would it appear so, were he to restrain his beams at the surface of the transparent element, and hold them back from throwing it into light. And what he does here he does in the next stream, and in that which is a thousand miles off, with equal ease; nor can any imaginable increase of their number or bulk lead us to fancy or believe that rays would be wanting, or light would fail, to scrutinise them all."

"Your theories are beautiful always, Syra, and, if true, most wonderful," observed Fabiola after a pause, during which her eyes were fixedly contemplating the fountain, as though she were testing the truth of Syra's words.

"And they sound like truth," she added; "for could falsehood be more beautiful than truth? But what an awful idea, that one has *never* been alone, has never had a wish to oneself, has never held a single thought in secret, has never hidden the most foolish fancy of a proud or childish brain from the observation of One that knows no imperfection. Terrible thought, that one is living, if you say true, under the steady gaze of an Eye, of which the sun is but a shadow, for he enters not the soul! It is enough to make one any evening commit self-destruction, to get rid of the torturing watchfulness! Yet it sounds so true!"

Fabiola looked almost wild as she spoke these words. The pride of her pagan heart rose strong within her, and she rebelled against the supposition that she could never again feel alone with her own thoughts, or that any power should exist which could control her inmost desires, imaginings, or caprices. Still the thought came back, "Yet it seems so true!" Her generous intellect struggled against the writhing passion, like an eagle with a serpent—more with eye than with beak and talons, subduing the quailing foe. After a struggle, visible in her countenance and gestures, a calm came over her. She seemed for the first time to feel the presence of One greater than herself, some one whom she feared, yet whom she would wish to love. She bowed down her mind, she bent her intelligence to His feet; and her heart too owned, for the first time, that it had a Master and a Lord. ("Fabiola," ch. xvi.)

PRESENCE OF GOD

BUT it is chiefly in our spiritual warfare that the sense of God's presence is our encouragement and strength. When Eliseus was besieged in Dothan by the army of the King of Syria, his servant was alarmed at beholding the host that encompassed the city with horses and chariots, and he exclaimed in his despair, "Alas, my master, what shall we do?" But the man of God well knew that the Lord encompasseth the just man as a wall of defence; he knew that there was an invisible protector beside him, who could laugh to scorn the forces of his adversaries. He prayed to God that the eyes of his servant might be opened and he too might see, "And the Lord opened the eyes of the servant, and he saw: and behold the mountain was full of horses, and chariots of fire round about Eliseus" (4 Kings vi. 17). Thus it is with the just in temptation. However encompassed by his spiritual foes, he knows that God has taken care to surround him with a force far superior to that which is against him. He knows that the tempter, before he could assail him, must have asked permission, as he did for Job, and that his power was limited to what God saw it was within his virtue to overcome. But above all, he knows, with that holy Patriarch, that the Lord considereth all his ways, and numbereth all his steps.

Had it not been this reflection, my brethren, what else could have animated the Antonies and the Fathers of the desert in their solitary conflicts, where no encouragement, no advice, and no dread of discovery could reach them. Their eyes wandered over nothing but the dreary and trackless sands of the desert; their ears were long disused to the voice of their fellow-creatures; their hands had no variety of occupation, but to be stretched out in prayer, and to work at a monotonous employment; their time was almost equally divided between prayer and contemplation. Yet they persevered sometimes for eighty years in this course, without relaxation, though no eye could have witnessed it; without alteration, though no tongue would have had a right to reprove it. But, my brethren, the great secret which maintained them in their primitive fervour was the recollection that even in that solitude they were not alone; that even there, every painful step which they took to the distant fountain was carefully counted by God; that every time they overcame their inclinations a new crown was prepared for them in heaven.

How would the early Christians have stood the conflicts they endured for their faith, had not the sense of God's presence inspired them with courage? Represent to yourselves the martyr standing in the midst of the arena, a spectacle to thousands, not one of whom pities him, not one of whom admires him, not one of whom even gives him credit for the sincerity of his belief. He stands unmoved, he hears the roar of the wild beasts without a shudder; of all the vast multitude he alone is without a passion, he alone is tranquil. And do you think then, that he sees the preparations of death around him, that his eyes meet the furious scowl of his tormentors? Oh no, his thoughts have created for him a very different and far more glorious scene. He considers himself a spectacle, not to men, but to angels; rank above rank he sees the heavenly court, in bright array, seated to witness the combat in which he is not the culprit, but the hero; in which he is not to be the victim, but the conqueror. He sees not the Emperor, in his purple, come to feast his eyes on the bloody spectacle; but he beholds the King of kings anxiously and affectionately looking down from His throne, upon the short conflict of His servant, and, like Stephen, he sees "the Son of Man standing on the right hand of God," and holding out a wreath of unfading glory, to crown the triumph of His champion. This glorious vision, which his thoughts create, alone fills his mind; every shout which follows each of his wounds sounds to him a burst of exultation and encouragement from his heavenly witnesses; and, notwithstanding the torments which he suffers, he scarce perceives the transition which he makes from the contemplation of God's presence upon earth, to His full and perfect vision in heaven. ("Sermons," iii. 165.)

GOD'S POWER AND WISDOM

BUT what an idea does His sacred work give us of His infinite power, when it describes in the fewest possible words the summary method of creation, "Quia ipse dixit et facta sunt, ipse mandavit, et creata sunt." By a simple command, by a will expressed, all these countless, and, to us, immeasurable beings came into existence. Were a man to labour for years, he could not produce a flower in all its organisation, much less make it grow, open, and produce seed. But the Word of God called forth from nothing this entire nature, with all its complicated laws acting in admirable concert. No experiment was required to see how the separate parts of this machinery would work, no progressive improvements were made, but, from the sun that shone forth to regulate the march of its attendant planets, to the mote that dances in its beams, a perfect code at once regulated every movement, and has required no modification since. And though this is proof no less of the wisdom of God, yet does it show forth His power, which by one *fiat* created in perfection so mighty a work. And in preserving and governing all these things is exhibited no less power than was displayed in creating them; for nothing ever fails from being unsustained, nothing goes out of place from want of renovation, nothing threatens decay from being worn out; but all is fresh and new as on its first production, and this without effort, without labour, on the part of God; but He, enjoying the happiness of an undisturbed repose, by the mere continuation of His will that these things should yet be, supplies vitality, energy, and beauty in an unfailing stream. What mighty power! What incomprehensible omnipotence! ("Meditations," p. 79.)

INCARNATION

WHEN the Jew was told that he should see the salvation of God, what idea would this phrase naturally suggest to Him? One great act of salvation or redemption, wrought by the hand of Almightiness, he held recorded in his annals, and it conveyed to him the idea of terrible and resistless power. Storms of hail, and darkness sensible to the touch; the fields blighted by devouring locusts, and the houses infested by intolerable reptiles; the rivers running with blood, and the chambers of all the first-born defiled with their corpses: such were the forerunners of the great salvation of God's people. The waters of the Red Sea divided; the chariot-wheels of Pharaoh overthrown; an army with its royal leader swallowed up in the billows: such was its conduct, and such the means whereby it was effected. Or if the same Jew sought for precedents in his history, of how a new law was to be presented to the world, he would find only the terrors of Sinai, its clouds and lightnings, and the voice of God's trumpet proclaiming His commands to an affrighted people.

But now that God is about to come and set free His inheritance, not from one tyrant, but, as the Jew supposed, from his numerous and far mightier oppressors, —now that His kingdom has to be established, not within the narrow limits of Palestine, but from sea to sea, from the river to the uttermost bounds of the earth, —now that His law has to be heard, not by a few thousand, that can lie prostrate round the foot of a single mountain, but by Greeks and barbarians, Romans, Parthians, Elemytes, and Medes, what new series of proportionate wonders and signs can He have in store that will fall short of the total destruction of visible nature! If before, He touched the mountains and they smoked, and the rocks melted away through fear, what will it be when He comes from the south, and the holy one from Mount Pharan, but that, as the prophet Habacuc describes it, nations should be melted, and the ancient mountains crushed to pieces, and the entire deep should put forth its voice and lift up its hands?

No, the understanding of man could have formed no estimate of that display of magnificence which consists in abasement, or of that exhibition of might which acts in silence and without sensible effort. Even in the visible world there is as much of power, and more of glorious, because beneficent, exercise thereof, in one drop of dew that refreshes and helps to form the flower hidden in the grass, than there is in the earthquake that overthrows the solidest works of man's hand; and yet the one passes unheeded, while the latter fills nations with amazement. And so is there more of marvel, of grandeur, and of glory in that silent descent of the Eternal Word on earth, "as the rain upon the fleece, and as showers falling gently upon the earth," than there could have been in the utmost extension of His almighty arm. ("Sermons," i. 3.)

DIVINE ABASEMENT

WHAT is a cross upon the shoulders of the man compared with the burden of the flesh united to the Godhead? What are blows upon His cheek, or thorns upon His head, compared to the humiliation of feeling, the cravings of human wants, in the person of a God-Man? What were nails through His hands, or a spear in His side, compared with the ignominy of submitting to the temptations of the Evil One? What was death compared with the imputation of guilt to which His Incarnation brought Him—yea, of the guilt of the entire world? No, when once that first plunge into the abasement of human nature had been made, when the entire abyss of its misery had thus been absorbed into Himself, the rest must be as mere drops and sprinklings, concerning which a loving heart will not condescend to calculate.

Nay, there seems to be something ungenerous and unkind in the attempt to establish anything like a proportion between our belief and our powers of comprehension, or our powers of love, when once we have seen that the very first stride went so infinitely beyond our measurement. There should seem to have been laid in the first mystery of Christ's earthly existence such a strong foundation of confidence as would allow a superstructure of any extent and of any mass. There should appear in His first words a promise of so much as should prevent all surprise at whatever might follow in fulfilment. Man should listen to its unfolding wonders, to its tale of love, with the simplicity of a very child, who, upon each recital of a marvellous incident, only craves and expects another still more strange, and is only disappointed and grieved when the history is closed.

And, in like manner, when a man with a heart disposed to love has learnt and believed that out of affection to him a God of infinite power and majesty has become a helpless infant, seeming completely as the children of men in a similar condition, yet possessing all the fulness of the Godhead; then that this infant, grown up to man's estate, has died an ignominious death, impelled by the same love, to save him lost, at the expense of His own life—will it any longer seem strange or incredible to him that, even after these efforts of incomprehensible love, this untiring benefactor had discovered and adopted a new, unheard-of way to complete His scheme of benefits—has submitted to a new act of humiliation, so as to become our food?

It would be, indeed, too inestimable a benefit for him to admit without proof; but against this his heart, at least, would not allow his reason to start objections. For any of us might be called upon to give satisfactory evidence that an affectionate Father has left him a magnificent legacy, but we shall think it nothing strange or wonderful if we were told that, being able, He had done so.

But the resemblance between the two mysteries of the Incarnation and Eucharist will bear a closer investigation. In both there is an outward veil, hiding from the eye of flesh a precious and divine deposit, visible only to that of faith. When the wise men came from the East, under the conduct of a miraculous star, there can be no doubt that they were but little prepared for what they were to discover at Bethlehem. The very circumstance of their inquiry at Jerusalem for Him who was born King of the Jews shows that they expected to find His birth treated as a public event, and His entrance into His kingdom hailed with festivals of joy. Yet they find Herod ignorant, not merely of the occurrence, but of the place where it was likely to happen, and obliged to summon the priests to meet their inquiries. What a shock was here to their expectations! Still, encouraged by the reappearance of the star, they prosecute their journey with undiminished ardour, and arrive at Bethlehem. Their miraculous guide points to a poor, dilapidated shed, not likely to be tenanted by any but outcasts of human society; yet, strong in faith, they enter in.

What do they discover? A little babe, wrapped up as the poorest infant would be, and laid upon a bundle of straw! And is this all that they have crossed the deserts to see? Is this all that they abandoned their homes and palaces to discover? When they set off from their homes, their friends derided them, perchance, for undertaking so long a journey, and on the guidance of a wayward meteor, that might abandon them in the midst of some frightful wilderness. Many, probably, thought it little better than madness to go so far in search of a foreign sovereign, only yet an infant. What an account will they have to give on their return of their success, and of the employment made of their precious gifts! Will not their very attendants ridicule them for their credulity, in coming so far to find only a child in a manger? Will they dare to report what they have discovered to Herod? In spite of all such obstacles, which pride must have raised, to a simple faith, without any new assurances to encourage them; without any miraculous splendour round the humble group they have found, to overawe them; without any evidences to convince them, they trust implicitly to the sure guidance of that star, which, having led them safe through all their journey, first to Jerusalem and then to Bethlehem, they do not conceive likely now to turn traitor and mislead them; they prostrate themselves before that child, they adore Him, and by their gifts do Him supreme homage, acknowledging Him as their Lord and their God.

If we, then, have in like manner been led by the light of God through all the obscure paths of faith, shall we hesitate to trust our guides to the utmost? If His Word, which told us how His Son became man, and has been believed, tells us no less that He has assumed another disguise of love, and shrouded His glories still further for our benefit, shall it not be equally believed? If His Church, which hath been our principal conductor through the mazes of early tradition, whereon alone the belief in the divinity of the Incarnate Word can be solidly built, fixing its directing ray, in the end, upon that humble tabernacle, assures you, with the same voice that till now you have believed, that therein dwells the God of your souls, your dear Saviour, no longer under the form of flesh, but with that same flesh, in its turn, concealed under the appearance of bread, why will you hesitate to prostrate yourself and adore? ("Sermons," i. 87.)

POVERTY OF OUR LORD'S BIRTH

YET reflect how much more becoming God and His Son was this manner of birth from any other that could have been imagined. What addition could the most sumptuous attendance and most gorgeous circumstances of Oriental pomp have been to His own proper splendour and glory? Suppose Him laid in a bed of state, as rich as gold and jewels and imperial purple could have made it. What would He have gained? He would have been more like an earthly monarch's son, destined to grow up a haughty, imperious tyrant. Men would have approached Him, though an infant, with a certain awe; they would have been more engaged in contemplating the dazzling objects that surround Him, than in gazing upon His own charms, and meditating upon His own glories. But, as we now see Him, it is Himself that we love and reverence. In the other case the tenderer feelings would have had but little room to play; what compassion, what interest, could we have taken in Him? What could we have called our own? He would have seemed to be able to give rather than to receive; we should have retired abashed from His presence, feeling that we could afford no service to one so magnificently attended. But as it is, He is indeed raised above all those circumstances which shed some lustre round the birth of the great, and we find Him upon His bed of straw, more glorious and majestic than an infant sovereign upon a gilded cradle. He is surrounded by His own glory, a glory which we feel is superior to the want of all outward aids. But then, in addition, He seems to us all our own. We may go in, together with the shepherds, and feel no timid reserve. We find none but Mary and Joseph there, both of whom we so well know and love. We salute them familiarly. The one, grave yet mild, seems to welcome us; the other, all gentleness, and smiling with the fondness of a young mother's heart, kindly encourages us to approach. She takes her veil from over the little straw bed, and shows us the face of her dear little babe, all smiling, and bright as heaven. She allows us to look upon Him with all affection, and admire His beautiful features, beautiful indeed beyond the children of men. ("Meditations," p. 83.)

OUR LORD, THE TYPE

As no nation or race of men could ever have gone out of their own physical characteristics for their type of ideal perfection in the beauty of form; as the Egyptian never could, by any abstraction, have generated a style of art in which the colour, shape, and features of his divinity should be purely European; nor the Greek have given to his hero the tawny hue, narrow eyes, and protruding lips of the Egyptian—for each to the other must have seemed deformity—so could neither they, nor the men of any other nation, have framed to themselves an ideal type or canon of moral perfection in character which arose not from what to them seemed most beautiful and perfect. A Hindoo cannot conceive his Brahman saint other than as possessing in perfection the abstemiousness, the silence, the austerity, and the minute exactness in every trifling duty which he admires in different degrees in his living models. Plato's Socrates, the perfection of the philosophical character, is composed of elements perfectly Greek, being a compound of all those virtues which the doctrines of his school deemed necessary to adorn a sage.

Now this hath often appeared to me the strongest internal proof of a superior authority stamped upon the Gospel history, that the holy and perfect character it portrays, not only differs from, but expressly opposes every type of moral perfection which they who wrote it could possibly have conceived. We have, in the writings of the Rabbins, ample materials wherewith to construct the model of a perfect Jewish teacher; we have the sayings and the actions of Hillel, and Gamaliel, and Rabbi Samuel, all perhaps in great part imaginary, but all bearing the impress of national ideas, all formed upon one rule of imaginary perfection. Yet nothing can be more widely apart than their thoughts, and principles, and actions, and character, and those of our Redeemer. Lovers of wrangling controversy, proposers of captious paradoxes, jealous upholders of their nation's exclusive privileges, zealous, uncompromising sticklers for the least comma of the law, and most sophistical departers from its spirit, such mostly are these great men—the exact counterpart and reflection of those Scribes and Pharisees who are so uncompromisingly reproved as the very contradiction of Gospel principles.

How comes it that men, not even learned, contrived to represent a character every way departing from their national type—at variance with all those features which custom, and education, and patriotism, and religion, and nature seemed to have consecrated as of all most beautiful? And the difficulty of considering such a character the invention of man, as some have impiously imagined, is still further increased by observing how writers recording different facts, as St. Matthew and St. John, do lead us, nevertheless, to the same representation and conception. Yet herein, methinks, we have a key to the solution of every difficulty. For if two artists were commanded to produce a form embodying their ideas of perfect beauty, and both exhibited figures equally shaped upon types and models most different from all ever before seen in their country, and, at the same time, each perfectly resembling the other, I am sure such a fact, if recorded, would appear almost incredible, except on the supposition that both had copied the same original.

Such, then, must be the case here: the Evangelists, too, must have copied the living model which they represent, and the accordance of the moral features which they give Him can only proceed from the accuracy with which they have respectively drawn them. But this only increases our mysterious wonder. For assuredly He was not as the rest of men, who could thus separate Himself in character from whatever was held most perfect and most admirable by all who surrounded Him and by all who had taught Him; who, while He set Himself far above all national ideas of moral perfection, yet borrowed nothing from Greek, or Indian, or Egyptian, or Roman; who, while He thus had nothing in common with any known standard of character, any established law of perfection, should seem to every one the type of His peculiarly beloved excellence. And truly, when we see how He can have been followed by the Greek, though a founder of none among his sects; revered by the Brahman, though preached unto him by men of the fisherman's caste; worshipped by the red man of Canada, though belonging to the hated pale race—we cannot but consider Him as destined to break down all distinction of colour, and shape, and countenance, and habits; to form in Himself the type of unity to which are referable all the sons of Adam, and give us, in the possibility of this moral convergence, the strongest proof that the human species, however varied, is essentially one. ("Science and Revealed Religion," Lect. IV.)

OUR LORD'S CHARACTER

REFLECT how, if man had been left to draw the outline of a character for the Son of God made man, he would have probably erred regarding the virtues he would have attributed to Him, as much, and in the same way, as the Jews did respecting His public character. We should have imagined to ourselves something brilliant, almost too dazzling. We should have supposed Him so wrapped up in sublime contemplation as to have scarcely condescended to treat of earthly things; so fenced round by the manifestations of unparalleled sanctity as to be approached only with dread or hesitation by the few with whom He conversed. We should have fancied Him walking through life with a grandeur of virtue, a certain magnificence of perfection, which no one could for an instant think of taking as his aim or model. Now, had Jesus been such as all this, and, consequently, a most rigid observer of the law, severe in fasting and other mortifications, He would only have appeared as supreme in the order of the Scribes and Pharisees, as perfect in the perfection of His nation, but not as the Saint of saints, the perfectest in the eyes of the entire human species. And this it is that He must appear to all who diligently and lovingly study His character. We are, indeed, astonished when we read how He was so affable that a sinner, upon his conversion, should have the boldness to invite Him to feast with him in his house, as did Zaccheus and St. Matthew. This little trait alone proves that, while He could by His superior power overawe transgressors and bring them to repentance, they lost none of their affection for Him by the complete abandonment of their ill-gotten goods, which He insisted on, and that they were under no apprehension of their admiration of Him being impaired through treating Him with such familiarity. The great beauty and perfection of our Saviour's virtue consists in its perfect appropriateness to times and persons. There is no strict line to which He seemed to have inflexibly bound Himself—no predominant virtue, so to speak, which severely ruled over the rest and kept them in the background; but each seemed ever ready for every occasion, one always appears as perfect as the other, and very little reflection upon any part of our Saviour's conduct will always convince us that He could not have there acted better than He did. Every alternation of zeal and meekness, of sternness and condescension, of devotion and intercourse, seems most seasonable, and His conduct in it the most perfect. He is as much the Son of God at the Pharisee's or publican's board as He is upon Thabor or at the tomb of Lazarus. In this manner is He distinguished from His saints, as from the rest of men. For among them He is pleased to distribute His gifts, that so we may the better contemplate separately those excellencies which were united in Him. Thus He made a St. Thomas of Villanova remarkable for his love of poverty, a St. Francis of Sales for his sweetness, a St. John of the Cross ardent for afflictions, a St. Philip Neri cheerful and kind-hearted. But in Him none of these virtues, though possessed in a degree which shows theirs to have been but faint copies, obtains such preponderance as to be a leading virtue to the disparagement of others.

Such was our dear Lord's character, made up of a thousand hues of bright perfection, but all blended together in exquisite harmony.

Reflect how our Lord's virtues have thus been made, however unattainable, at least imitable. We can study them without being dazzled, and in reference to circumstances, and thus can make them a model for our own conduct. For His virtues never seem to have been practised merely for the purpose of making an act of virtue, but because the time and place required Him to act just as He did. We have thus a key for ascertaining His motives, and can lay up a collection of moral axioms as to how we ought to act in the like circumstances, axioms which never can mislead us when practically applied. He is thus to us a living model—not a mere picture of possible perfection, but one which we feel we may in some degree copy with hopes of success. It is, in fact, remarkable that some of the sublimest virtues seem more imitable in Jesus than in some of His servants, though far superior to them. I think I could more easily copy the meek silence wherewith He endured indignity and cruelty than the eagerness with which some martyrs ran to their sufferings. And so may we say of His other perfections. They all seem practicable, because they are never intrusive. We can easily copy them, because in their occasions we can discover their reason. ("Meditations" p. 40.)

OUR LORD'S TEACHING

REFLECT how our blessed Saviour is described to us as teaching "as one having authority, and not as the Scribes and Pharisees." What dignity and grace, then, must we not suppose to have been exhibited in His person, what majesty in His countenance, what impressiveness in His gesture, what solemnity in His tones, and what sweetness and unction in His words! When we read that great multitudes followed Him into the wilderness, and for days forgot their homes, their worldly interests, and their daily sustenance, in hanging upon His words, what an idea must we not form of the marvellous charm that invested His sacred person and played in His accents? When we see men abandoning their nets, their parents, and their homes at His simple call, or leaving their worldly concerns, as Matthew did, to follow Him, upon a simple invitation to do so, we may form some notion of what His look and voice possessed of grace and power. What must these have been when eloquently expatiating upon the precepts of love, or the sublime revelations of the Gospel? With what authority must He have taught, with an energy how far beyond that of the Scribes and Pharisees, when He lashed their vices and made them quail under His reproof? But, further, He taught not as these men, because He taught with meekness and condescension. These arrogant men repelled from themselves with scorn the poor and sinners, and treated the rest of mankind as far their inferiors, especially in all that concerned virtue and perfection. Not so Jesus. Although He was truly holy and pure unto all perfection, He was always most humane and gracious, condescending and affable. He received the most flagitious, when penitent, with open arms, and ate and familiarly discoursed with them; He mingled among the poorest as one of themselves; He instructed the ignorant with patience and assiduity. None were afraid to approach Him and learn from Him. How delightful must it have been to have and to hear such a Master! Lastly, Jesus taught as one having authority, and not as the Scribes and Pharisees, because He did not, like them, lay intolerable burdens upon men's shoulders, which they touched not with a finger of their own; but He practised all that He taught, was an exemplification of all His maxims, the model of all His school. Did He teach men to be poor in spirit and to despise earthly comforts? He was as poor as they, when He might have been richer than the Roman Emperor, by a wish; and He chose not to have where to lay His head. Did He tell them to be meek under calumnies and persecutions? Well, He suffered the most severe, and He suffered with unconquerable patience. Did He forbid the requiting of evil with evil, and command us to pray for those who injure us? This, and even more, did He fulfil under the greatest aggravations. Thus was His conduct a living commentary upon His precepts, and He taught more by His actions than by His words. ("Meditations," p. 61.)

OUR LORD'S MEEKNESS

OUR Saviour at once displayed His full perfection, nor was it possible to add to the degree which He first exhibited. His humility was not only born but perfected in the crib of Bethlehem; we can conceive it in no way augmented beyond what it there appears. His submission to the law was demonstrated to its full in His circumcision on the eighth day after His birth; His wisdom was manifested in unrivalled splendour in His twelfth year when He disputed with the doctors, and then in its last degree upon His first manifestation to Israel; His obedience was most perfectly displayed when He lived in obscurity in Nazareth; His strength under temptation and His mortification increased not after His forty days' fasting in the wilderness; His charity and His power broke forth together in full splendour at His first miracle. But His meekness was manifested gradually and by marked advances; it kept pace with the great work of our redemption, and it secured perfection with its accomplishment. It seemed as if He wished to lead us from step to step up so new, so unexpected, so uninviting a path. First, it was the simple declining from all contests, the shunning the occasions of collision with His enemies. Then He meets their rage, through all the fury of reproachful and menacing words, meekly chiding and reproving until they proceed to violence, when He retires before the storm, hides Himself and goes out of the temple (Jo. viii. 59). As His end approaches, He enters upon more formal possession of this virtue, and rides into Jerusalem upon an ass, as the meek king whom Zachary had foretold. At every stage of His passion He advances in meekness. First He exhibits it to a treacherous friend: " Judas, dost thou betray the Son of man with a kiss?"—then to the officers who arrest Him : "You are come out as it were to a robber with swords and clubs to apprehend Me; I sat daily with you teaching in the temple, and you laid not hands upon Me" (Matt. xxvi. 55). Next comes the dreadful scene of His last night, when the mind is lost in contemplating the endurance of the Lamb of God. Hitherto He had displayed the meekness to be practised by the Christian, by the martyr—henceforth it is the prerogative of the world's Redeemer, and that Redeemer an immaculate God. ("Sermons," iii. 72.)

THE SACRED HEART

WHEN our Divine Lord said to us, that "out of the abundance of the heart the mouth speaketh," He at once suggested to us how we may judge of the emotions and impulses of His own blessed Heart. In Him there was no deceit, no double heart ; but all was sincere, and plain, and just in Him. Then out of His Heart He uttered His words (Job viii. 10, "loquuntur de corde"), and they are but the overflow of the abundance treasured there. From His sacred lips you descend to His blessed Heart; and you cannot be deceived.

Then, when He first appears on earth, He speaks

The Sacred Heart

those few but pregnant words, "Behold, I come." They were the utterance, not of the lips, but of the heart; they were expressed by the first breath that passed inarticulate from His humanity, unheard even by the attentive ear of Mary, which conveyed thus early to her immaculate heart whatever proceeded from His. "To the world which hates Me," those words say, "to a people that knows Me not, to a generation obstinate and hard-hearted; to earth reeking with sin detestable to Me, to creation perverted from all its beautiful ends and enslaved to the devil; to a barren desert compared with My Paradise above; to a dismal land overspread with the darkness of sin and the shadow of death; to direst poverty, distress, cold, hunger, and toil; to contradiction, ingratitude, scorn, and calumny; to disappointment, abandonment, treachery, and denial; to ignominy, pain, anguish, and agony; to buffets, scourges, to the cross, and death—O man! for *thy* sake, behold I come." Willingly, deliberately, lovingly, the words are breathed from that infant Heart, the first incense rising from that living temple of divinest charity. And must not that Heart have needs been full of mercy, full of pity, and full of kindness, to have given them utterance? Good measure, indeed, and well pressed down, shaken together, and running over, was that charity which, in His very incarnation, was poured into His bosom. Those words began that overflow which ceased no more; but, like the waters of Jerusalem, which, issuing from the upper fountain, gathered to themselves, as they passed, those of the lower one, and so ran on, still increasing, till they became almost a torrent, so do these thoughts of charity take up in their course so many others, spoken at every step of our dear Redeemer's life on earth, till we are overpowered by their strength.

Whence proceeded those words of compassion, in which we all have such a part: "I have come to call not the just, but sinners to repentance; I am sent to the sheep that have perished of the house of Israel; there is more joy in heaven for one sinner that doth penance, than for ninety-nine just that need not penance"? From what source came forth the words which He spoke to Zaccheus or to Matthew, the publicans, to the sinful woman brought before Him for judgment, to the paralytic sinner laid at His feet, to Magdalene of her own accord prostrate there: words of gracious self-invitation, or of a generous call to apostleship; words of kind forgiveness of past sin, and encouragement to persevere in grace; words of most tender and soothing pardon, full of charity, that filled even a Pharisee's house with a sweeter savour of that unknown virtue than did the broken alabaster-box of spikenard? Whence? do you ask? It was from that same gentle and loving Heart, which, pure and holy itself, had ample space enough in it to hold and embrace there, even sinners, and the whole world of sin.

From what source came out those wonderful words of pleading, "Father, forgive them, for they know not what they do;" or that sweetest of forgiving reproofs, "Dost thou betray the Son of man with a kiss;" or that mildest of just expostulations, " Many good works I have done; for which of these works do you stone Me?" or that sweetest of rebukes, "If [I have spoken] well, why dost thou strike Me?" or that almost maternal consolation, "Weep not over Me, ye daughters of Jerusalem, but over yourselves and over your children;" or, in fine, the eloquence of that silence, which went to the heart more than words, as He stood before the priests or Pilate; and the mute power of that look which spoke to the heart of Peter and made it overflow in tears? Whence? do you ask again? Oh no! Your own hearts tell you, better than our words can do, that all these and many other such words came surging forth from, not a well-spring, but an ocean, of love for man— for man the worthless, for man the reprobate—that lies deep and wide, and ever heaving, in that most amiable Heart of Jesus. What an abundance, indeed, and a superabundance of charity was required to give truth and reality of feeling to such words, so spoken as they were! ("Sermons," i. 349.)

OUR LORD AND THE CHILDREN

Now it was of such a crowd [of the poor] as this that we are told that "they brought Him young children that He might touch them"; and of the children of such parents, when the disciples rebuked them, He said, "Suffer the little children to come unto Me." But He was not content with doing what those poor people asked. St. Mark tells us that He went far beyond this: "And *embracing* them, and laying His hands upon them, He blessed them." More pointedly still, when He wished to place before His apostles and disciples—His fishermen, His sailors, His publicans—a type of perfection, and representative of those who were fit to enter into His Church, He Himself "*calls* unto Him a little child." What sort of a child? He did not send for him, He calls him, one at hand, one of the poor, a child from the crowd, the rude, vulgar crowd.

Intending to show them what they must *become* to enter the kingdom of heaven, would it not have been almost harsh and ungentle to put in the midst of them one whose entrance into it was likely to be as difficult as the passage of a camel through the needle's eye, a child bright with beautiful health, sleek, and clothed in soft garments, a type of earthly prosperity, training, and happiness? "Alas!" would they not say, "nothing can ever make us like that child." But let us rather imagine a little child called there and then from amidst those who habitually followed and admired Jesus—a wan, emaciated, sickly child, neglected and uncared for, poorly attired, perhaps in tattered raiment, with bare limbs and uncovered head: one in whom the poor would see little unlike themselves outwardly, little to mortify them or humble them, nothing in fact different from themselves, except in the innocence and simplicity of its age—and we shall understand the full beauty of this passage in our Lord's life, and the sublimity of its lesson.

Now what doth Jesus with this poor little thing, picked up in the street or the lane? Does He merely, perhaps authoritatively, call it, and set it in the middle of His followers, scared or insolent, to be lectured on, like a model or a machine? Surely not. Listen once more to St. Mark: "And taking a child,"—*taking* it, mind, not ashamed of handling or caressing it,—"and taking a child, He set him in the midst of them, whom when He had embraced, He saith to them: Whoever receiveth *one* such child as this in My name, receiveth Me." It is with this little poor and perhaps outcast child in His arms that He spoke those words of grace, the motto inscribed on the charity of to-day. But this is not the whole mystery of the act; for it comprises the entire scheme and principle of Catholic education.

Jesus *embraced* that little child, His representative on earth: that is, He pressed it to His own living, warm, and palpitating Heart; to that Heart which, by every pulsation, sends salvation and eternal life through the frame of the whole Church, which darts, with irresistible thrill, the price of redemption to the utter bounds of earth. It was a dearly-bought distinction to holy Simeon, earned by a long life of hope and prayer, to hold in his arms his infant Saviour, to whom he could nothing give. What an honour for *this* child to be taken up into His arms who could give him all things. But no, this is not enough : that poor little creature has forestalled the place of John, the place of honour and of love; that place far beyond what John's mother had dared in her maternal presumption to ask, which was only that he might sit on the right or left hand of Jesus. When He rejected her petition He reserved for him much more—that he should recline upon His glorious bosom, the tabernacle of His self-immolating Heart. But the child had climbed up there, had nestled there before even the beloved one, and had come down again educated as the contact with that adorable Heart alone can educate—the very God-child of Jesus. So necessary a consequence was this, that in the ancient Church it used to be thought that this chosen child grew up to be the holy Martyr and Bishop Ignatius, the most like to John, in burning love, of the early saints.

But as we said just now, in this sweetest incident of our Redeemer's life we have the whole theory of Catholic education.

First listen to His words and learn: "He who receiveth *one* such child as this in My name, receiveth Me." How easy a thing it is, then, to receive Jesus! How easy, especially in this metropolis! Come! two need not receive the same. Our Lord asks you to receive one apiece, to enjoy the stupendous privilege of receiving Him. We have them ready. Come ten thousand strong, ye rich! come twenty thousand in ranks, ye who are not in want! We have one at least for each of you, in the streets and lanes, in the courts and corners, in the garrets and cellars of luxurious London. And how will you receive these tender ambassadors from your Lord, these delicate and frail little images of God Incarnate? Will you be harsh and ungracious to them, or haughty and imposing? will you be repulsed by their rags, their uncleanliness, their rudeness, or their stolidity? Or, rather, will you be kind and gentle, generous and handsome, in your dealing with them? will you warm them at *your* hearts, give them rest on *your* bosoms? It was thus, at least, that Jesus treated them, when He received them, and asked you to receive them.

And now, dearly beloved, in our love for Him, you will ask us how is this to be done? Simply and easily. Every child whom you will provide with a Catholic education, you bring to the very Heart of our Lord and educate there. Science and letters, if taught in His spirit, may indeed be as His two arms, which raise the child from the earth and its grovelling thoughts; but religious and moral truth alone puts His seal upon all other teaching; and that seal is the pressure of His sacred Heart, of its diamond strength and brilliancy, on the yet soft wax of the childish heart. By this holy impulse is the one clasped close upon the other, and the infinite graces of the one are inhaled, as was man's first breath of life, by the awakening intelligence and expanding feelings, from the living fountain of all-redeeming love! ("Sermons," i. 383.)

TRANSFIGURATION

WHO hath not often longed, with the eloquent Chrysostom, that he could have beheld the Apostle Paul addressing his defence to Festus, or preaching before the wise men of Athens? Who hath not wished that his happiness it had been to witness the divine power of our Lord's appeals when crushing under His indignant eloquence the pride of the Pharisees, or when mildly unfolding to His apostles, in their charming simplicity, the moral doctrines of His law? Nay, so natural does this superiority of the living testimony to the written appear, even where no proportion exists between the authors of the two, that the rich glutton in hell, pondering on the experience of his own impenitence, hesitates not to say that his hardened brethren will be sooner brought to faith and repentance through the preaching of the ulcerous and ragged Lazarus returning from the dead, than through the reading of Moses and the prophets. How much surer, then, would he have felt of the desired conviction could he have carried his presumption to such a pitch as to hope that Moses and the prophets themselves might be allowed to break their cerements and testify in person to his obdurate generation.

And precisely such is the evidence here given of our Saviour's dignity, authority, and character. When addressing the Jews He had appealed to these very witnesses as speaking through the organ of the written Word. But, alas! they had ever read them with a crooked mind, forestalled by preconceits concerning the temporal glories of their Messias and the worldly conquests which He should achieve. They misunderstood their evidence, and remained in unbelief.

But to the chosen few it was given to know the mysteries of God's kingdom in the full and clear light of living evidence, and to hear them speak whom others had only read. For here their most extravagant desires were more than fulfilled; their most unreasonable hope of proof must have been incredibly surpassed. Moses, whose face had shone so brightly as to terrify his countrymen, now standing overshone and eclipsed, as the lamp before the mid-day sun, by the presence of their Divine Master, whose countenance truly rivalled the source of earthly light! Elias, who had ridden, of all men alone, upon the fiery chariot of the Lord of Hosts, and whose cloak imparted to him that inherited it prophecy and miracles, now receiving a light and splendour from the dazzling brightness of *His* garment! These two, the greatest men, without exception, whom the arm of God had ever strengthened for the manifestation of His almighty power, now as humble attendants, ministers, and servants, honoured and privileged by standing at His side, must have produced a briefer, deeper, and more indelible conviction of His superiority than the painful and repeated perusal of whatever prophecy had written. They seem to say that the law and the testimony are now sealed up, and all the mighty things accomplished which they had foretold and foreshown. They stand as shadowy forms beside the reality of Christ's presence, as faint, indistinct, and dusky images, receiving light and reflecting glory from the brightness of His truth.

But in the choice of witnesses thus called in, there were personal considerations which greatly would add to the interest of their testimony. Both of them had been purified before God by a fast protracted through forty days, even like our blessed Saviour's not long before. Both had been admitted to a closer view of the Divine countenance than any other of the human race. In this manner did they approach nearer to His perfection, and were far livelier types of His surpassing excellence, than any others among the Fathers of the Old Law. And that the figure might afford still fuller measure of comfort to the disciples who witnessed it, they had in their generation, like Jesus, been lovers of their people, zealous for their fidelity to God, and unwearied in doing good.

Such are the great and holy men who return to earth to confer with their Master and Saviour, as though deputed by it and its inhabitants to hold solemn council with Him touching their dearest interests. And ah! how truly does their discourse prove whose representatives they are, and what little else than pain any embassy from our fallen kind could bear Him! No glad tidings do they bring of His chosen people's being repentant and seeking reconciliation; no promise or hope of His reception among them as their King and Redeemer. No; they too had been liberators of their people, and were familiar with its reward: it is concerning His decease at Jerusalem, from the hands of *His* people, that they come to treat. Oh! who can imagine the shame and sorrow that hang on their countenances, struggling with their kindling gratitude, admiration, and love, which a topic so disgraceful to their nation, yet so necessary to man, must have excited in their bosoms! But think, on the other hand, what a new idea of the grandeur of Christ's redemption must have flashed upon the wondering apostles' thoughts on finding that subject, which was their scandal and distress, chosen as the meetest theme of conference at this unusual and magnificent meeting. How must the ignominy of the cross have, for a moment at least, been forgotten on hearing it the subject of praise and thanksgiving, chosen by such men, at the very instant that heaven itself seemed opened visibly before them. ("Sermons," i. 107.)

THABOR AND OLIVET

DID I wish to convince one whose feelings are alive to the noble, the beautiful, and the perfect, but whose belief in Him was weak, I would by no means take him to Mount Thabor, where the spectacle was meant for friends; but I would sooner lead him to the other scene of the Mount of Olives. The idea of one who is considered God-man, represented as arrayed in glory, is too analogous to natural apprehension to have so convincing a force. But the conception of such a Being presented to us, bowed beneath sorrow till His pale forehead chilled the earth, with a body bedewed with blood, and a soul steeped in unutterable anguish—the conception of such a One honouring the inferior nature which links Him with sorrow, by assuming its characteristics as fully as He ever bore those of the sublimer, embracing and caressing the cruellest realities of His manhood with equal love and earnestness as He did the magnificent prerogatives of His Godhead: surely this is a thought, an idea, which the boldest invention never could have dreamt, and which none but one truly possessed of the two could ever have practically realised.

No; had the Redeemer of man been Himself but man, He would have been screened from every infirmity of His nature. He would have required the investment of every outward attribute of perfection, even in appearance, to raise Him above the rest of men, to make Him seem worthy of His immense elevation, and give Him a claim to the love, the obedience, and the veneration of His fellow-men. Only One, who was truly God as well as man, could afford to sink beneath the lowest level of human wretchedness, and hope to secure love and admiration by becoming, to appearance, even less than man. ("Sermons," i. 115.)

THE PRECIOUS BLOOD

WHATEVER is good, whatever is holy, whatever is perfect upon earth, has come to us from, and through, and by the most precious Blood of our Divine Lord and Saviour Jesus Christ. This, from the beginning, was more variously and more abundantly symbolised to us than anything else in the New Testament; though its excellence is manifested by the contrast in which it stands with its types. It was to be innocently shed like Abel's, that it might be shown to plead better and

The Precious Blood

more efficaciously than it for mercy, not for vengeance. It was poured out in sacrifice, that it might be proved infinitely superior to the blood of oxen and of goats, which had no power to cleanse the soul. Finally, the paschal lamb, the noblest type of our redemption, by the anointing with its blood of the doorposts of the Israelites, scared away the destroying angel, and made Pharaoh relax his grasp on God's captive people, and so freed them; only to prefigure how the Lamb that taketh away the sins of the world would baffle and overcome the prince of darkness and of eternal death, and force the tyrant of earth and hell to let His own people go free, to offer sacrifice even in this wilderness.

And how was this? The posts of the gate which alone leads to life immortal, the cross under which all must stoop who desire to enter into Paradise, are richly streaked, nay, thickly painted, with the Blood of "our immolated Pasch," more terrible to His enemies than the brightest flash of Heaven's lightning. And so, when we partake of the Divine Mysteries, the threshold of our mouths, our lips, are dyed with the same rich drops that fell so copiously on Calvary.

With what devotion, then, should we not commemorate this shedding of our Saviour's precious Blood, at the very mention of which the Church makes her ministers bend their knees, in awe and adoration of a mystery so profound and yet so sweet, so fearful and yet so tender. As the more deep and terrible is the gulf that opens beneath us, the more we feel drawn towards it, and tempted to plunge into it, so is this abyss of wonderful and unfathomable goodness, awful to contemplate, yet inviting our love to dive into it fearlessly, and taste unsated of its delights.

To think that God should have taken flesh, the very body of man, with all its lowliness of nature but wonders of construction, merely that He might die, and that He should have blood to shed, for man's ransom, salvation, and nourishment; to contemplate by what harrowing and afflicting ways this outpouring should have to be made, by what stripes, buffets, wounds, gashes, piercing and transfixing of every part of that thrice-holy Body, to the very rending of its divine Heart; to meditate on the overwhelming truth that God, the Father who loved Him with an infinite affection, should have been pleased, propitiated, soothed, and turned to love from just anger, by this tremendous atonement, baffles and sets at naught all our estimates, and all our reasonings on the eternal and infinite ways of a divine dispensation. Yet how bright this depth, how richly lighted by every tender hue of love! How meekness and gentleness, mercy and forgivingness, disinterestedness and self-sacrifice, bounty and liberality, affectionateness and familiarity, parental fondness and brotherly caress play through the abyss, as profound, and as measureless, and as incomprehensible as itself! How unsearchable are the ways of God's love, as much as those of His might! Who hath been His counsellor but Himself—the infinite goodness urging on the infinite energy of the Divine in all things.

But what multiplies beyond the bounds of a limited conception the immensity of this love is, that it is individual and singular. "Sic totum omnibus quod totum singulis." Every drop of blood so unreservedly poured out on Golgotha, was gathered into one cup, the whole contents of which every soul may drink and make its own. The entire price was paid for each: the value of each soul is the equivalent of the whole ransom. The treasure is not divided and paid out in single coins, but the entire sum is lavishly given to each prodigal. Who can penetrate to the depths of this almighty mercy? yet who can forbear to love it and do his utmost to be worthy of it? ("Sermons," i. 376.)

OUR LORD'S AGONY

SUPPOSE, then, that wicked Judas, when he rushed out of the supper-hall, had brought in the satellites of the priests, and had seized Jesus in the midst of His apostles, there would have been something unbecoming the majesty of His sufferings to be thus surprised, as though unprepared, amidst the calm enjoyment of society with those He loved. The whole Passion would have appeared to us a deed of violence, and that spontaneous assumption of pain and death which is its leading characteristic would have hardly appeared. It was right, therefore, that a separation from the rest of mankind should take place, that Jesus should calmly and deliberately prepare Himself for all that was to follow, and give Himself up to His sufferings, as chosen by Himself. Hence, when His enemies came to seize Him, He is pleased first to throw them thrice upon the ground before He surrendered Himself to their power. He showed in His agony and in His prayer, that He foresaw what was to ensue, and submitted to it all.

But, moreover, it was unbecoming that men should strike the first blow upon the Victim of sin; for whatever they inflicted was but in consequence of a just and stern decree. It was the Eternal Father who must first lift His hand upon this His Isaac, and by investing Him with the character of the universal oblation, give Him up to the cruelty of man for the consummation of the mysterious sacrifice. And here, indeed, He laid His hands upon His head, as did the High Priest upon that of the emissary goat, laying upon Him the iniquities of us all, and holding Him responsible for their enormity. During the rest of His Passion our thoughts are distracted by the harrowing spectacle of bodily torments, and by the detestation inspired by the conduct of His enemies. Here we are exclusively occupied with the consideration of inward grief; we see Jesus alone with His own personal sorrows, and come to consider those as so essential a part of His sufferings, so deep, so overwhelming, as that whatever He afterwards endured in the body shall seem but as an addition and appendage to them.

For observe diligently the awful expression of the sacred text: "And being in an agony, He prayed the longer;" and His own words: "My soul is sorrowful even unto death." These expressions suggest to us the only comparison that will illustrate the anguish of His spirit—the last struggle between life and death, when in ordinary men the latter conquers. They represent to us the convulsions of exhausted nature, resisting in vain the wrestling of a superior destroying power, that gripes it closer and closer, and presses out by degrees its vital energy, till it sinks crushed and hopeless within its iron embrace. They give us an idea of the heart smothered in its fitful throbs by the slow ebbing of its thickening streams; of the chest rising against a leaden weight that oppresses it; of the limbs stiffening and dragging one down like icy lumps; of the brain swimming and reeling in sickening confusion. But, then, when we stand by such a spectacle on the bed of a dying friend, awful and painful as it is to our feelings, we have the consolation to know or to believe that the feebleness of nature which causes it is a security against its severity, that the sense is already dulled, and the mind brought down almost to the verge of unconsciousness. But here is one in the very prime of youth, in the vigour of health, without a stroke from man, or a visitation of evil fortune, or a domestic bereavement, so seized upon in one instant by inward sorrow, as to be cast into this death struggle, through its intensity. Oh, who can imagine the fearfulness of the conflict! To be assailed by such grief as is capable of causing death, and to have to grapple with it, and resist it so as to prevent by endurance its fatal effects; to feel death, in the very pride and fulness of life, attempt usurpation, by strong and armed hand, against the wakeful and resisting powers of vitality! And to wrestle through the dark hours of night, as Jacob did with the angel, unaided, unsupported, alone! Good God, what a conflict, and what a victory! When you stand by one reduced to his last struggle, you see with compassion how the cold sweat settles upon his brow; you see in it the last symptom of the intensity of his pain; and if he were your bitterest enemy you would not refuse to wipe it gently away. Look, then, at the agony of your Saviour, and see how in it that sweat is blood! yea, and blood so profusely shed, without wound or stroke, as to flow upon the ground!

There are plants in the luxurious East, my dearly beloved brethren, which men gash and cut, that from them may distil the precious balsams they contain; but that is ever the most sought and valued which, issuing forth of its own accord, pure and unmixed, trickles down like tears upon the parent tree. And so it seems to me, we may without disparagement speak of the precious streams of our dear Redeemer's Blood. When forced from His side in abundant flow, it came mixed with another mysterious fluid; when shed by the cruel inflictions of His enemies, by their nails, their thorns, and scourges, there is a painful association with the brutal instruments that drew it, as though in some way their defilement could attaint it. But here we have the first yield of that saving and life-giving heart, gushing forth spontaneously, pure and untouched by the unclean hand of man, dropping as dew upon the ground. It is the first juice of the precious vine, before the wine-press hath bruised its grapes, richer and sweeter to the loving and sympathising soul than what is afterwards pressed out. It is every drop of it ours; and alas, how painfully so! For here no lash, no impious palm, no pricking thorn, hath called it forth; but our sins, yes, our sins, the executioners, not of the flesh, but of the heart of Jesus, have driven it all out, thence to water that garden of sorrows! Oh, is it not dear to us; is it not gathered up by our affections, with far more reverence and love than by virgins of old was the blood of martyrs, to be placed for ever in the very sanctuary, yea, within the very altar of our hearts! ("Sermons," i. 207.)

THE REDEMPTION

HERE, as in the noblest tragedy, action becomes equivalent to suffering, and our Redeemer may be said to do for man whatever man does against Him. Now, to our minds there is nothing more decisive of the respective claims of Catholic and Protestant to be the religion of the New Testament than the manner in which they treat its most solemn portion, that which records the final act of redemption. The very essence of modern Protestantism is to regard this greatest act as a mere abstraction. The mind is concentrated on the sole apprehension of an accomplished atonement, and its instrumentality by death. By a process eminently selfish the price and its purchase are transferred to the individual soul, appropriated by it, and thus viewed extraneously to Him whose they really are. There is no contemplation in the Protestant view, it is one of mere self-application. To contrast it with the Catholic idea, and so illustrate both, perhaps a simple parable may be useful.

Let us imagine to ourselves two spendthrifts for whose debts a loving father has given bond. The day of reckoning arrives, and the surety comes willingly to pay the ransom. One son stands by, grateful indeed, but cold and calculating. He looks not at the huge sum that is counted out, but is eagerly waiting for the last coin to be told, and then exultingly cries out, "I am free," and goes his way. But there is another beside him, who watches with the intensest gaze every particle of the precious offering, because he knows what it has cost his father to procure it. In every piece he recognises the fruit of some privation undergone or some cruel humiliation endured. On one he reads his father's hunger, on another his abject toil. He remembers, as one portion of the store is brought out, that it was gained at the expense of calumny and hatred from friends; and when another is produced, that it was earned by the loss of those most dear to him. At every instalment he looks into his dear parent's countenance, and sees its manly sorrow and its varying emotions as these same recollections pass over his heart; and though the smile of love is on his lips, as the last golden drachma falls from his hand, at thought of what he has achieved for his children, even this is but more heartrending to the tender one of the two, and he almost loses all sense of his own liberation in the anguish inflicted by its price. He thinks not of himself, for love is not selfish. He goes not away singing, "I am ransomed, I am free,"

The Redemption

but he rushes to his father's feet, exclaiming, "Thou hast purchased me, I am thine!"

Such we believe to be the true difference between the Protestant and the Catholic mode of considering our Saviour's Passion. The one looks at it with an acquisitive eye, the other with the eye of love. To the Protestant it would have been the same if the simple act of death had been recorded, and its preliminary and accompanying sufferings had been suppressed. Not one emotion would have been lost to him, any more than, in his system, any advantage. What does the cruel agony in Gethsemani give him? It does not redeem him. What does he gain by the welts and gashes of the Roman scourges? They do not ransom him. What profits him the mock coronation and its insulting homage? It does not save him. And then, what can Mary and John do for him at the cross's foot? He declares he does not care for them. What matters it to him if the seamless garment be diced for or rent? It bears no deep mystery of faith to him. No; only let him secure that moment when the last breath passes over the Victim's lips, and it is enough, for it is the atonement.

Yet all that we have briefly enumerated was suffered for our sakes and recorded for our profit. Although the last piece completed our ransom, all that preceded it composed the sum. For surely our Divine Redeemer did naught in vain, nor aught superfluously. He was generous, indeed, but not wasteful. The Catholic, therefore, treasures up in his heart every smallest gift of love, where the smallest is immense. From this minuteness of Catholic perception springs a sense of reality, an approximation of feeling, which makes that not merely vivid, but present, which is separated from us by ages. On the other side is a mere hazy and vague generality, merging in a conception of the mind, instead of a real fact. And from this unreality easily springs up a lurking infidelity that saps the foundation of Christianity. The mind comes to think it unnecessary to trouble itself about details so long as the one apprehended truth is certain. "Christ died for us, no matter how," is the whole needful dogma of an evangelical mind.

But there is another view from which the Protestant eye habitually shrinks, but one which the Catholic boldly contemplates: it is that which completes the circle by joining the beginning and the end of the Gospel together, steadily uniting the Incarnation and the Death. The first of these great mysteries receives but little prominence in modern Protestantism, because this lacks the daring of faith to believe that He who died was the Word Incarnate; and it is this feebleness of belief that leads to that vagueness and generalisation in doctrine which we have described. Say to a Protestant, "God was struck in the face, God was scourged, God was crowned with thorns," and he dares not trust himself to look upon the doctrine. The eagle eye that can gaze upon the sun belongs not to his system; it is but a craven bird. He feels himself unable to grasp the awful mystery. If he deny the divinity of our Lord, his atonement is gone. But he dares not contemplate the dogma through its various applications, and he shrinks

The Redemption

from such phrases as we have given with a misgiving terror—they sound shocking and almost profane—and thus he is driven to suppress in his thoughts those detailed sequels of the Incarnation, and dwell upon only obscure perceptions of two doctrines, which he has not heart to firmly combine. Socinianism thus becomes the refuge of a vacillating attempt at faith.

The Catholic Church is a stranger to this wavering. She pursues one doctrine through all the mazes of the other, and combines the two inextricably. The Infant and the Victim are equal realities; nay, a unity, beginning in God, and in God ending; God throughout, in feebleness as in might, in obscurity and in brightness, in suffering and in glory. Nothing in Him is little, nothing unworthy: the fool's garment on Him is as sacred as the snow-bright vesture of Thabor; the scourge of cords in His uplifted hand is as mighty as the thunderbolt; the first lisping of His infant tongue as wisdomful as His sermon on the mount; a bruise upon His flesh as beautiful to angels' eyes, as adorable to man's soul, as His first smiling radiance shed upon His virgin mother. Thus does the Church believe, thus realise her faith. She alone understands the true doctrine of her Saviour's death as He Himself expounded it; for none other has learnt this lesson from His actions—that love is an essential condition of forgiveness as well as faith, and love it is that will linger over every detail of love. ("Essays," i. 640.)

THE HOLY NAME OF JESUS

When the prophets spoke of old, they contented themselves with the simple preface, "Thus saith the Lord of Hosts." Seldom was it a prologue to words of peace or comfort, but rather to menaces, and warnings, and woes. And yet they that heard them looked not on the meanness of the speakers, but considered the majesty of the God who sent them, and they rent their garments before them, and humbled their souls with fasting, and covered their bodies with sackcloth and ashes, and did penance.

And when the minister of the New Law stands before you saying, "Thus saith the Lord Jesus," shall there be less heed taken of his words because he speaketh in the Name of One who is gracious and full of mercy, and comes to communicate "thoughts of peace and not of affliction"? No. Did we come before you in our own names and speak to you "of justice and chastity, and of the judgment to come," you might, like Felix, send us back and say, "For this time go thy way." Did we as of ourselves preach to you the resurrection of the dead, ye might, as they of Athens, mock us to scorn. If, in fine, we presumed to command you to be continent and chaste, meek and forgiving, penitent and humble, to distribute your goods to the poor, or to afflict your bodies by fasting, you might, perhaps, resent our interference with the concerns of your lives, and chide us, not unreasonably, for exacting duties hard

The Holy Name

and disagreeable. But when we speak unto you these things by the power and in the Name of Him who is King of your souls and Master of your being—when we claim from you docility and obedience for Him whose livery we wear and whose heralds we are, refuse ye at your peril to receive our words and honour our commission.

But, good God, what do I say? Shall I misdoubt me of the power and virtue of the Name of Thy beloved Son—of that Name at the sound whereof "every knee shall bow, of things in heaven, of things on earth, and of things under the earth"? Shall I fear that the neck of man redeemed will be more inflexible than the knees of Thy vanquished enemies, and refuse to take up Thy gentle yoke? Shall I apprehend that the soul of the captive who hath been ransomed by the power of this Name, will adore and love it less than the angels, to whom it brought no tidings of salvation?

No, my brethren, from you we hope for better things. For know you not that we are engaged together in a holy warfare, for which we have no other strength than that of this holy Name—in "a wrestling, not against flesh and blood, but against principalities and powers, against the rulers of the world of this darkness, against the spirits of wickedness in high places"? And if you fight not under the Name of the God of Jacob, how shall you prevail? Anciently when armies rushed to battle, a name was put into the mouth of each, as a watchword and cheering symbol of the cause in which they struggled. Glad was the heart of the commander, and flushed with confidence of victory, when one unanimous shout of the name of their king or their patron rung clear and joyous from his men as they rushed to the onslaught, and drowned the feeble response of the rival host. And so in the Name of Jesus will we strike boldly at our spiritual foes; and bravely will we sound it forth together, to the terror and discomfiture of hell, and the overthrow of its might.

It is the Name of ten thousand battles and of countless victories. It echoed of old through the vaulted prisons of this city [Rome], and filled the heart of the confessor with courageous joy. It broke from the martyr's lips when nature could no longer brook silence, and was as "oil poured out" upon his wounds. It was the music of the anchorite when in the depths of the desert the powers of darkness broke loose upon him, and it dissipated his temptation. And so it shall be the signal of our combat, the watchword of our ranks. See, it is written in broad letters upon the standard we have followed, "Jesus of Nazareth, King of the Jews." Shame and confusion to the dastard who deserts his banner, or refuses to follow where that Name leads! Victory and glory to the chosen ones who shall confide in its power and combat in its cause! ("Sermons," i. 73.)

SWEETNESS OF THE NAME OF JESUS

REFLECT how the Name of Jesus is yet more excellent by reason of its sweetness than of its power. It is a heavenly Name, first pronounced on earth by an angel, and fit only for angels' lips to utter. Let us conceive

Sweetness of the Holy Name

how it sounded when first spoken on the eighth day, when, being asked what name should be given to the child, His blessed mother answered, "Jesus." With what affectionate reverence did she utter the word! With what devotion did she dwell upon a Name of which she alone and her holy spouse, St. Joseph, understood the full force. How others, perhaps, wondered that she found such a peculiar delight in pronouncing it! But to her how sweet a Name! It was, indeed, peculiarly *her* Name, that whereby she knew Him. She called Him not Lord, nor Master, nor Son of David, nor Christ; she knew Him by no other name than that of Jesus! He was her Jesus, her babe, her child, Jesus! How often was that word pronounced under the blessed roof of Nazareth, and how did it awaken thoughts tender and loving beyond all words! What to Mary was poverty, contempt, or any human grief, so long as she had that Name on her lips, and Him whom it designated on her virginal bosom or at her side? And is it not, then, a sweet Name to our hearts? Will it not bring to our souls the thought of our dear Saviour in His infancy, and enable us to dwell upon Him with delight, loving Him as our own Jesus, manifested as an infant for our sakes? And in this meditation of Him shall we not again and again, yea, unceasingly, repeat this pleasant and most sweet Name? Then after this let me go to Calvary, where I shall see One lovely beyond the children of men hanging upon a cruel cross, pierced with painful wounds, overwhelmed with sufferings, anguish, and abandonment (and I know that

He undergoes all this of His own accord for my sake); and let me ask any of the spectators, "Who is this? by what name is He known?" That bystander will tell me He is called "Jesus of Nazareth." Such is His only Name, in His Passion as in His infancy. All titles of honour disappear at these two seasons. The only Name whereby we can think of addressing Him is that of Jesus. Is it not, then, the Name that of all others I should love and most frequently utter? ("Meditations," p. 246.)

VISION OF JESUS

REFLECT how St. Paul ardently "desired to be dissolved and to be with Christ." This idea in him included the great joy of heaven. He had not conversed with or known Jesus upon earth, though in vision he had been allowed to see Him. He longed, therefore, to come into His presence, and enjoy that happiness which his fellow-apostles had once possessed; and that, too, in the character of a faithful servant rather than of a feeble disciple. Do not we feel some small portion of this earnest love when we contemplate the glories of the everlasting tabernacles? Oh, how delightful will it be, when for the first time we pass over the threshold of their gates, and dart forward our sight, far beyond the bright and beautiful array of saints and angels that surround us, and seek out Him who has been the great and Divine object of our gratitude and love during our probation here below! Undazzled by the glory that meets our eyes on every side, we shall fly forward on wings of eager haste to reach the Feet of Him who has been the desired of our souls, the fairest and most lovely of the children of men. He needs no badge or distinction whereby we may distinguish Him from His saints—no palm of victory, no white robe of triumph. All the riches which adorn that splendid City He has, like a generous conqueror, distributed among His companions and followers. Five jewels alone He has reserved for Himself, which neither the sun can equal in brightness nor the rose in hue. Each hand and foot bears one enchased in His sacred Flesh; and upon His side, close to His heart, He wears one larger and more brilliant—far more glorious, and to us dearer, than those decorations which monarchs have to bestow; for it has been won in deadly conflict against sin and death, fought for our salvation. Who will not recognise Jesus his Saviour by these tokens of mercy, by these characteristic badges of an unalterable love? And even without them, who knows Him not by the mildness of His heavenly countenance and the sweetness of His address? How shall we restrain ourselves, even for a moment, from falling down at His Feet and worshipping them? Have you not often, in your sorrowful repentance, envied the Magdalen, who was allowed there to pour forth her grief and express to Him her love? And have you not said to yourself, "Well, my turn too will one day come, and I shall, as truly as ever she did, prostrate myself there and indulge my grateful affection"? The time is now come; and here you may fulfil in reality the aspirations of your most loving meditations, when, after receiving Him at His holy altar, or while offering up His adorable Sacrifice, you wished you could truly see and embrace Him whom your soul loveth. There you will feast your eyes with the sight of that very Jesus whom you have so often thought of as an infant in the manger of Bethlehem, or as in the arms of Mary, the benign Child of a benign Mother. There you will see that very Body from which virtue went out on every side; those Feet that carried Him on His missions of mercy from city to city; those Hands that blessed you and bestowed good on you so freely; those Lips from which such heavenly wisdom flowed. But oh! above all, there you will see that Sacred Humanity which paid the dear price of your redemption, in stripes and buffets, in gashes and wounds; that Body which was given up to the striker and the executioner; those limbs that, nailed to the cross, held Him on that altar of agony whereon we were ransomed. Who shall describe or conceive the raptures of love and gratitude with which we shall thus, for the first time, give full scope to our best affections towards our Divine Redeemer? What a moment of ecstasy that will be; worth a life of penance and pain! Yet that moment is only the first of an eternity of equal delight.

Reflect how this joy and beatitude felt by the soul on its first meeting the Lord Jesus will not merely consist in looking upon Him, but will derive great increase from the interchange of loving sentiments which will ensue. For, first, He will open His lips to give an eternal welcome to His own soldier and follower who, having fought the good fight, has now come to claim his crown. "Well done, good and faithful servant: enter thou into the joy of thy Lord." Oh, what will a life or a world of wrongs and sorrows, of toils and mortification, appear, considered as the merit which has gained us these words, and the smile of approbation that accompanies them! How insignificant will the labour appear, put beside this reward! "Too little have I done for Thee, O blessed Saviour," we may imagine the soul to say; "too little have I suffered for Thee, to be greeted thus! Fain would I have come before Thee with better gifts in my hands, with something worthier of Thine acceptance than my imperfect desires to love and to serve Thee." And, having once found utterance, how much shall we not find to say to our Saviour? how many thanks to pour out, how many declarations of affection to renew? We shall never weary of repeating again and again how much we owe to Him and how much we love Him; and for all eternity our ears will not be satiated with hearing His reply, so merciful and so loving, to the protestations which we shall for all eternity continue to make. This will, in truth, be one of the principal joys of heaven, and one which even our imperfect minds can in some sort apprehend, to live eternally before the light of the countenance of Jesus our Lord! It will not be with us as with the three upon Mount Thabor: we shall not ask in vain to make tabernacles upon the mountain of God's glory, where we may see Him exalted, honoured, and glorified; nor will it be only a passing radiance we shall then be allowed to behold; but for ever and ever we shall dwell with Him in bliss, enjoying the sight of Him, placed where He ever should be, above angels and thrones and dominations, and surrounded by splendour and glory. Hence the Lamb slain from the foundation of the world is represented to us in the Word of God as forming the chief brightness of the heavenly Jerusalem: "And I saw no temple therein. For the Lord God Almighty is the temple thereof, and the Lamb. And the city hath no need of the sun nor of the moon to shine in it. For the glory of God hath enlightened it, and the Lamb is the lamp thereof" (Rev. xxi. 22, 23). ("Meditations," p. 500.)

OUR LADY, A WITNESS

LET us then imagine the "glorious choir" of these holy men about to spread over the whole earth to preach the Gospel, and collecting together the great facts which they must proclaim as the basis of their doctrine, and to which they must bear witness, even by the shedding of their blood. There is as yet no written word of the New Law, and this meeting is therefore the very first source of universal teaching. Each one comes to pour into the common fountain his jealously guarded store, thence to well forth, and flow unfailingly, as the stream of tradition through the Church—the life-bearing river of the earthly paradise. Some bring less and some more; while those who have been born after-time into the faith, receive almost with jealousy what into their eager ears, by the more favoured ones, is poured. John and his brother, and Peter, attest the anticipation of celestial glory on Thabor. The first of these alone can recount, while others hang down their heads and blush, what took place on Calvary and on its rood; and the last bears witness against himself of his triple denial in the high priest's hall. Nicodemus has a hidden treasure which he brings out in the mysterious conference that he held with Jesus; and Magdalen may be the only one to tell the history of her forgiveness. But when each one has contributed his all, miracles, and parables, and gracious words, and wisest discourse, and splendid acts, they have but furnished materials for a history of three years of a life of three-and-thirty. Where do the remaining thirty lie hidden? Who holds their annals? Who is the rich treasurer of that golden heap of blessed words and acts divine? One, only one. Let her be entreated to enrich the world by participation of her recondite knowledge. She comes to pour, into the bright waters that flow from the apostolic fount, the virginal cruse which, queen of wise virgins, she treasures in her bosom. Yea truly, and the lamp which *it* feeds cannot be extinguished. A few drops, indeed, only will she give, for by those thirty years it may be said that she mainly was intended to profit; they were *her* school of perfection. But every single drop is most precious—is as a peerless and priceless pearl. "Oleum effusum nomen tuum." The very Name of *Jesus*, that Name of blessing and salvation, she makes known as a divine revelation to her, and with it all the promises of what He should under it accomplish, and the proclamation of what by it He was declared. While apostles surrounded Him to witness His wonderful works, while multitudes pressed in admiration to listen to Him, she hung at times on the skirt of the crowd, or stood outside the door, the solicitous, because loving, mother. But the maternal heart naturally flies back to the days of infancy, which are there laid up in vivid recollection. The woman will most gladly remember the hour of her purest joy, when she rejoiced that a man was born into the world. What, then, if He was the "Wonderful, God the Mighty." And such are the precious and most soothing manifestations which Mary will make for the comfort of devout souls, even to the end of the world. She will lay the very groundwork of the evangelical narrative. Whatever gratitude the Church bears towards the collectors and preservers of our first sacred records, is due in signal manner to her. Whatever of credibility, authority, and truthfulness is warranted by Christian belief to the witnesses of what constitutes the basis of faith, must be peculiarly extended to her. Nor may we doubt the justness of her title in the Church—*Regina Apostolorum*.

This, our obligation, is further enhanced by a consideration to which we have alluded, and which has often struck us in reflecting on a passage in the Gospel. May we be allowed to add, that its beauty, as well as its importance, seems to us to have been much overlooked. From Matt. i. 18-24, it is clear that the angel's visit to the Blessed Virgin was by her completely concealed. This would have seemed almost impossible. It was a subject for the purest yet intensest joy; for an exultation of spirit that would beam forth from every feature, would quiver on the lips, betray itself by involuntary gestures of bliss. Then, to be so exalted and not show consciousness of it; to be raised above every attainable dignity; to find oneself become the theme of prophecy, the fulfilment of types, the term of the Old Law, the dawn of the new day, the mother of the world's life—in one word, the Mother of God—and not by look or word hint it; to be as calm, as simple, as natural the next time she spoke with Joseph as if nothing had occurred,—this gives us a truer estimate of the beauty and perfection of her character than almost anything else that is on record. And, further, that naturally foreseeing or knowing, as time went on, Joseph's tormenting perplexity, she should have preferred to bear its pain—the most grievous possible to her pure and affectionate heart—to a manifestation of her lofty privileges and heavenly maternity, proves both a humility without parallel, and a confidence in God's providence worthy of it. But now, is it rash to say, that if even such strong motives as were here presented did not suffice to overcome her humble modesty, and induce her to manifest her hidden glory, there must have been a reason stronger still to influence her when afterwards she gave minute details of Gabriel's interview and the circumstances of the Divine Incarnation? And this will be supplied by the same power which impelled St. John, in extreme old age, to record his remembrances of our Lord's discourses; the Holy Spirit's prompting to a work important for our instruction, and so for our salvation. ("Essays," i. 596.)

THE ANNUNCIATION

THERE is no mystery, perhaps, in which grace, not merely in its inward and highest nature, but in its exterior and corporeal form, or in its oral expression, is more admirably and amiably set forth. Yea, and running through all its compound forms of speech, be it gracefulness or graciousness, it is all there. Where has art found a richer vein, a lovelier theme, a fairer rivalry between grace terrestrial and grace celestial, than in the meeting of Mary and Gabriel? From the first dawn of pictorial art it has been seized upon as one which lent to the pencil the fittest subject for graceful representation. Around the angel could be thrown all the charms of a heavenly nature clothed in the human form, a benign yet majestic countenance, a commanding but still a reverential mien, ease and dignity not unmixed with admiration and respect. For in the ancient type of this sacred mystery we see not a fantastic shape, half-clothed in flying drapery, making a descent on a rolling cloud, or perched on it in an academic attitude, and waving the hand with significant gesture as if about to make a set speech ; but the idea that the angel was in this, his errand, one of "God's ministers" ("Qui facit ministros suos ignem urentem"), suggests

The Annunciation

at once that he should appear as such are wont to be clothed on earth. Accordingly, he is almost unfailingly represented in ecclesiastical array, never in that which belongs to the celebration of the most sacred rite, but either in the sacerdotal cope or the diaconal dalmatic. . . .

We may easily conceive the painter, who felt his subject as the old masters did, baffled by what remains. Modern notions would lead us to think more about the angel, and less of the angel's queen. How beautifully does the tradition respecting the picture of the Annunciation in Florence contrast with this feeling. The artist had completed the rest of his task, had finished his archangel's head with exquisite feeling, had given to it grace and beauty more than human, had exhausted all his powers, and despaired of giving expression to his conception of the Holy Virgin, whom the angel was saluting. He knew that he must surpass all that he had done, and produce a countenance more radiant with celestial charms than even he had given to the angelic messenger. In vain he tried to reach the type of grace which he had framed in his imagination; every effort seemed more abortive, till in sheer hopelessness he gave up the task, and fell, through weariness of mind, into a slumber. But when he awoke, to his amazement and delight, he found the figure painted, with such dignity and beauty, and in so wonderful a manner, and in so short a time, that no human hand could have achieved it. Hence it came and has continued to be considered as an angel's work. Now, let the reader think what he pleases respecting this legend, it will remain a faithful record of an artist's feelings at a time when art was the handmaid of religion; it will show how pure, how sublime, was the conception which his mind could form of that virtue which the angelic salutation set forth, "Hail! full of Grace! the Lord is with thee!" How transcending, not merely earthly, but heavenly beauty in its outward manifestation! Nor was the difficulty only there. The heathen artist had an easy mode of raising his hero or his goddess above humanity, by giving the features an unimpassioned beauty which seemed incapable of interest in sublunary concerns. But the expression of countenance which the scene under our consideration required, was very different. To stamp upon the face and attitude the maidenly bashfulness which startles, without loss of dignity, at the unwonted approach of a visitor; the humility which shrinks, without baseness and cowardice, from the proffered dignity; the radiant joy which receives, without ruffling the serenity of soul, the glad announcement of salvation; to represent a woman superior to an angel, not merely in body, but in soul, unconsciously filled with the richest outpourings of Divine blessing, the handmaid in mind, in dignity the queen, might well have seemed superior to the power of art, even when ennobled by the highest motives and supported by the holiest inspirations. Who that has contemplated this subject as represented by the Blessed John of Fiesoli, so justly called "the Angelic," has not felt that it requires a saintly mind to enter into the

The Annunciation

depths of artistic as well as theological mystery involved in this theme?

The same feeling which suggested the propriety of giving every superiority in it to her in whom "the mystery" was wrought, in place, in character, and in expression, naturally inspired the respective attitudes of the figures; the angel often kneeling as he delivers his message, while the Blessed Virgin is indifferently either seated or standing, or kneeling in prayer. Protestant minds are sometimes shocked at this relative position; but a Catholic heart seizes its propriety at once. Before the angel's errand is completed, she whom he addresses has become the dwelling of the Incarnate *Word*, consubstantial to the *Father* and true *God*. Him there enshrined he must adore, independent of her superior dignity, well worthy of such reverent salutation. While all that meets the eye in this scene is graceful in the extreme, every other sense seems no less greeted with its corresponding gratification. The flowering lily, which almost invariably springs from an elegant vase in the modest chamber, seems to diffuse a pure fragrance through it, as well as to symbolise the virginal purity of the atmosphere we breathe; and the scroll which waves in the angel's hand, guides the ear to the sounds that proceed from his lips, the gracious salutation of her "full of Grace." ("Essays," i. 516.)

MARY, ALL-MOTHER

IT is, indeed, remarkable, my brethren, how completely that motherhood of the Blessed Virgin, which the woman in my text so loudly blessed, has been delineated in the Gospel. Almost all the other persons connected with our Saviour's history undergo extraordinary changes. John the Baptist, from the solitary anchorite in the wilderness, becomes the herald of the Messias, the baptizer of Israel, the reprover of Pharisees and even of kings. Magdalen first appears as the woman tenanted by evil spirits, and is soon changed into an ardent follower and dauntless servant of Jesus. The apostles begin as fishermen and publicans, to be transformed into workers of signs and miracles, even before their Master's Passion. But Mary never appears in any character but that of a mother, solicitous and suffering only for her Son. She is first seen receiving the heavenly messenger, and, according to his promise, conceiving and bearing the Eternal Word made flesh for man's redemption; and soon becomes an object of persecution to His enemies, so as to be compelled to abandon her native land. Amidst the flattering and glorious scenes that surround her at His birth, we find it simply recorded of her by St. Luke, that "Mary kept all these words, pondering them in her heart." After this did God reveal to her, through holy Simeon, the piercing grief which, as a sword, should pass through her soul. We meet her not again until twelve years later, the solicitous

Mary, All-Mother

mother wandering about the streets of Jerusalem, seeking her lost Son, sorrowing. And when she has found Him, and understands not perfectly the deep, mysterious answer that He makes her, we have the same description of her conduct, which in one stroke sketches her mild, unobtrusive character, that "His Mother kept all these things in her heart." After this we have total silence in her regard, during eighteen years of a life the most blessed which can be conceived upon earth, under the same roof with the Son of God; till she comes forward once more to initiate Him into His public life by inducing Him to work His first miracle at Cana. Through the three years of His wonderful public ministry, while all Judea rung with His praises, while crowds pressed round Him to be healed, while priests, and Pharisees, and doctors of the law listened with respect to His doctrines, and men would have set the royal crown upon His head, she takes no part in His triumphs and His fame, and only once approaches Him, in tender solicitude, to call Him from the house where He was surrounded by the multitude.

But so soon as we come to the last perilous trial, when disciples have fled, and apostles have denied Him; when friends have abandoned Him, and relations are ashamed of kindred with Him; when He is surrounded by a ruffianly mob, whose brutality seems equal to any outrage; when He is hedged round by the cruel array of soldiers and executioners—*then* may she, the mild, retired maid of Nazareth, but still the mother, be seen pressing through every obstacle to share in His sufferings, and catch His dying breath.

This, then, is the only character in which it is meant that we should know her, as the Mother of Jesus. And are not *we* the brethren of Jesus? Did not He Himself assure us so much; did not St. Paul, did not St. John, repeat the same consoling doctrine? And to us, my brethren, who believe that every tie which connected us with Him on earth is not broken, but strengthened in heaven; who believe that a holy union does exist between those who upon earth are fighting for their crown and those who in heaven have received it already; who believe that every claim which we can make to the interest and intercession of those who have reached the goal is gladly acknowledged and made good—to us who so believe, yea, and who so feel, this is not matter of vain boast or empty parade. For, if such is our faith, this title which we have received has gained a mother for us in heaven, who will often plead in our behalf. ("Sermons," i. 317.)

OUR LADY AT THE CROSS.

THERE was one heart in which all that was to come was faithfully treasured—hers who had listened to the wonderful and mysterious words of the venerable old man that told her, in the days of her motherly happiness, that the sword of affliction would pierce her heart. Oh! she had often, no doubt, conversed on the painful topic with her Divine Son. She knew too well what was the course He had to run. She knew wherefore He had come into the world, and how every breath of His was an act of obedience to the will of God. She knew well that He had bitter food, indeed, to take, which was not prepared for Him by her hands. She had lived, by anticipation, in the suffering which naturally resulted from this knowledge communicated to her; and she well knew the time was come when, at the last passover with His disciples, He was about to cast aside this world, and enter into the kingdom of His Father. Then did she know that another cup, besides that of His paschal feast, was to be placed in His hands, to be drained by Him to the dregs. She knew that well—so well that it is hardly necessary even to have recourse to the pious tradition that she saw in a vision what passed in the garden of Gethsemani. But certain it is that the morning dawn saw her hasten to her Son, in order to carry out that conformity which she had preserved with the will of God during the whole of her life; that conformity which had been so great that her Son, in obedience to her will, anticipated the time for the performance of His first miracle. It was right that this conformity should at length be transmuted into a perfect unity, incapable of the slightest separation; and that could only be done, as it was accomplished, on Calvary, at the foot of the cross.

My dear brethren, why was Mary there? That simple question in its answer solves a great problem. Why was Mary there? It was no part of the sentence on Jesus, as if to increase or to enhance the bitterness of His death, that His Mother should stand by; and it never was commanded in any nation, however barbarous, that the mother should be at the scaffold when her son expiated what was, rightly or wrongly, imputed to him as his guilt. It was not compulsory on Mary to be at Calvary; she was not driven there, nor was it usual in her to seek publicity. She followed Him, indeed, through all His mission in Judea; but she used to stand without, and the people who surrounded Him would say, "Your mother and brethren are outside." She did not claim the privileges of her rank to be close to Him when He was disputing with the Pharisees or instructing multitudes. When He went into a house to perform His miracles, or to a mountain to be transfigured, He took Peter, James, and John. We read not that Mary presumed to follow Him, and exult in the magnificent exercise of His Divine power, or the manifestation of His heavenly glory. No, she followed at a distance; she kept near Jesus, watching over Him. But she knew that it was not her hour; that it was not yet the time when her parental duty was to be associated with her parental rights. She had lived the whole of her life in retirement, first in the Temple, then in the cottage at Nazareth. And she, who naturally shrunk from the assemblies of men, came forth at the time most trying to her feelings, to be present at the execution, the brutal execution, of her Son, in that form of suffering which was most revolting, and most fiercely rending of her tender heart. Mary came forth to witness the death—of whom? Of her only beloved

Devotion to Mary

Son, of her only child, whom she remembered once an infant in her arms. She will draw nigh to see those hands cruelly pierced which she had so often pressed to her lips; she will stand by to see that noble, that Divine countenance — the first look from whose eyes beamed upon her, the first smile of whose lips shone upon her heart—bedewed with blood, streaming from the thorny crown; to see Him still bearing the marks of having been beaten, and buffeted, and defiled by spittle, and mocked by His persecutors. She came to seek Him at the hour of this suffering. And why? Because the heart of the Mother must be near that of the Son, in order that they may be both struck together, and so endure most perfect union of suffering, that she may be said truly to co-operate in sympathy with the Divine work of salvation. ("Sermons," i. 339.)

DEVOTION TO THE BLESSED VIRGIN

WHATEVER, therefore, Catholics may say or do in regard to our Blessed Lady, it is nothing more than a simple giving of reality to belief in her motherhood; nor is it easy to see, on what principle bars or limits can be put to stop the flow of those feelings towards her which this view necessarily sets in motion. We must either not love her at all, or we must try to love her as her Son did and does, for His virtues are to be our measure. Now, who can ever reach the affection of such a Son towards such a Mother? Again, she must either have no influence at all, or it must be boundless.

If she have a throne anywhere, it *must* be at her Son's right hand; and if she be allowed to open her mouth, the Son cannot "turn away her face."

In this simple view we have at once the key to all the affectionateness and all the confidence which devout Catholics entertain for her. We have, moreover, the explanation of another general rule of a devout life—that the more holy a person is, the more warm and tender will his feelings be towards her. Perfection consists in the imitation of our Lord's virtues; the closer the imitation, the greater the perfection. As His love for His mother was doubtless a virtue, and as we are bound to love all that He loved, the nearer we come to Him in this, the more we advance towards His perfection. And as all growth in perfection is general, —that is, cannot be in one point and not in another— so must this virtue increase along with every other.

We will only add a few words more, words which perhaps some Catholic experience can alone make intelligible. The most effectual antidote to the seductions of sense is perhaps the spiritualising of their natural tendencies. He who is brought to hunger after and to labour for spiritual food, cares little for the meat that perisheth. They who covet treasures in heaven soon learn "perituras calcare divitias."[1] And nothing will more purify the affections of the soul, and make them proof against the taint of a corrupt and sinful nature, than the fixing of them early upon objects which, on the one hand, brook no association with frail and perishable

[1] "To trample underfoot perishable riches."

beauty, and yet, on the other, can feed, and fill, and absorb all the power of love. Blessed indeed is the heart of him "qui pascitur inter lilia"![1] Now, there is no other object so able to effect this as the affection which Catholic devotion — that is, the realisation of Catholic faith — inspires for our Redeemer's virgin-mother. It fills the mind with an image of loveliness so pure, so chaste, so ethereal, so transcending all earthly combinations of the beautiful, that all else seems but gross and paltry. For it is the beauty of holiness that it reflects upon the soul, in which there is naught of worldly levity or of remorseful pensiveness, no such mere comeliness as painters or poets can express; but there is that grave and calm sweetness which tells of humility, and meekness and modesty, and tender-heartedness and love for all, mingled with that unspeakable majesty and sin-reproving earnestness which become the mother of a God-made man. It is an image which ever comes before the soul, not surrounded with the alluring accompaniments of worldly forms, but enshrined in a soft atmosphere of light celestial, warm and glowing, but too holy to be nearly approached. No carved and gilded frame sets off its fairness; but cherubs smiling from golden clouds, and gazing in wonder at the miracles of grace in which heaven and earth first met, surround and adorn it. And then, to make good her title of mother, upon her bosom rests that wondrous babe, with arms expanded, and wide-open eyes, as though to show that

[1] " Who feedeth among the lilies."

every dart of holy affection from our souls must pierce both hearts, and finds not its way to hers except through His. Fill, we say unhesitatingly, the youthful imagination betimes with the chaste love of beauty such as this, and he that bears it will walk through life in safety, treading on the asp and the basilisk of a treacherous and a poison-breathing world. It will prove a charm to foil every spell of this brutalising land of Circe. (*Dublin Review*, January 1847. "Essays," ii. 427.)

OUR LADY'S DOWRY

IN Catholic countries you might see the poor and afflicted crowding round some altar where their pious confidence, or experience of past favours, leads them to hope that their prayers will best be heard through the intercession of our dear Lady; and you would mark their countenances glowing, and their eyes raised upwards, and perhaps streaming with tears; and would be struck with the heavings of their bosoms, and the eager whisperings of their prayer, and the deep sobs that escape them. Then, perhaps, some stranger who knew them not would scornfully remark to you, as Heli did concerning Anna, that those poor creatures are intoxicated with a lying spirit of superstition, or even idolatry. But God hath looked into their simple hearts and judged far otherwise. Even if that confidence which leads them to a particular spot be unfounded, it has drawn from them such deep-breathed sighs of devotion as are elsewhere scarcely to be seen; it has, for a time at least, driven the world and its follies from their hearts, annihilated all thoughts of earth within their souls, and raised them upon wings of love towards heaven, into the company of saints who see God, there to make interest with her who is best by Him beloved.

Oh that the time had come when a similar expression of our devout feelings towards her should publicly be made, and all should unite to show her that honour, that reverence and love which she deserves from all Christians, and which so long have been denied her amongst us! There was a time when England was second to no other country upon earth in the discharge of this duty; and it will be only part of the restoration of our good and glorious days of old, to revive to the utmost this part of ancient piety. ("Sermons, i. 323.)

HONOUR DUE TO SAINTS

REFLECT how agreeable it must be to God to witness this interchange of good offices between His children upon earth and those who reign with Him in heaven. He has destined us, as we humbly hope, to be one day their happy companions and friends in the joys of His kingdom; and He is well pleased to see us, during our time of preparation, on terms of friendly and brotherly intercourse with them. He is glad to see us find pleasure in conversing with them, and paying them that honour which their dignity merits. King Assuerus commanded that the person whom the king desired to honour should be presented to the public homage of the entire city, and led about with a state little inferior to his own. So, having Himself honoured His saints, Almighty God wills them likewise to be honoured by His servants on earth, openly and magnificently. He knows, moreover, that in this case the honour flows on to Himself. For what do we bless and praise in the saints, and what causes us to feel devotion towards them, but the splendid gifts and prerogatives wherewith God has crowned them, and which, after all, are only the fruits of His graces and mercies? " Deus in nobis sua dona coronat." When we call upon His apostles to intercede for us, why do we so but because it pleased Him to choose them from among men to be the instruments of His extraordinary favours and blessings? And do we not honour His choice and give glory to Him, when in consequence of this His partiality to them we offer up to them extraordinary homage, and address them with peculiar fervour? If our devotion is particularly excited towards the martyrs, it is because we admire their constancy in the midst of torments endured for God, and therein the power of grace which triumphed over the weakness of nature. So is it when our feelings of reverence and devout affection are moved to address the virgins whose chastity made them the spouses of the Lamb. So far from resenting such feelings, He must be pleased with the confidence we place in His saints, as resulting from our belief in the love He bears them and the readiness with which He rewards His servants. ("Meditations," p. 177.)

OUR GOOD ANGEL

REFLECT what should be our feelings towards that pure and loving spirit himself whom God has deputed to have charge over us. Our ancestors, happy in their choice of words to express religious and devout ideas, have summed up these pious feelings in one word: this our keeper is called, in simple and affectionate terms, "our good angel." It is not difficult to say how we should regard one who deserves to be thus called. The epithet signifies that his errand to us is one entirely of kindness and friendship, and that as he is so engaged we cannot but love and esteem him. We do not know him as yet, but one day we shall. And we should anxiously long for this pleasure. Imagine a poor family reduced to grievous distress, in constant want of food and medicine, but most generously relieved by an unknown benefactor. When they know not how to hold on any longer, a seasonable succour is sure to be received from him; when sickness attacks them, the needful remedies are supplied as by his viewless hand. Oh, how often they talk of this their unseen friend, and wish they could see him, and know him, and thank him face to face! And how they paint him to their imagination as kind and amiable in countenance, speech, and behaviour! Just so should we feel towards this good angel; only we have the full certainty that one day we shall see him, and that we shall surely find him as lovely and beautiful as our poor imagination can in any way represent. If thus we love him, we shall no less reverence him. For he is truly a *good* angel; not merely kind to us, but holy and venerable; a friend of God, adorned with the choicest and sublimest gifts of heaven, full of excellences, and admitted into God's own counsels. He is raised immeasurably above us; so that, however we may love him, a certain degree of awe and respect should mingle in our affection. In truth, this should be of the nature of an affectionate admiration, knowing that so sublime a being, and so perfect, condescends to minister to us and bear us up in his hands. This reverential feeling will greatly strengthen the restraining influence which his presence will exercise upon our roving or dangerous thoughts. Nor will our confidence be less than any other feeling towards one so good. For, on the one hand, he must be good to us; and, on the other, his goodness makes God to love him, and willingly to hear him. He is powerful, and able to overcome our foes; for he has once proved himself valiant and victorious against these, under the guidance of the blessed Michael, his prince. The first time that we shall see this blessed spirit will be the instant after death, when he will stand beside us at the tribunal of Christ. How miserable would it then be to see him turn away his face from us in sorrow, and reject our attempts, if we have forgotten him in life, to find refuge under the shadow of his wings. Let us make him now our friend, that so he may then take us by the hand and present us to his Lord and ours as good and faithful servants. ("Meditations," p. 450.)

PART III
MORAL

SIN AGAINST THE JUDGE

YOU have God at your side, and against that very God do you sin. Can insult go farther, can provocation be more malignant, can rebellion be more atrocious? Why, even the Jews, unfeeling and audacious as they were, on that last dreadful night of our Blessed Saviour's Passion, blindfolded Him at least before they struck Him on the face and loaded Him with their insults; you are more audacious and more unfeeling still, for you outrage Him, and insult and mock His sufferings, while you know that He is steadfastly noting all that you do, not as He did then, that He might pray for their forgiveness on the cross, because they knew not what they did, but that He may repay—avenge them when your time shall come. For, my brethren, if even the view I have taken of the presence of God be not sufficiently strong to check you and preserve you from transgression in the moment of temptation, there is another still more awful and appalling.

"What seest thou?" asked the Almighty of Jeremias; and he said, "I see a rod watching." Then said the Lord unto him, "Thou hast seen well, for I will watch over My word to perform it" (Jer. i. 11, 12). Such is His presence to sinners, as a waking and watching rod, to punish their faults, and hastening to perform the threat which it holds out; for they presume to insult Him, not only as He stands beside them, but even at the very moment when He is sitting in judgment over culprits like themselves who have outraged Him in the same manner. Raise up your eyes to heaven, O sinner, when on the brink of offending the majesty of your Creator, and you will see that God whom you are going to insult, while His all-searching eye beams bright and clear upon you, and you will see Him at that very moment sitting upon His judgment-seat to execute justice and judgment, each in His proper time, upon all the sinners of the earth. You will see at every instant criminals like yourself, or even less guilty, whom the eye of the Judge has long been following in their course of iniquity, dragged before His bar and receive their sentence of condemnation for the very sin which you are going to commit. See the minister of vengeance only waiting for His consent to snatch up the next victim who has completed his career; the accusers of the human race pointing, perhaps, to yourself as one just going to complete the prescribed number of crimes through which the Almighty's patience has to endure. See the balance in which your offences are weighed against the graces God had allotted for you; see how fearfully its beam already trembles and hesitates which way to incline—perhaps it is only mercy which kindly supports for a few instants longer your weight of guilt—the very act you are going to commit may press down the scale of condemnation and determine unalterably

Sin against the Judge

your lot of woe. It is at the bar of a tribunal thus arraigned, it is in the presence of a Judge thus seated, that you proceed to commit your crime.

It is with an insulting defiance that you mock this Lord of all things, in the presence of the myriads of ministering spirits who surround Him on His throne, burning with zeal for His honour and glory; in the presence of those accusers who appeal to the justice of the Judge, whether so crying an insult deserves not instant award of punishment. And if He but gives the signal, how many instruments of vengeance obey His rod, and render your escape impossible. The sword of the Lord will leap from its scabbard when it has to drink the blood of those who have dared to rebel against Him. Disease in every variety, from the awful stroke of God which fells the sinner, root and branch, in all the verdure and beauty of his youth, and in all the ripeness and exuberance of his crimes, down to the lingering illness which sucks out his health, and parches up the blood in his veins—these are but agents at His command, to execute His mandates and drag the culprit to His tribunal. The lightning of heaven would rejoice to strike the head that has been raised to insult its Maker to His face; the sea, if he flies to it, like Jonas from the face of the Lord, would raise its storms and billows against him; the very earth, if He command it, would gladly open and swallow him, like Core, Dathan, and Abiron. And is it then aught but madness and frenzy to commit your crime in the very presence of that tribunal which will one day judge it, and which may, at the very moment of its commission, pronounce its sentence as it daily does on thousands, execute it without appeal or reprieve, and plunge you for ever in a dungeon of unspeakable torments and woe? Does impunity through so much previous crime render you callous and fearless of such a visitation? Oh, remember that every additional step in your guilty ways renders it, on the contrary, more probable, more near, more certain; for every addition to the catalogue of your crimes is carefully registered, the few blank leaves which remain will be soon filled, your turn will then arrive, and your fate may be quoted to future sinners as a warning example that God's justice does not slumber, but sooner or later avenges the insults directed thus outrageously against it. ("Sermons," iii. 153.)

WHAT THE SINNER RENOUNCES

Oh that I had words, my brethren, to describe or bring down to your comprehension the treasures of grace and the inheritance of glory which we renounce by sin! A soul just regenerated by baptism, upon which its Creator, looking down with complacency, sees His image and likeness stamped fresh, and as yet unsoiled; in which the Son beholds the fruits of His redemption full and ripe, without the smallest blight or taint; in which the Holy Spirit dwells in the plenitude of grace and divine favour—is a thing almost too precious for this world of iniquity to be allowed to hold. It deserves a sanctuary apart, in which to be enshrined from the approach of the profane and from the very look of the wicked. It should be served, as in truth it is, not by an earthly priesthood, but by the ministry of angels. For it is an ark of divine covenant, far more beautiful to His eyes, far more valuable in His estimation, than the one which Moses made of setim-wood and gold. That soul is the bride of the Lamb, decked out with a magnificence of precious gifts becoming her rank. She is the beloved, the darling child of the Most High, and as such entitled to an inheritance in His kingdom, rich beyond calculation, vast beyond measure, enduring beyond all computation of time. God having repaired in it, as far as possible, the mischiefs of original transgression, is willing and intends to bestow upon it every good thing it can require to make it happy. As its period of probation here below advances, it receives fresh instalments of its rich inheritance in the knowledge of God, in His love, in the use of His sacraments, so that nothing remains that He can do for it, till the time shall come to accomplish its happiness by taking it into His eternal rest.

Now all these privileges, blessings, and rights, present and future, the lover of iniquity deliberately casts away. I say deliberately. Not that he calculates in the heat of his passion, but still it is with full previous consciousness of their worth and of his interest in them. He is as Esau, who, when fatigued and hungry, in exchange for a mess of pottage, renounced his birthright with the glorious inheritance of promises made to his fathers. He is like the prodigal who gives up the advantages and joys of his father's house for the chance of pleasure in the riots of a distant land. Each was borne away by the impulse of passion, but each lost, notwithstanding, the blessings which he before enjoyed.

When Adam transgressed, it was at least against the chance of an improved condition that he threw his stakes. He entertained hopes of a sublimer happiness by being as a god, knowing good and evil. There was a bold presumption in the cast, but there was no consciousness that he was flinging himself into the arms of misery. He knew not well what death might be; he had not seen it. He was not aware that there was another earth beyond the bounds of Eden, which produced thorns and briars, into which he could be banished. But we, when we offend God and resign His gifts, understand to the full the terms of our bargain. We know too well what that death is which becomes our due; we know well what the place will be to which we shall be consigned when driven from this miserable substitute for our lost Paradise.

See, then, this wretched soul, a few moments ago so comely, clothed in righteousness, laden with spiritual gifts, endowed with most abundant graces, in dignity little less than the angels, and crowned with glory and honour, able to hold up its head before God, and be caressed by Him as a child entitled to look up to the heavens in all their splendour and say, " Ye are mine," —see it, by one spontaneous act, disfigured and defaced, as though it had been plunged from that moment into an ocean of destructive evil, and drawn thence, base and poor, naked, trembling and hiding itself at the voice of

What the Sinner Renounces 139

God, degraded to a lower condition than that of things devoid of reason, without power of defence, without a plea of mercy, without a title of grace, stripped of the very name of God's child, divorced for ever from His love, to wander like Cain from before His face, without a home or an inheritance! But yet, not without some inheritance.

He has exchanged, he has not barely renounced, what he enjoyed. He has acquired new possessions, new titles, new rights. He is now "a child of wrath," instead of being, as before, a child of grace. If before, he had the abundant good things of his father's house, he has now the husks of swine in his chosen master's bondage. If he had a place prepared for him in heaven, a throne of light and glory, "Topheth is now prepared for him, prepared by the king, deep and wide. The nourishment thereof is fire and much wood: the breath of the Lord, as a torrent of brimstone, kindling it" (Isa. xxx. 33). And now let me ask you, did the robbers who met the wayfarer between Jerusalem and Jericho, robbed him of all his goods, stripped him of his fair apparel, and disfigured and disabled him with wounds, leaving him half dead—did they act towards him with a hatred less deadly than we have shown to our souls every time we have so plundered and reduced them to utter wretchedness by sin? Could any other being give proofs of bitterer hatred to them than we ourselves do thus display? ("Sermons," ii. 203.)

STATE OF HABITUAL SINNER

As our bodies, even when full of health and vigour, have lurking in their very constitutions the germs of disease, ready to break out at every fitting opportunity, and take, according to this, a varied form; so is the soul the seat of every evil propensity, hidden, indeed, so long as the living power of grace keeps them in subjection. But if, even when controlled by its superior strength, they are as chained enemies that rebel and ever strive to acquire mastery and dominion, what must they be when sin has expelled from the soul the grace and power of God? Their irons are now broken, and eager to make up for the time they have been kept in bondage—finding, too, the soul an unprotected prey at their mercy—they run riot within it, spreading everywhere waste and devastation. Every irregular desire is lord of the moment, till chased by some wickeder and baser usurper. The soul, which before used to govern, is now the slave under the command of these thousand tyrants. And if this state of abandonment to the passions be suffered to strengthen into habitual vice, every faculty, every power of man becomes tainted with its respective evil. The heart, once pure and simple, changes to corrupt and designing, full of evil desires, and of devices to gratify them; the imagination is abandoned to every train of foolish or wicked thoughts which happen to enter it; the reason becomes perverted, to the disregard of the awfullest truths, and the belief of the vainest delusions; the will gradually loses its desire of good, till it actively joins in the pursuit of what is bad; and only one faculty in the entire man, memory, remains faithful to the trust of its great Giver, and faithfully, too faithfully, treasures up the recollections of the past. Thus does the poor victim, first plundered of all its rich possessions and glorious inheritances, stripped of God's favour and friendship, with the deadly knife that has inflicted a mortal blow standing in its heart, stagger on a few more paces in its blind career, and then falls heavily to rise no more. Yes, that sin, so brief in its duration, so unsatisfactory in its expected results, was yet a stroke of death, begun here indeed, but to be completed by a hand of juster power; for the Word of God has assured us, that after this first, the sinner shall suffer a second and an eternal death.

In what a strange and most unnatural state must the soul be while placed between these two events, dead in truth before God, but waiting another and a final destination! It would be a frightful and a hideous spectacle, were one who had been laid in his shroud to return to the functions of life, yet so that he should ever bear about him the traces of his dissolution: to see his glazed, unmoving eye, that never sparkles with tidings of joy, nor moistens at the deepest distress, and features devoid of passion or expression, that relax not into a smile of pleasure; to touch the hand ever damp and icy, and find the heart motionless and cold; and yet, to behold this living death partake in the business and pastimes of men, and speak their flattering speeches, and talk of its feelings—oh! how it would poison every joy in which it mingled, and how men would shrink and shroud themselves from the hateful apparition! Not less odious, unnatural, and disgusting to those beings that can behold the spiritual part of man, must that soul appear which is truly dead to God as the corpse in the grave is to man, yet animates a human frame, and drives it through the functions of its worldly life, and discharges the other offices of a rational being. A soul without an impulse of grace, without a throb of love for God, without a noble emotion, without an aspiration to heaven, without a virtuous desire, yet holding place among living men, is an animated corpse, a hideous spectre haunting the abodes of men. ("Sermons," ii. 209.)

SOUL MURDER

REFLECT how, if the murder of the body be so horrible a crime in the eyes of men, the murder of a soul must be infinitely greater in the eyes of God. The body, at best, is created frail and perishable; there is no violation of the law of its nature when it dies, and it is only a point of time and circumstances if it be destroyed by violence somewhat before the end of its natural course. But the soul of man is created immortal, and not intended at all to die. Its final end is eternal happiness with God. Its life is His grace and favour, deprived of which it is deprived of all hope of attaining its final purpose. If, then, the loss of this favour constitute the

Soul Murder

death of the soul, the destruction or deprivation of it must constitute its murder. By how much, therefore, the soul is in the eyes of God more precious than the body, by so much more heinous must its murder be. We can imagine the feelings of a murderer when he stands alone over his victim, after having seen him sob out his last breath with the blood he has shed. How his heart must be wrung with despair as he sees the features become blanched and set, and the limbs motionless and stiffen! What would he not give to restore life to that corpse; unless, indeed, his hatred was of the most deadly character? How he would almost wish that he could infuse his own life into it; pour half his own blood into his veins, and breathe his own breath into his nostrils! He feels like Cain, and fancies that the earth may open and swallow him up. Hence does it so often happen that this crime is followed by the self-murder of the assassin. What, then, ought to be the feelings of one who has inflicted a deadly wound on the soul of his neighbour, and plunged it at once into the abyss of perdition? Oh, it is unfortunate for us that the object of such a crime is concealed from our view; for, dreadful as the sight would be, it would, if once seen, effectually save us from committing an act so terrible. To see a soul, fair and innocent as the loveliest child, smiling in grace and the favour of God; then, while our words of deceit and seduction are poured into its ears, or our evil example placed before its eyes, writhing in a mortal struggle between death and life—that is, between duty and temptation—even as though strangled and stifled by our hands, and agitated convulsively beneath our grip; then, as it yielded to our evil persuasions, to see it drop a livid corpse from our hands, every feature hideously distorted; to see it blackened and shrivelled, its beauty utterly destroyed; to see the angels shrink from it as though its infection tainted the air, and the evil spirits like vultures surrounding it, ready for a word to pounce upon it and bear it to their horrible abode; and to feel all this work of hateful devastation, this frightful change, to be the work of one's own hands! This must be a sight, could it be witnessed, unutterably fearful, but permanent and efficacious as a warning. Yet how faint a representation is this of the havoc committed upon a soul by one who leads it into sin!

Reflect now how much more terrible and harrowing this imaginary spectacle would be, were the object of the ruin some one particularly dear to us. Suppose the murderer we have imagined to be one who, in a moment of passion, had stabbed his dear friend; or that the scene we have represented to ourselves had been of a father who, under a passing frenzy, had strangled his own child; how much more horrible does the idea become, how much more rending must be the remorse excited by it! Now, in the commission of such spiritual murder this is unhappily too often the case; it is inflicted by those who stand most closely to one another in relations of love, and who have the strongest mutual obligations. We seldom draw a stranger, much less an adversary, or one that dislikes us, into sin. But it is the companion and the friend who is in most cases drawn aside from virtue by the force of evil example or the influence of loose conversation. It is the superior entrusted with the souls of his disciples, the priest who has to render to God an account of his flock's salvation; these are, alas, so often the cause of their ruin! It is the parent who, by a love of dissipation or neglect of duty, sows the seeds of vice or irreligion in his child. For let us not deceive ourselves. Not merely by some overt act, or persuasion, or enticing to sin, may we destroy a soul as one would the body by driving a knife into the heart. No; we may poison it by the most subtle processes—by simply instilling into it one false maxim, which, like a drop of venom in the veins, first seems to produce only a local and temporal derangement, but is gradually taken up into the system, and spreads throughout the frame, and so ends in destroying life. Nay, the infection which may cause this fatal result may be but breathed, so to speak, upon the soul; it may be a glance of the eye or a casual word that may destroy it for ever. And how dreadful, again, to think that by *neglect* we may be the cause of a soul miserably perishing! As we should be guilty of murder if any one confided to our care died from want of nourishment, medicine, or anything which it was our duty to provide him with, so shall we surely be called upon to answer before God for the spiritual death of any one who falls into perdition for want of that sustenance which it was our duty to give him: the Sacraments, instruction, reproof, or advice. ("Meditations," p. 361.)

DEATH

TRULY a mine of rich and precious meditations is the grave! and the churchyard is a field wherein is hidden a pearl of great price for those that apply themselves to its discovery! Take but a handful of its mould and consider whereof it may be composed. It was once, peradventure, a heart that throbbed or writhed, as yours may do, with the best or most evil passions, the centre of much love, and joy, and hope; and withal of much grief, and hate, and disappointment; something as warm, as bounding, as lively, as uncontrollable as is now beating within *your* bosoms. Into that dust, too, have been resolved eyes which once sparkled like yours with expression, with intelligence, with life; tongues that cajoled the multitude, or charmed the circle of domestic listeners; features which the ancient chisel would have transformed into marble, that their impress might be unperishing; athletic frames and well-built limbs which seemed to defy the power of destruction. And see what they have all become, since all nature has been at work upon them! The worms of the earth have curiously dissected them, the strange alchemy of their own disharmonious elements has transmuted their very substance, the winter's damp and summer's heat have macerated and dissolved them, the rains of heaven have filtered through them; till, crushed, and crumbled, and mouldered, they have been turned up as dust, to be fanned abroad by the four winds

Death

of heaven. And from this change may we not augur another, more feelingly involving ourselves? Will not future generations moralise over our scattered remains, even as we now do over those of our forefathers? Will not they say, Those graceful forms which in those days inspired such admiration, and appeared to all who saw them worthy of immortality, what were they, after all, but dust? Those supple and powerful limbs, which bore the youth of that age through all the bright and interesting scenes of their time, what did they prove in the end to be but dust? Yes, my brethren, such shall we too be shown to be no less than the generations that have preceded us—slime of the earth, that which ye tread upon with scorn, that which ye shake as defilement from your skirts—dust—dust!

We fly, I know, habitually from these reflections; but in spite of ourselves they will not be shaken off. This groundwork is, indeed, within ourselves; the savour or seasoning of death, which this body of ours hath in it from its formation in the womb, accompanies it through life, and must, in its various evidences and increasing manifestations, too often remind us of the frail and worthless materials whereof we are composed. What else are our almost daily indispositions, our hourly ailings, our perpetual uneasiness in one part or other of our system, but germs and out-buddings of that noxious, creeping parasite, death, which entwines itself the stronger round us in proportion to our very growth, and will one day suck out the last sap of life from within us?

In fact, strange as it may seem, the principle of death penetrates so completely the operations of life—the complicated machinery by which these are conducted tends so essentially to fret itself in pieces, that we can hardly conceive the body's constitution before the Fall, nor how it ever existed otherwise than as destined to dissolution. In other words, the principle of vitality is the principle of death; and sufficient cause of our final end is involved in the simple fact of our having lived. The flood of life, which bounds so briskly through our frame, diminishes at every beat the moments of our existence, and exercises a wearing influence, however imperceptible, upon the channels through which it flows. That shaping power which it possesses, of gradually forming and consolidating the bony structure in the infant and youth, which power alone can give consistency and strength to the body, perseveres with obstinacy in its action after it has ceased to be useful: stiffens and hardens the joints, ossifies the softer textures, and becomes the cause of aged decrepitude, the weakener of the frame, the preparer of its dissolution. That genial heat which gives to youth its most beautiful glow, and imparts energy and warmth to all its enterprises, is a fire that cracks and corrodes the walls of its furnace, and disposes it to its final overthrow.

While the operations of spirit know no limit, but are capable of perfectibility without measure, and always go on in the line of their peculiar destination, not contradicting themselves, nor involving their own annihilation, it is precisely the contrary with the body's vital functions. The over-exertion of any organ produces its decay—the palate palls, the eyes are dimmed, the stomach fails, the lungs waste away, the very brain will sear and pine, by the excess of action in those functions whereunto they have been ordained. Their sum is evidently their own overthrow; their strongest effort a fatal blow to their own existence. Justly, then, did the Apostle call this our earthly tabernacle the "body of death," inasmuch as it is made up and held together by deadly principles, engaged in constant conflict which of them shall in the end achieve the destruction of this brittle frame. ("Sermons, ii. 221.)

DELIRIOUS DEATH

BUT it may be thought that such a representation [of remorse] is contradicted by experience, inasmuch as the last hours, or even days, of the most reprobate are generally passed in a heavy senseless torpor, hardly capable of feeling and reflection, and interrupted only by transitory gleams of consciousness. And yet I doubt whether even so the view is more consoling; whether the indefinite sense of pain, the raving incoherences of the last dream, made up as it must be of fragments from a worthless life, and refreshed by short glimpses of bitter realities, are not more frightful and oppressive than the collected look upon the most appalling dangers. For we can imagine faintly the condition of a man who, having fallen into a deep water, first plunges and struggles fearfully, astonished and amazed at the obstruction about him; how his ears are stunned by the moanful murmur of the deeps; how his eyes stare upwards at the pale horny light that gleams upon him; how his feet beat about impatiently for a standing-place, and his hands grasp and squeeze in vain the oozy and slippery element; how his chest and throat gasp and strain in agony, and all the flesh of his body creeps and trembles with exhaustion. Then, when his senses are becoming bewildered, and his perceptions confused, and the holy spark of existence just extinguished, he is borne up by the buoyant spring of life once more to the surface, and whirled round for a moment above the waters; and in that moment he sees the clear blue sky gazing upon the calm mirror around him, and the green hills, and the pleasant fields, and the habitations of men, all standing quiet and at peace; or he hears the little birds singing in the trees, and the fisherman in his skiff; and all the love of life returns with its images, and seems to tie his soul to the meanest bulrush upon the bank. Then does he stretch forth his hand for help, and utter a faint scream of agony, and takes one long draught of air as he feels himself dragged downwards again, and plunged and tossed more wildly in the pathless deep; and the waters seem now more bitter, and his abandonment more complete, and his life more hopeless, from the renewed images thereof which he has borne with him to this his final struggle. Even so may we imagine the sinner, in those long intervals of fancied unconsciousness, tumbling in the waves of an ill-defined existence, trying in vain to grasp and seize hold thereon by each of his senses, with all his confused recollections, of hideousness and beauty, of pain and delight, of childhood and old age, of virtue and lewdness, swimming around him in the bewilderment of a nightmare; with all the sorrows of domestic mourning days, and the savage hours of youthful debauch, the altar and the gaming-table, the banquet and the charnel-house, staggering before his amazed sense. Then comes one of those momentary gleams of recognition, a fitful upflaring of life's lamp, in which a clear view is once more caught of the world and its attachments, the domestic walls, the weeping friends, the tabernacle of the flesh; and withal the consciousness of past evil and the dread of future uncertainty, the sense of responsibility and the terror of doom, flash once more upon the mind and renew all its remorses; yet without the time or power to receive help or comfort: and so again the sense is hurled back into darker and more fantastic dreaming, into a gloomier lethargy, and a more frightful forestaller of death's final sleep. ("Sermons," ii. 233.)

DEATH UNHEEDED

EVERY hour that we live we are approaching or drawn nearer to that fatal term. Our occupations, our amusements, our framework, expose us daily to accidents that may hasten it. We daily hear and read of others perishing in circumstances in which there could be nothing dangerous, and in which we have been a thousand times placed; some while travelling in the pursuit of their innocent occupations, by casualties which no prudence could avoid; some in the bosom of their homes, by occurrences which no foresight could have predicted. We instantly remember that we have repeatedly stood in the same situation; sometimes we too have had our narrow escapes. But this recollection only gives ground for a pleasant security, never for a reflection how frail and brittle a blessing is our life. The delicate formation of our organs, the complicated operations which life requires within us, the conflicting principles which struggle for victory in every throb of our pulse, make its enjoyment still more precious. Almost from our infancy the seeds of our future dissolution begin visibly to unfold. Disease, generated from our own substance, developed with our growth, strengthened upon our nourishment, broods within us, a lurking enemy, slowly but unceasingly filing away the stamina of life, till our constitution is undermined, and we sink unresisting victims of its power. Almost every year we receive some intimation of this constant action. Some complaint every now and then attacks us, occasionally, perhaps, sufficiently strong to excite the alarms or the despair of our friends, at others merely reminding us of our weakness and mortality; while we feel that the slightest additional irritation, perhaps a current of air, had it accidentally played upon us, might have aggravated our disorder, and even rendered it fatal. But these warnings, too, pass over us unheeded and

Death Unheeded

without profit. The weakness and danger of relapse which they leave behind them are not considered as any proof that death has gained upon us, and that a few attacks thus repeated may suffice to complete our fall. "Waters," says holy Job, "wear away stones, and with washing, the ground by little and little is washed away: so in like manner Thou shalt destroy man. Thou hast strengthened him for a little while, that he may pass away for ever: Thou shalt change his face, and shalt send him away." While life is yet in its vigour, these warnings are repeated at certain intervals; as it declines, and our danger becomes more imminent, they are more frequently renewed, and at length become completely habitual. But they are hardly the less disregarded on this account. Year after year imprints deeper wrinkles upon our brow; old age gradually impairs our senses, and blunts the power of enjoyment; continual use paralyses the limbs; but, in spite of all, the old man, covered already by the badges of death, totters towards his grave with as little care or reflection as if he confidently expected some miraculous renovation in his shattered frame.

Oh! blind indeed, my brethren, must we be, thus to delude ourselves, and to close our eyes to these evidences, which daily meet us, of our ever-approaching dissolution. You pass not your threshold but a funeral procession crosses you; you enter not a church but the monuments of the dead environ you; you tread not the soil but it is enriched by the ashes of the deceased; wherever you stand you press the grave of departed empires. Within, a principle of destruction is creeping through your veins; at every step you take your enemy has gained upon you. The dominion of death is on every side and within you, and yet you feel not that you are in its reach. All around you speaks of death; and it stalks beside you as constant, but, alas! as unheeded an attendant as your shadow.

After all this, was it necessary that religion should interfere to remind us of our mortality? Was it necessary that a prophet should remind man that all flesh is grass, and all his glory as the flower of the field? Was it necessary that the Son of God should so often tell us that His last visitation will arrive when we least expect it, and that He will come upon us like a thief in the night? Was it necessary that year after year a solemn day should be observed to remind the children of clay that they are mortals, and that they should be summoned to the foot of God's altar, and be there ordered to remember that they are as weak, that they are as crumbling, that they are as easily dispersed from the face of the earth, as the kindred ashes with which this lesson is written on their foreheads?

If, with all these admonitions, it must be the height of infatuation not to live in the constant apprehension of death, by what name shall we call this blindness, when we reflect upon the dreadful evils attendant on an unprovided death? By an unprovided death I mean not only that tremendous judgment of God when, for the public terror of the wicked, some signal sinner is struck down in the fulness of his iniquity; not merely when the impious sensualist, like Baltassar, receives his doom in the midst of his excesses; not merely when the irreligious scoffer is struck, like Herod, by the angel of God while profaning and bringing blasphemy on the name of his Creator. These are the thunderbolts laid up in the "storehouse of God's wrath" for rare and terrible lessons; and yet His justice daily surprises unprepared and unthinking Christians. It surprises the man who, passing his days in the ordinary rounds of dissipation, scarcely ever affords himself time to think that he has a salvation to secure, or a God to propitiate. He hears, indeed, whenever public decency obliges him to observe the outward forms of religion, that there is some object of greater importance to man than the gratification of passion, the accumulation of wealth, or the study of ease. But the truths of God make no practical impression on his soul, and he is accustomed to dismiss from his mind every serious thought and every religious counsel, as the Roman governor removed the terrifying preaching of the Apostle—"For this time go thy way; but when I have a convenient time I will send for thee." ("Sermons," ii. 245.)

ON SALVATION

"WHAT doth it profit a man if he lose the whole world and gain his own soul?" Such, my brethren, is our second inquiry. Methinks that, instead of answering and dilating upon it, I might send you to meditate upon it in the silent catacombs that undermine this city

[Rome], where you might ask the spirits of the martyrs, whose venerable sepulchres surround you, what has been their gain? You might ask an Agnes and a Cecilia, what it profited them to undervalue beauty, youth, fortune, life, and to endure fire and the sword, and if they were content with the exchange? You might interrogate a Pudens, or a Eustachius, or a Sebastian, what he profited by the loss of rank, of wealth, of military repute, of imperial favours, of life by painful execution? And all would reply, and the crowded dormitory of saints would re-echo, from end to end: "Gladly we trampled on all these things; exultingly we not so much lost as flung away the world, and we preferred the rack and the sword, because they were the instruments of our salvation. Or you might ask an Helen, a Constantia, or Pulcheria, or, in later times, our own Saxon monarchs Offa or Ina, wherefore, despising their thrones, they cared only to build or enrich pious foundations in this city, and lay their bones before the martyrs' shrines? and they will answer you, Because thrones and sceptres are as nothing in the Christian's mind compared with the securing of the soul's health and eternal salvation. Every sacred edifice in this city, every stone in its walls, seems to proclaim this truth, that to save the soul, everything else must be sacrificed, for that this is the sole occupation worthy of man. ("Sermons," iii. 40.)

CHRISTIAN ATHLETE

IN two things doth the Apostle seem to propose to us this example of those engaged in a race, for our imitation in the affair of our salvation. First, inasmuch as, even when not actually engaged in it, they never lost sight of its difficulties or disqualified themselves for meeting them. "Every one," he writes, "that striveth for the mastery, refraineth himself from all things" (1 Cor. ix. 25). And as we should always be in a state of preparation for the effort wherein we must be often engaged, never relaxing in watchfulness. Then, secondly, inasmuch as when actually engaged in their decisive effort, they made it the sole occupation of all their powers. "I therefore so run, not as at an uncertainty; I so fight, not as one beating the air" (1 Cor. ix. 26). The first is the perseverance of watchfulness to prevent or remove all that can impede our progress; the second is the perseverance of energy in doing all that can advance it.

The ancients have left us an account of how they trained themselves who devoted themselves to the occupation of the games. Their diet was spare and simple, their beverage but water; they forbade themselves all domestic comforts, they denied themselves more than necessary sleep; their lives were more chaste than those of the philosophers; they reduced their bodies more than an anchorite; they toiled more arduously than slaves condemned to the mines. And this went on for years, almost unremittingly. It commenced in early youth, with the first dawn of ambition; it went through all the term of growth to manhood; it was an education apart, for training the body to the standard of just vigour and suppleness; the age of the passions was passed over unheeded, because all of them were absorbed in one alone—ambition. And ambition for what? "They indeed, that they might gain a corruptible crown!" For the chance of one branch plucked from the nearest palm-tree, for the hope of one wreath woven from some neighbouring laurel grove, for the prospect of one round of vociferous applause from a multitude that twenty times had hissed them, for the sake of having their names trumpeted about till the next lucky champion's dins them out of men's ears and memories—for this, and nothing more, that was endured, without relaxation or grudge; the tenth part of which would have secured a crown unfading if done for God! Nay, for less than all this, for the risks were immense that not one of those prizes would be attained.

Now we, my brethren, have dedicated ourselves from infancy to this nobler combat; our names were entered among the candidates for heaven, in golden letters, upon God's own book, when we received the adoption of His children through baptism. Asked what we expected to obtain by the faith we were about to profess, we replied, "Life everlasting." This was our goal—towards this we started clothed in a white robe, emblem not only of innocence but of victory. And was there nothing from which we were told we must refrain ourselves, nothing we were called upon to renounce, and actually did renounce, as necessarily arresting, or delaying, or risking our progress towards the end we must reach? Yes, a threefold enmity, not of rivals who might use a fair advantage to trip up our heels or pass us on the way, but of foes leagued in that triple cord of conspiracy which is not easily broken, to overthrow, to confound, and to disappoint us: the world, the flesh, and the devil. These are the forbidden things from which we must restrain ourselves, over which we must never relax in our watch, if we wish to be saved.

You will say, But are we not always engaged in the race itself? Are there, then, times when we are only preparing for our endeavours? Certainly from the first moment that we offered ourselves to Christ till a happy death shall crown our efforts, there is no interval of absolute relaxation. For it is when the hour of prayer returns at its regular intervals, it is when the day recurs for the discussion of the charges which conscience has collected against us or for the happier duty of nourishing the soul with the Living Bread that comes down from heaven, it is when the frequent period of temptation comes, it is when trials of our virtue from men's follies or malice reach us, it is when adversity or sickness strikes us,—it is in times like these—and they will be found each day—that the more eager and active attention is required which turns the thoughts towards one absorbing subject, an actual striving for salvation. But if there be thus times when we are actively engaged with salvation, there are others when it is less directly and engrossingly our occupation. When we mingle with the world for the discharge of our public or private duties, when we solace ourselves with necessary relaxation, when we refresh our bodies with their becoming nourishment—when, in fact, we descend from the order of duties which immediately brings us before the face of God, to those of a lower and homelier sphere, it is then that we need that perseverance of vigilance which can alone secure us from surprise, fatal to our endeavours. For if in these more frequent intervals the enemy is allowed to prevail upon us, if we are seduced into the commission of any one thing interdicted to the champion of Christ, our strength will be broken, our courage will fail, and when next called to trial, our efforts will prove vain. Our watch, then, must be unremitting; nothing must surprise us. ("Sermons," iii. 79.)

FICKLENESS

In reading that painful series of reproaches which form the great body of the prophetic errand to the house of Israel, one can hardly fail to be struck with the imputation of a twofold perversity, one species whereof is seemingly at variance with the other. For, on the one hand, they are ever denounced as a generation obstinate and stiff-necked, bent towards evil with an incorrigible propensity, and at the same time as fickle and unsteady in every purpose; now returning to God in sackcloth and in ashes, then once more listening to the first seduction, and giving their worship to Astaroth and

Fickleness

Baal. Yet in all this is no contradiction; for these men belonged to that lowest and most degraded class of pretended followers of religion in whom the occasional practice of duty and of virtue may well be considered a departure from the perversity of their habitual conduct, and an unsteadiness of purpose in their natural proneness to evil. Through their sojourn in the desert they required a course of almost unceasing wonders to keep them even outwardly attached to the God who had freed them from Egypt: a temporary absence of Moses from the camp was enough to excite a mutinous call for the idolatry of that country; a casual scarcity of water was sufficient to rouse them to blasphemous murmuring against the Most High. And so ever after is their history but a repetition of similar unsteadiness in their fidelity to God; while under the government of their judges they are alternately the champions of His justice against the idolatrous tribes of Chanaan, and their slaves and fellow-worshippers, and this is their commoner lot; now they will have no ruler, but each tribe and house cares for itself; then they become clamorous for a master and king; and when they have obtained one to their cost, it is only that they may still more conspicuously display the fickleness of their character. Fasting and weeping with Ezechias, rioting and revelling with Achaz, slaying false prophets with Elias; stoning Zacharias, the son of Joiada, to death in the very court of the Temple; trembling at the menaces of Isaias, and despising the tears and counsels of Jeremias; purifying the Temple only to defile it anew; consulting alternately the ephod and the idol of Accaron—such is the history of the people which God had chosen to be His peculiar care upon the earth.

And when the Son of man came into His own He was again provoked by them, even as He had been in the desert of Sin, by the inconstancy of their affections. The very men who to-day have followed Him into the wilderness, and forgot their homes and their daily bread to feed upon the Word of God, will to-morrow take up those stones, which would have made better children of Abraham than they, to cast at Him; the same miraculous exercise of His power is necessary, one time to avoid being perforce proclaimed king, and at another to escape being hurled over a precipice; the same crowd which on the first day of the week gives Him a triumph, on the fifth votes Him an execution; and they who on the first bore in their hands the palm-branch that symbolised His conquering might, on the last thrust into His the ignoble reed, the emblem of their own base inconstancy!

Well might Jesus, sickened by the heartless degeneracy to which the fickleness of His people had reduced them, proclaim him more than a prophet who was free from its reproach. Well might He, in dismissing the messengers of John, after having charged them to inform him how the blind and the lame were cured, and the dead rose again, add these humbling words, "And blessed is he that shall not be scandalized"—that is, offended—"with Me!" Gracious God! and is this

Fickleness 163

credible—that He who might have asked for so much in return should place His estimates so low? Might He not have exacted that the widow of Naim should ever have a room apart for Him in her house, as His prophet had at the Sunamitish woman's? and that the ruler and the centurion should stand His friends, and oppose their influence to the machinations of His enemies? Might He not have claimed as His, every limb restored to health and every sense re-endowed with activity, and demanded that the feet which, crippled, He had strengthened, should rush forward to His rescue, and the arms to which, withered, He had given life and nerve, should be stretched out to snatch Him from His foes? Ah! He knew too well the weakness of man's wavering, reed-like heart to place upon it so heavy a load of gratitude, and He is content if any of those who have sworn to Him eternal fidelity and love, in requital for so much kindness, shall refrain from being His enemy and finding in Him cause of offence. And so, in truth, we may say, that after having for three years journeyed over the length and breadth of Palestine, and having wherever He went healed *all* their sick, He must have had collected at Jerusalem at His last passover such an army of indebted followers as might, had they raised their voices, have drowned the priestly yell for Barabbas, and might, by but lifting their hands, have overawed the Roman president into justice. But their fickle hearts had been turned aside, and they had forgotten their benefactor and their obligations.

Do you, my brethren, stand astonished at such inconstancy of good feeling in these men, and does your indignation burn at the baseness of their heart? Then look into your own and see if this counterpart be not there. Do you discover fainter evidences of loving-kindness and of a watchful care over you than Israel received in the wilderness or the promised land? Has a shorter arm rescued you, or from a bondage less severe than that of Pharaoh? Have you been baptized in waters less marvellously prepared than those of the Red Sea, or drunk of spiritual drink, waters less precious than trickled down the figurative rock, or been fed with bread of angels that came down from heaven less than the manna? Have you been borne from the cradle, even till now, in any arms but those of your God, or has any one loved you more than He? He, moreover, hath done for you what in the days of His flesh He did for His people: He hath cured your soul when sick, and restored it to life when dead in sin. And, in return, where has been the steadiness of your fidelity and virtue? You were young, and as yet innocent, and you seemed to flourish as a green plant set by running waters; your growth tended upwards towards heaven, and your healthy branches spread on every side. A perfumed breeze of pleasure came, soft and enervating; it played and dallied with you, and scarcely had you felt its touch but you bent beneath it; its poison reached your core, the sap of your virtuous energies was parched up; and when it had passed away, you found that you were but a hard, dry reed which the wind had shaken! You fancied yourself strong and powerful, as the cedars

Fickleness

of God; you believed you had twined your roots round the clefted rock of divine revelation, and had lifted your head till it seemed to hold communion with the regions of heaven; you had defied the assaults of temptation to shake you from your proud standing. But the storm came, the winds blew and the rains fell; the hour of tribulation proved your hollowness; you crouched down, powerless, your virtue bent down, and you discovered yourself to be no better than a feeble reed which the wind had broken!

But will you say that never have you been thus rudely shaken and clean overthrown, but that those virtuous purposes wherein ye began, in the same you have persevered till now? Truly, then, you are not of the race whereof it is said that "all flesh is grass." Can we remember a month of steady perseverance in resolutions taken at its beginning, or a week of fervour without relaxation? How often have we recommenced, as we flattered ourselves, a virtuous life, and imagined that we had changed our hearts, but after a brief course have fallen back into torpor or cold neglect? And what hath so quickly turned us aside, but a breath? The sneer of a worldling hath baffled our resolves of prudence, the invitation of a friend has overthrown our plans of temperance, the prolongation of amusement has shortened our allotment of prayer, a trivial disappointment has blown away our patience, a hasty word has blighted our meekness, a silly shame has made us deny Christ! Oh, surely in the best of our purposes we are but as reeds shaken by the wind!

And even in the little, often fancied good which we do perform, how feeble and wayward we are! One time we are in love with some peculiar practice of devotion, and then it is cast off for another. Now we are all alive to this scheme of charity, and after a time another becomes the favourite in its stead. One year the peculiar views and suggestions of popular guides, or fashionable theories, fill our minds, which the next will banish to make room for something new. By turns we are indulgent and rigorous: we retire from the world, and we mingle in its amusements; we serve our God by caprice, and not by law; we have a changeable idol of self-love ever placed beside His altar, and it is often hard to say which we adore; and we may one day be surprised to find, that, however solid the foundation whereon we have built, there hath been much wood, or hay, or stubble laid upon it, and fashioned into some seemly form, which "the wind shall carry off, and the breeze shall take away." ("Sermons," ii. 366.)

PERSEVERANCE

THIS is a clear truth, delivered in the Word of God, that only "he who perseveres to the end shall be saved," that only he who is faithful unto death shall obtain the crown of life. To the beginning of our virtuous course no term is unalterably fixed. At all times God calls upon such as have not yet commenced, and such as having commenced, have proved unfaithful, to delay beginning no longer. At whatever hour the wicked

Perseverance

man shall detest and abandon his way, God will receive him to mercy. Whenever the Lord of the vineyard summons us to His task, we may date the day's work. But to the end of our course of virtue He has fixed an invariable term: for it to be acceptable it must end only with our lives. If it be one hour shorter, the difference is eternally fatal. The sinner must be found a saint by the Son of man when He knocks at the gate. The labourer must pursue his work till night, or he will not receive his wages. This truth is the basis of that salutary fear and trembling in which alone our salvation is to be wrought out. It is the motive of that terrible exhortation of the Apostle immediately after our text: "Wherefore he that thinketh himself to stand, let him take heed lest he fall" (1 Cor. x. 12). It is the ground of that fearful apprehension which he therein expresses, that while he preached himself to others he might himself become a castaway (1 Cor. ix. 27). What an awful thought! One whom God had miraculously taken in hand, first to convert and then to bring to the apostleship; one who had been beaten with rods, and stoned, and shipwrecked for Christ's sake; one who had founded churches and converted thousands; yea, one who had been rapt into the third heaven, and looked almost into the very face of God—yet left in the horrible anxiety of uncertainty of salvation, humbly compelled to avow, that still his race might have all been run in vain, and his name been blotted from the book of life! And we, miserable creatures, who have not suffered an ache or a reproach with patience for Christ's sake, who have despised and rejected graces innumerable and immense, who have grovelled in the world's lowest mire, wallowed in its basest thoughts, will still persevere to speak and act as though we held salvation in the hollow of our hands, and had a law of life established in our behalf. No; Christians, be ye who you may, there never was a more baneful, soul-killing doctrine palmed upon God's law than this, that any term shorter than life is ever appointed for any one's strivings after salvation, or that assurance can be given to man of a certainty of eternal life.

There is one, only one course which can give such security—that of unlimited perseverance, considering nothing gained until the whole is possessed; the never risking a sufficient time—and that is only an indivisible moment—in which death can strike us while out of God's grace by sin; the living so each day, each hour, as though upon it individually depended the allotment of our eternal destiny. Let every act be so performed in the presence of the all-seeing Judge as though the next moment He should have to pronounce sentence upon it; let every prayer be said as fervently as if it should be our last supplication for mercy; let every confession be made as though it were our last act of reconciliation; let every communion be received as though it were the last Pasch which Jesus had destined to eat with us, the viaticum for our last eternal journey. In a word, let not time, at least future time, be an element in our calculation concerning our prospects of salvation; but let the present ever find us in a state fit for heaven.

For in this doth a race differ from a mere journey,

Special Providence

that he who is engaged in the former calculates not in how long or short a time it may be convenient to him to pass over his allotted space, but he strives to do it in the briefest imaginable time, and thinks none too short in which he can do the entire task. And so we, who are hurrying on towards our goal of eternal salvation, must feel that our interest consists in this, in doing in the shortest possible time the most possible work of God. For if our life has been passed in constant transgressions of God's law, and we feel that much is required to repair it, we will not say, "I will employ so many years in tears, and sighs, and fasting like the royal Prophet," but I will at once so repent, and so entreat heaven, and so do penance, as that, should but one day be granted, the work shall be found done, and yet if years shall follow, I shall not be found to have in anything essential relaxed. ("Sermons," iii. 91.)

SPECIAL PROVIDENCE

THE grandeur of Divine Providence in the care of individual man cannot be better expressed than through that feeling which makes each one to himself the centre, and, as it were, the pivot round which its dispensations seem to move. Had the doctrine of Christianity that to each of us is appointed a guardian spirit who watches over him with unceasing assiduity possessed no ground in revelation, it would have been the truest and purest expression that could have been conceived of that feeling which we separately entertain, that a particular kindness from birth has made our welfare its exclusive care. At first sight this feeling may seem to partake of pride—nay, to be only its expression in a preference which we give to ourselves before others, as though standing above them in the sight of God. But quite on the contrary, when carefully discussed, it shall seem rather to stand opposed to it, and to form the best and surest foundation of humility. For pride takes away from God and forswears His gift, and presumes upon some proper and personal perfection; whereas this feeling rather magnifies His bounty and increases our thankfulness, and strongly impresses those awful words, that "to whom more hath been given, from him more shall be required"; and placing His mercy in strongest contrast with our return for it, makes us judge more severely of ourselves, who have received more than others, and have, perhaps, done less. And thus pride never can fall upon the exaggeration of God's kindness, but rather only upon the pretensions of our return. ("Sermons," iii. 123.)

PRESUMPTION

Such as the past year hath been, it will appear, and you must answer it at the bar of divine justice. Ye know not that another year will be granted you, so that possibly this may have to be pleaded by you as the crown and finish of your life for God, as the consummation of that perfection at which you aimed. Will you stand the test? Will you abide the issue of a final, fatal, irrevocable decision upon the good deeds of the

Presumption

last year, upon the balance of virtue over vice, upon the triumphs of grace over nature? Do you shrink in terror from the idea that this last year should be the evidence whereon your doom is to be pronounced by an inexorable Judge? Then, let me ask you another question: Has this year been *worse* than those which preceded it? Is it peculiarly disgraced by evil, that it must not go before the Judge unexpiated? Nay, is it not because it is *too like* the foregoing that you will not trust it with your eternal lot—because it has their negligences, their dissipations, their crimes stamped upon it? And if so, if you are not satisfied that the elapsed year hath been happy, because it is the type of all your others, miserable creature, on what do you rely for salvation? For the past alone is yours, and the accumulated deficiencies of several years cannot possibly make a balance in your favour.

Ah, yes—I know too well where you have laid up your hope: there, where every mortal will unhappily stake it—on the visionary future! Ashamed as we may be to own it, there is not one of us who looks not on heaven as a prize yet to be won, and who founds not his prospects upon the great things which he fancies he yet shall do. Let us then bid farewell to the past and its discouraging recollections, and stretch our view into the mist of the coming year, to descry, if possible, the probabilities of its promise. When we rely for anything on the future as future, there is essentially and necessarily a delusion. It is only inasmuch as it shall have become the present that it can work us weal. Mere future good is but like that deceitful appearance in the eastern deserts, where the faint and thirsty traveller sees before him at morning the lively image of a distant lake, so clear and distinct that he can distinguish, as he fancies, the rippling of its waters, and around it, and reflected in it, tall trees and green shrubs that promise refreshment; then, as with his parched lips outstretched he journeys towards it, he finds it remain, indeed, but ever stationary and ever as distant from him as at first; till after he hath been wearied unto death by the pursuit of the phantom, the vision trembles and waxes faint and vanishes, leaving him only deeper in the pathless desert, and farther removed than ever from all human help. And so it is with us if we pursue the promised refreshment of a future moment, still left to the vague indecision of its own natural state. If now, at the present moment, I see the earnest preparation commenced, that so when the future shall have succeeded to its name it shall also have proved the inheritor of its advantages, then indeed will I encourage you in hope; but it is no longer to the future that you trust. If, on the other hand, you continue inactive at present, and insensible to the advantages of the passing hour, I tell you unhesitatingly that you are trusting to vanity and deceit when you imagine that futurity will enable you to do what you now neglect.

For your hopes of salvation must depend upon grounds whereof no one hath assured you or can give you certainty. It may arise, in the first place, from a sort of vague, presumptuous idea, that God will certainly not allow us to be lost. You see perhaps in the history of your past life tokens innumerable of His exhaustless mercies towards you, care over your infancy and youth, the blessings of a virtuous education, preservation from many dangers of body and soul, and you think that you are the favoured of God, the special object of His providential benevolence. God forbid that I should say one word to weaken this amiable and sacred feeling; but may He no less prevent its being to us a snare and a pitfall. For, my brethren, if every one of us feel thus, as I doubt not most do, it can give no evidence of more than an ordinary carefulness and interest, which with sweet ingenuity suits itself to each, so as to appear unto him surpassing. But if all or most men reason so, and if of most men but few, as He assures us, are chosen, it follows that to the majority such a feeling is no warrant of salvation; why then to us? Are we the only ones who may not be deceived? Nay, furthermore, I would say to you: I trust that all you imagine may be true, and that God hath each of you in His especial keeping; what follows thence? Why, only that your debt is greater; that your talents have been ten instead of one or five; that it is so much the more shameful and unhandsome of you to tamper with a goodness manifested to you beyond others; in fine, as a motive for deeper and oftener meditation upon the awful words, that "to whom more hath been given, from him more shall be required."

For I would ask you, Doth Holy Writ hold out encouragement to such as place reliance upon such a motive, and not rather exhibit frightful examples of its fatal fallacy? Did the Almighty ever foretell your birth by prophets, and promise that you should be the pride and glory of nations? Did He say in particular of you that you should call Him Father, and be by Him called in special wise His son? Hath He appeared to you and given you all the desires of your heart—wealth, and dominion, and fame, and wisdom, such as none other hath ever possessed? And if He hath done all this and more for you, it comes not up to what He did for Solomon; yet He allowed him to become a vicious old man, and an apostate to every silly idolatry. Have you been educated to virtue under His own eye; have you learnt religion from His own lips; have you been chosen as the minister of His words and the dispenser of His graces? Oh, tremble then the more; for it was just such a one as this that was suffered to betray Him with a kiss! Fly then from so treacherous a ground for relying on the future for your salvation, and turn not the goodness of God into a curse by your presumptuous assurance. ("Sermons," iii. 271.)

FASTING

BUT, in the Word of God, and the belief of our forefathers, there is still another advantage attributed to this exercise [of fasting], to believe in which might, in the present state of ideas, subject us to the charge of weakness and superstition. It is indeed, my brethren, a grievously afflicting thought, that in proposing and inculcating the practice of many Christian exercises we should have to appeal to the belief and examples of ages past; that we should have to speak of fervent and unabashed religion as of something which did once exist amongst us, but is now numbered among many other ruins of man's mental greatness. But it was the persuasion of the early Church, in conformity to the inspired pages, that the public and private calamities which oppress us in such frightful succession are the visitations of divine justice or divine providence, sometimes punishing, sometimes trying the world, and that these calamities may be averted, suspended, or mitigated by the exercise of fasting and penance. When the scourge of God had desolated the land, the prophet Joel, by His command, enjoined the priests to "blow the trumpet in Sion, to sanctify a fast, and call a solemn assembly." "Then the Lord answered, and said to His people: Behold, I will send you corn, and wine, and oil, . . . and I will no more make you a reproach among the nations." The same pious confidence went even further: men hoped by these means to obtain counsel and assistance from God on important occasions. The Israelites held solemn fast before they proceeded in war against the tribe of Benjamin. Esther requested the Jews to fast, to ensure the success of her hazardous undertaking. Esdras and his companions fasted and besought the Lord in their difficulties, and it fell out prosperously unto them. The apostles fasted whenever they imposed hands in ordination, so to draw the blessing of God upon the heads of His new ministers.

But, alas! the sword of the Lord might be stretched over the whole land—its produce blighted, its inhabitants exterminated—yet who would now think of humbling himself before His mighty hand; or, like even the impious King Joram in similar circumstances, tear his garments in sorrow, and show the sackcloth of penance on his guilty flesh? The judgments of God might visit us in our domestic sanctuary, and blight our most tender hopes, but who would now think of averting them by fasting and prayer, as did King David, when the agonies of death seized his child? ("Sermons," ii. 100.)

NON-FASTERS

YES, my brethren, if any one ought to feel downcast and afflicted during the Lenten season, it is the man whose infirmities prevent him from uniting in the austere and devotional practices of the Church. Seeing himself disabled from joining the sacred ranks of fervent combatants who are fighting the battles of the Lord, he should feel a holy envy at their happier lot, and consider himself degraded by his rejection. He should think himself, like the lepers, separated from the congregation of the saints as they gather round the tabernacle of the Lord, and obliged to beg for a place in their acceptable intercession. Then would he compensate for his inability to join the holy rigours of his brethren by additional prayers and alms, or by such works of piety and penance as come within his reach. Instead of this, how differently from St. Paul do such as these "willingly glory in their infirmities" at the approach of this time of penance! Then are weaknesses searched out and discovered in their health and constitution, which never once prevented them from plunging into amusements, and standing out the far greater fatigues of society. Then are motives for relaxation seriously studied and artfully exposed, which had never interfered with any other occupations but those of Lent. But you, my brethren, when you fast, be not as the hypocrites—sad. Endeavour to comply with your obligation to its utmost extent—once more to quote the words of the Epistle, "in watchings, in fastings, in chastity, in knowledge, in sweetness, in the Holy Ghost, in charity unfeigned, in the words of truth, in the power of God, by the armour of justice." Then will you, at its term, approach, like Elias after his forty days' fast, God's holy mount, to behold Him, not as heretofore, in the whirlwind and raging fire, but in the gentle whisper of reconciliation and peace. Then, like the Son of God, at the expiration of the same period, you too will be fed at a celestial banquet, and receive with the bread of angels a pledge of admission to that true home where forty days of penance will be repaid you by an eternity of bliss. ("Sermons," ii. 109).

CHARITY DINNERS

WE know that we still retain old-world ways, exploded in the more refined modern plans of charity, and if the latter could be made to answer, and answer better, we have no objection to substitute them. But unfortunately, whether through want of practical lessons, or from defect in the materials we have to work on, every attempt to depart from those ancient methods has signally failed. One great advocate for the education of the poor says: "I am opposed to all charity dinners on principle, so I regret I cannot support your charity, which depends on one." Another is averse to an excursion, another to a tea-party. This gentleman will not subscribe where there is no inspection, that one will not where there is. Here one has a scruple about giving his money, unless the rooms are better ventilated; there another will do nothing till the starving priest has nuns. In fine, principles rise up, upon secondary details, always sufficiently strong to strangle the master principle, that children must be educated, and the poor maintained. Were this made the primary law, *suprema lex*, the contribution would come in and do its good, even though wrapped up in a protest against its being expected to subject the giver to the dyspepsia of a public dinner. But let it be remembered that the great body of our contributors, by an immense majority, is composed of those who genuinely represent the Anglo-Saxon race; whom every witness to their propensities, before the Normans enervated them, from St. Augustine to Froissart, attests to have been solid feeders, whom St. Gregory advises his disciple to humour in their natural taste, by letting them have a beef-feast on great festivals, and who alone identify in their vocabulary the two ideas of expansion of soul and plenitude of body, in the phrase "good cheer." To "be of good cheer" and to "have good cheer" naturally go together.

Yet more seriously, let it be remembered that the great bulk of these generous alms-givers are men whose day is given to work and toil, and who never sit round tables bright with light and silver, and offering more than homely variety of viands. A social evening, in an ample decorated hall, where they meet many friends, where all is copied, however imperfectly, from aristocratic usages in look and in attendance; where they are in company with a few high-born but meek-minded persons, who yet condescend, in these days of supposed equality, to dine with the artisan and the citizen; where they are addressed by some one of superior station as friends and fellow-Catholics; where, after all, they are in no danger of their hearing anything hurtful, but may occasionally have a tear brought to their eye at the tale of sorrow and poverty that is told them, and certainly their hands guided to their purses by their own best feelings—an evening thus occasionally spent by honest men of this class will not surely be one of those convivial scenes that will embody itself, at the last hour, in a dance of hobgoblins, painted by Turner.

We acknowledge that there is something heroic in submitting to be tortured by evil food, and poisoned by bad wines, at a tavern, and more so occasionally, *entre nous*, in being doomed to listen to lame speeches that hobble on, supported by the crutches of occasional cheers. But, after all, the thing is bearable, and not worse than a *table d'hôte* abroad, or an old stage-coach dinner in England, or, oh! worse than all, a meal half way between Dover and Ostend. And really charity is worthy of an occasional act and display of heroism. But if any of the gentlemen who so dislike the system of a charity dinner, that they will rather see the poor starve than eat one themselves, would for once stoop so low, we believe that the sight of many honest, earnest faces expanding beneath the gentle influence of charity, and the sound of their applauding voices whenever a sentiment is spoken on what is dear to a Catholic heart —the Pope, the bishop, the clergy, the nobility, charity, virtue, education, the child, the old man, the sick—would thaw the prejudices of another school in which propriety held a higher place than humility, and orderly dispensation is more esteemed than somewhat tumultuous charity. We believe that many who went this year as guests would consent to go next as stewards.

However, we have transgressed our limits in this Apician excursus from our main object. The system, good or bad, is that by which thousands of children are educated, and hundreds of orphans clothed and fed, and hundreds of aged men and women warmed and supported. Alms-houses have been built by it, orphanages have been erected, churches and schools in part raised. And this great, or rather necessary work falls upon the shoulders of the industrious middle class, aided, indeed, by those whose names have for many years headed their subscription lists with solid donations, and whose fathers before them saw the same assistance afforded to the same unperishing cause.

And thus we fear the work will have to continue for one generation at least to come, in spite of the liberal counsel which we constantly receive, in rather vague terms, of how much better everything might be, or ought to be, if the present system were wholly given up, and we only instead of it—ha! that is just what we want to know, but can never get told us. (*Dublin Review*, December 1856, p. 459.)

TRIBULATION

WHILE all goes well with the sinner, while the world smiles upon him, while his schemes are successful, what shall awake the conscience from its heavy lethargy? Nothing but some visitation of God's justice. It is a case where nought will do but cutting deeply, and searing with fire, to excite sensibility. Nay, if blessing can attach to God's enemies, blessed may we say is the sinner who knows not rest of heart or ease of body, rather than the one who sins without a warning or a check. Yes it is, in truth, a fearful thing for a man to have the Almighty his declared enemy; to be visited by Him only by calamities and remorses when waking, and by hideous dreams when sleeping; to be given up during life to the tormentors till the last farthing be paid on the rack of conscience, and under the whips and scorpions of persecuting misfortunes. It is a fearful thing for one to be thus kept in mind, while he continues to sin, that there is a just God, and an avenger beyond all partialities, and a judge above all bribes; one who neither sleepeth nor forgetteth; one whose right hand can bring back from the extremities of the earth, and can bury in the depths of hell. It is fearful, too, to be kept continually in the prospect of a miserable death, whether it be one of surprise without the time, or of stupidity without the sense, or of obduracy without the grace, or of circumstances without the opportunity, of making a penitent end. But in all this there is matter, however small, of hope. While God visits us at all, it is a sign that He thinks of us. The present life is not the time for punishment devoid of mercy. While the debtor is on his way to prison he may agree with his adversary and escape the messenger's hands. While the sick man feels pain there is vitality and activity in his constitution, and he may recover. And therefore, I think, it must be a much more fearful thing for the sinner to be forgotten of God, and never to feel a sting in his bosom, or to see a cloud over his pleasures. It must be a terrible thing to have one's perdition sealed; to have the process already closed, both depositions and sentence, and laid up in God's chancery, as an irreversible doom; and so him who is its object troubled no further, but allowed the full choice of his pleasures, as one permits to a man between sentence and execution his choice of viands, in full certainty that when his hour hath tolled the terrible law will take its course! How smoothly glides along the boat upon the wide, unruffled, though most rapid stream that hurries it onward to the precipice over which its waters break in thunders! How calm, and undisturbed by the smallest ripple, slumbers its unreflecting steersman! Oh! for one rock in the midst of the too smooth channel, against which it may be dashed and whirled round, to shake him from this infatuated sleep! It is the only hope that remains for him. Woe to him if to the end his course be pleasant! That end will pay it all. . . .

When God wishes to purge His servants of even slighter imperfections, He visits them with sorrows, sometimes more severe than what would be employed to chastise the most profligate vice. He has removed sovereigns from thrones which they had honoured by their virtues and charity, and sent them outcasts to beg the alms of their own subjects; He has allowed the foulest calumny to blacken before the entire world the character of the most innocent and spotless; He has wrung the hearts of the most devoted to His love with frightful anguish till they almost reached the borders of despair. And by the searching trials of these visitations He has probed their reins, and peered under every fold of their hearts, till the most concealed defilement was scoured away, and the soul burnished to beauty and splendour. But what a tribute is here to the wisdom and mercy of God, and what noble homage thence results to Him! For where would have been the wisdom and the power, where the glory or the magnificence, to have made men happy only where they have what they desire, and loudly thankful when all things succeed according to their wishes? Do not the very heathens and publicans do this? It is only a wonder that the sounds of praise and hymns of gratitude ever cease ascending day or night from the houses of the prosperous and rich or from the fertile fields. But it was a splendid design and splendidly executed, and only by God to have been designed and executed, to make songs of jubilee ascend from dungeons; to raise up thanksgivings from the bed on which one lies racked with exquisite tortures; to make benedictions be invoked on His name from the dunghill, whereon a leper, once rich and powerful, is obliged to sit. "The Lord hath given, and the Lord hath taken away: blessed be the name of the Lord." Such is the greeting with which the accumulation of every possible calamity short of death is welcomed by the patient Job; for in his history God hath recorded for us the noblest example of that process whereby men acceptable to Him are brought unto perfection. ("Sermons," ii. 390.)

PART IV
DEVOTIONAL

HOUSE OF PRAYER

TO all, to the sinner and to the just, the House of God is a house of prayer. And what does this imply? Why, that here is, as it were, the hall of audience wherein God sits day and night to receive the smallest petition of His lowest subject; that this is the court of the Most High, where all are equal in His sight—where the poor and the rich, the despised and the honoured, the base and the noble, the servant and the master are heard with equal attention and regard, and equally receive the objects of their petitions. That it is the council-chamber in which He condescends to consult in a manner with us on the subject of our desires; where we are allowed to expostulate with Him if He seem too severely to afflict us; to propose to Him whatever we consider for our advantage; to suggest such courses to His providence as may appear most suited to our wants. That it is His treasury and storehouse, where are laid up graces and blessings innumerable and most varied, which He unlocks at our request, and deals out to us according to the measure of our earnestness and perseverance. And how do men on earth prize and value the power of having such near access to the majesty of an earthly monarch, mortal and feeble as themselves; and how do they reverence the place where from time to time he condescends to show them but a passing attention! Who, then, will not revere the Holy Temple in which the King of kings is well pleased to admit the most unworthy of us into a familiarity such as scarcely any sovereign of earth ever showed to his nearest favourite? When King Ezechias received a bitter and insulting letter from Sennacherib, "he went up to the house of the Lord, and spread it before the Lord: and he prayed in His sight." So likewise when Anna had been taunted with keen words by her rival, so that she wept and could not eat, she went alone into the Tabernacle of the covenant in Silo, and having "her heart full of grief, she prayed to the Lord, shedding many tears." Thus did the saints of the Old Law, in public calamity and in private affliction, fly to the House of God as to a refuge and protection; thus did they there pour out their sorrows into His bosom, sure that their cause would be attended to and their petitions heard. Nor were they disappointed; for God sent His angel to rout the huge armies of Sennacherib, and gave Anna more than she desired—not only a son, but a prophet and judge in Israel. And in the New Law He promised that such should be the character of His Sanctuary, that "there shall be a Tabernacle for a shade in the day-time from the heat, and for security and a covert from the whirlwind and from rain." On occasions even of barbarous and reckless invasion the conqueror has been known to order the churches of God to be respected, and those who had taken refuge in them to be spared. But from our spiritual enemies they are, by God's own appointment, a shelter and pro-

Adoration

tection. How is the proud spirit calmed and brought to peace when it has been humbled before God's altar in the prayer of repentance! How do we rise nerved for the battle, and resolved to persevere, from the refreshment of a loving and confident supplication! How soon are we convinced, by a few moments' meditation in the House of God, of the vanity of human applause, of the helplessness of our own nature, of the worthlessness of all that has not a value in His sight! And all these consolations and blessings you here receive ought surely to form a strong and additional hold upon your affection and respect. ("Sermons," iii. 314.)

ADORATION

ADORATION is not what may be considered the privilege or possession of any one who believes in God; it does not consist in an act of worship whereby we acknowledge Him as God, whereby we express our gratitude to Him or entreat His mercies. It consists in an awful, yet sweetest feeling that you are in the immediate vicinity, in very contact of God, yea, of God in the flesh, like as they felt of whom we read that they cast themselves down at His feet and worshipped Him. It consists in the annihilation of the very powers of the soul, which leads to the prostration of the body, its natural representative, on the very ground beneath Him. It consists in the assurance that His hand is extended over us, that His eye is fixed on us, that His heart darts rays of compassion and love to our hearts as if they were beating the one on the other. Then we feel as St. John must have felt at the Last Supper; or as St. Peter when he begged Him to depart from him a sinful man; or as the wise kings when they kissed His feet, an infant in His mother's arms, with a love which burnt up self in sacrifice pure and unreserving. ("Sermons," i. 43.)

FORTY HOURS' ADORATION (1)

IF the principle of private devotion among Catholics be that of coming as near as possible to the feelings in faith and love of those who lived in our Blessed Redeemer's society upon earth, the great idea and principle of public worship in the Catholic Church is to copy, as faithfully as may be permitted, the homage paid to Him and His Father in heaven. With the Church triumphant she is one, and their offices in regard to praise and adoration are the same. Now, if we look up towards that happier sphere, we see the Lamb enthroned to receive eternal and unceasing worship, praise, and benediction. How beautifully has the pencil of Van Eyck transferred this scene to earth, in his splendid picture at Ghent of "The Adoration of the Lamb." In it all the tribes of earth and all estates of men, united in the Catholic Church, are represented as engaged in admiring, in praising, and in worshipping the Lamb that was slain from the foundation of the world. And this universality of homage only requires perpetuity, an unceasing perpetuity, to make it a counterpart to the scenes which opened upon John at Patmos. In the Catholic system this could not be wanting. The Church would not be content with opening her sanctuaries all day to such chance worshippers as devotion might lead to them, even though she might know that no hour or minute would elapse during which some one or other in her vast dominions would not be engaged in such exercise of prayer. She would not even leave this duty of perennial homage to those communities who, distributing the day and night into various portions, some at one hour, some at another, no doubt fill up the entire space with holy services. Through every season and through every day she would have ever going on a direct, uninterrupted worship of her Lord and Saviour as the adorable victim on His altar-throne.

For this purpose, in large towns, where there are a sufficient number of churches, the entire year is portioned out among them in spaces of eight-and-forty hours, an interval which has given the name to the devotion of the *Forty Hours' Prayer*. No expense is spared, no pains neglected, to make this sacred rite as solemn and as devout as possible. The church is richly adorned with tapestry and hangings, while the daylight is excluded—not so much to give effect to the brilliant illumination round the altar, as to concentrate and direct attention towards that which is upon it, and make it, like the Lamb in heaven, the lamp and sun, the centre of light and glory, to the surrounding sanctuary. After a solemn mass and a procession, the Blessed Sacrament is enshrined and enthroned above the altar at the same moment that, with similar pomp, it is reverently taken down in some other church. Around it is disposed, as it were, a firmament of countless lights, radiating from it, symbolical of the ever-wakeful host of heaven, the spirits of restless life and unfading brightness, that keep watch round the seat of glory above. At the foot of the altar kneel immovable, in silent adoration, the priests of the sanctuary, relieving each other day and night, pouring the prayers of the people as fragrant odours before it. But look at the body of the church! No pews, no benches, or other encumbrances are there; but the flood of radiance from the altar seems to be poured out upon the marble pavement, and to stream along it to the very door. But not during the day will you see it thus; the whole, except during the hours of repose, is covered with kneeling worshippers. Looking at the scene through the eye of memory, it comes nearer to the contemplation of a heavenly vision than aught else that we know. It seems to us as though on these occasions flesh and blood lost their material grossness, and were spiritualised as they passed the threshold. Softly and noiselessly is the curtain raised which covers the door, and passed uplifted from hand to hand, in silent courtesy, as a succession of visitors enter in; they who in the street just now were talking so loud and laughing so merrily, how they steal in, with slow pace and gentle tread, as though afraid to break upon the solemnity of the scene! For before and around them are scattered, without order or arrangement, persons singly or in groups, as they have entered in, all lowly kneeling, all reflecting upon their prayerful countenances the splendour from the altar; and as they pass among them to find place, with what careful and quiet step they thread their way, so as least to disturb those among whom they move; and then drop down upon their knees too, in the first open space, upon the same bare stone floor, princess and peasant, priest and layman, all equal in the immeasurable distance between them and the eternal object of their adoration. In no other time or place is the sublimity of our religion so touchingly felt. No ceremony is going forward in the sanctuary, no sound of song is issuing from the choir, no voice of exhortation proceeds from the pulpit, no prayer is uttered aloud at the altar There are hundreds there, and yet they are engaged in no congregational act of worship. Each heart and soul is alone in the midst of a multitude, each uttering its own thoughts, each feeling its own grace. Yet are you overpowered, subdued, quelled into a reverential mood, softened into a devotional spirit, forced to meditate, to feel, to pray. The little children who come in, led by a mother's hand, kneel down by her in silence as she simply points towards the altar, overawed by the still splendour before them; the very babe seems hushed to quiet reverence on her bosom. The hurried passer-by, who merely looks in, cannot resist the impulse to sink, if only in a momentary genuflection, upon his knee; nay, even the English scoffer, who will face anything else, will not venture to stalk, as elsewhere, up the nave, heedless of others' sacred feelings, but must needs remain under the shelter of the doorway, or steal behind the shadow of the first pillar, if he wishes to look on without partaking. But more forward, or in the recesses of the aisles, how many you will find who have not merely entered in to pay their passing evening visit, but who have spent their hours in that heavenly presence, where they seem to breathe the pure air of Paradise. To them it is, indeed, "the house of God and the gate of heaven!" It does one's spirit good even to look again upon such hours, through years of distance and miles of space; it recalls to mind emotions deeper and tenderer than we may hope for here; it makes one almost envious of those whose privilege they are. Never shall we forget the first evening that we were admitted to enjoy it. It was, indeed, a sumptuous church, though its rich marbles were draperied over, in one of the fairest cities of Italy.[1] But though we have since seen many more costly and more spacious, it has retained in our memory a charm peculiar to itself, a distinctive character impressed by the solemn circumstances under which we first saw it, an affection and interest, which none other has been able to supplant.

But we must hasten on. As night closes in, will there not be danger of this worship ceasing? The last visitors have retired, the sacristan is locking the gates, the poor who have the privilege of asking alms at the door have ceased their pious appeals—for it is right that charity should be exercised at such a place; and where should the lame and the blind sit to ask it, rather than at that gate which of all others best deserves,

---

[1] Santa Maria della Vigne at Genoa.

for the time, the title of "the beautiful"? Still the piety of the faithful is neither exhausted nor fatigued. While equipages are rolling through the streets, conveying the worldly to and from places of entertainment, and long after they have ceased their din, there is one carriage, at least, which is busy all night with a better errand, which at stated hours may be seen to set down at the church a relay of night watchers, and to take to their homes those of the preceding hour. Pious confraternities devote themselves to this as well as to other deeds of piety, and carry on the godly work for centuries, night after night, without newspaper advertisements, dinners, or steam excursions. ("Essays," i. 483.)

THE FORTY HOURS' ADORATION (2)

BUT it is not your Saviour, "as the hidden Manna" of which you partake, that you have here to reverence and love; it is your Lord, your God, triumphant over death for you, yet shrouding from you His overpowering glory, to whom you have to pay your open and solemn homage—not enshrined in His poor tabernacle, where, because unseen, He is often unhonoured, but enthroned, as in heaven, above His own altar, Lord of His own Sanctuary, centre of all surrounding splendour, challenging, with love, deep adoration. Around Him shall flame the hallowed tapers, by whose pure ray the Church symbolises, however feebly, the bright spirits that shine around His heavenly throne. At His feet earth shall scatter its choicest flowers, as its graceful tribute to Him that bloomed so fair from Jesse's root. On all sides shall be arrayed whatever of richness and splendour our poverty can collect, to adorn the chosen abode of Him who hath said, "The silver is Mine and the gold is Mine," and does not disdain any manifestation of our reverence. Hasten then, dearly beloved, to bring whatever may be necessary to enrich the solemnity of that happy day when your Lord, in His kingly progress, shall visit your own temple, saying, "I will fill *this* house with glory," and, whether it be splendid or lowly, shall there abide in special state. Give proof to all that come there to visit Him, that you prize, you cherish, you love this privilege which He bestows, and that, like Solomon and the people of Israel, you have "gladly offered all those things" which are requisite to its becoming, and even splendid enjoyment. And "presently the Lord whom you seek, and the angel of the testament whom you desire, shall come to His temple."

Oh! then go forth with joyful hearts, to meet and welcome Him; and leave Him not alone, so long as He shall condescend to dwell in the midst of you. From that lofty mercy-seat whereon He hath been placed, from that bright radiance in the midst of which, as a peerless and priceless gem, He hath been set—beauty Himself, essential Light, and matchless Splendour—there go forth on every side, not scorching rays of glory, not burning shafts of might, but a mild and constant flow of holiness and grace, which fills the entire space from roof to pavement with the very breath and air of heaven. Silent and soft, as wave impelling wave of fragrance, goes forth, and diffuses itself around, that savour of sweetness, that balm of life, that virtue which, emanating from the sacred humanity of Jesus upon earth, healed all diseases. And from the threshold of this, His palace now no less than His temple, it will pass abroad, and spread itself on all sides, till it reach your dwellings; and, more powerful than that blessing which the Ark of the Covenant (type whereof you now possess the reality) shed over the house of Obededom, it will impart to them peace and grace, and welfare spiritual and temporal. " I will fill this house with glory, saith the Lord of Hosts . . . and in this place I will give peace, saith the Lord of Hosts."

But now it is that you will practise that angelic worship, lost and unknown out of the Catholic Church, the worship of pure adoration. For, beyond her pale, men may praise God, or address Him, or perform other religious acts, but they cannot know nor make that special homage which His presence, as we possess it, inspires; when, without word spoken, or sound uttered, or act performed, the soul sinks prostrate, and annihilates itself, before Him, casts all its powers, and gifts, and brightest ornaments as worthless oblations before His altar, and subjects its entire being, as a victim, to His sole adorable will. When first, then, you approach the place where He is solemnly worshipped, as you humbly bend your knees and bow your heads, let this deep and silent adoration be your first act. Speak not in words, forget all selfish thoughts, repress even all eager longings of your hearts, and receive the benediction of your mighty Lord in solemn stillness; while you, reputing yourselves but dust and ashes at His feet, a nothingness before Him, tender Him the homage of loyal vassals, humbled as the clay before the potter, as the creature before its God. Then raise up your eyes, those keen eyes of Faith, which, through the veil of sacramental elements, see, as John did, "in the midst of the seven golden candlesticks, one like to the Son of man," yea, the adorable Jesus, the king of your souls, and there feast long your sight upon that sacred Humanity which love hath given Him, and with it kindred and brotherhood, and ties of tenderest affection with you. And now speak to Him, but with outpoured souls, with the unrestrained familiarity of warmest friendship, face to face—no longer with the awful Lord, like Moses or Elias, on Horeb, but with them, and Peter, and John, on Thabor, where you see Him radiant with His own light, but mild, and inviting love.

Pray to Him now for your own salvation and for that of all mankind. Pray for the exaltation of His holy Church, for the happiness and prosperity of the supreme pastor, our holy and afflicted Pontiff. Pray for the propagation of the true faith, and the conversion of all in error, and especially of our own dear country. Pray that God will mercifully remove from us the scourges and judgments which we have deserved by our sins, and remember no longer our offences, nor those of our parents, but rather show us mercy, and give to us His good gifts, but principally His grace, holiness of life, and perseverance in His divine service.

And then, oh! never think of rising from before Him without thanking Him from your hearts for this miraculous institution of His power and goodness, this sweetest pledge of His love. Adore Him now again as the Treasure of your souls, the Food of life, the living Bread that cometh down from heaven, your Consoler, your Strengthener, your surest Hope in life and death. Speak to Him of the kindness, of the self-abasement, of the immense condescension which He here exhibits; of the untiring affection for poor man which He displays in bearing with so much coldness, ingratitude, and even sacrilege, as this blessed memorial of His death exposes Him to; of the still more incomprehensible excess of love which makes Him communicate Himself daily to us, frail and sinful creatures, as our food, and thus brings our very hearts and souls into contact with His! And offer Him your humble tribute of reverence and love, in reparation and atonement for those scoffs, contradictions, and blasphemies to which He has long been, and is daily, subject in his adorable Sacrament, and nowhere so much as in this unbelieving land. ("Sermons," i. 394.)

VISITS TO THE BLESSED SACRAMENT

THE terms which Catholics soon come to apply to religious practices are no unapt keys to the interpretation of those feelings with which they are to be accompanied. Thus, the familiar expression "*a visit* to the Blessed Sacrament," so well understood in Catholic countries and Catholic communities, contains a depth of faith and of love which long descriptions could not so adequately convey. It declares at once the simple, hearty, practical belief in the Real Presence; not a vague, surmising opinion, not an uncertain hope that the Lord of glory may be there; but a plain conviction that, as surely as a king dwells in his palace, and may there be found by those who are privileged to enter in; or rather, that as certainly as He Himself dwelt once in a stable, making it His first palace upon earth, and was there "visited" by kings from a distance, and by shepherds from the neighbourhood; that as truly as He abode in the houses of His friends, and was "visited" by Nicodemus for instruction, or by Magdalen for pardon; so really does He now dwell amongst us, in such sort as that we may similarly come before Him and have recourse to Him in our wants. Nothing short of the liveliest faith in the mystery could have introduced or could keep up this practice.

But the term is likewise the offspring and expression of love. It implies a certain intimacy, if one may use so homely a term, with him to whom it is applied. It gets us beyond the dark regions of awe into those of glowing affection; it raises us up above the crouching attitude of Israel's children at the mountain's base—nay, carries us straight through the clouds and lightnings at its side, to the silent, radiant summit, where God and man meet face to face, and discourse together as friends are wont to do. Yes, chamber devotion is doubtless good; the still domestic oratory at home, with its little tokens of loving piety hung around—trophies often from a holier land—is very composing, soothing, and devout. But the great and generous thoughts of Catholic heroism are conceived, or rather inspired, at the altar, where the adorable Sacrament reposes; there, depend upon it, in silent prayer, the noble damsel in heart rejects the world and its vanities, and plights her troth to the spouse of her chaste heart; there the young ecclesiastic, bowing in meditation calm and sweet, muses on the triumphs of his schoolmates over the swords and red-hot pincers of Tonquin, and resolves to share their crown of martyrdom; there whatever is planned for the Church of God that requires earnest zeal and persevering energy, is matured and resolved. And there, too, is the heart unburthened of its daily load of sin and sorrow, anxiety and distress, with a fulness of feeling that comes not elsewhere; sacrifices seem easy which in any other place would be hard; and the Catholic soon learns to feel and utter those words which are there most applicable: "Etenium passer invenit sibi domum, et turtur nidum sibi . . . altaria Tua, Domine virtutum, Rex meus, et Deus meus."[1] ("Essays," i. 480.)

THE BANQUET HALL

THE Church is not merely a teaching, but a feasting place; not a lecture-room, but a banqueting-hall. And which Church exclusively is this? Enter the Catholic Church (the type of the Church in the abstract), and

[1] Ps. lxxxiii. 3, 4.

you find not only always a table, but, if one may speak in so homely a way, a table with the cloth spread, which tells you that to-day there has been already a feast, and to-morrow there will be another, and the day after, as there was yesterday. If a Catholic found it otherwise, if he saw the altar uncovered and naked, and its furniture removed, and its tabernacle, in which the feast lies ever prepared, open and empty, he would conclude at once that the place was not in use; that, in fact, it is not actually used as *a church:* he cannot dissociate the two, the Church and the feast. Where else is this to be found? In the meeting-house, we trow, the pulpit reminds one not of feasts. And in an Establishment church, though the piscina may have been restored, and two new oak carved chairs may be beside the communion-table, *this* is but as a piece of furniture covered up when the family is from home. Nor can we believe that in the mind of an average churchman there is any obvious and natural connection between his religion and the communion-table, nor that by any instinctive association does he think of the latter when he speaks of "going to church." No one, we again repeat, can fully realise this parable but a Catholic. For, as our Saviour spake it to the Jews of His kingdom, consequently of the Church, it is to this it must be applied. But when applied as by a Catholic heart it necessarily is, every part is coherent, the figure is perfect, and the details full of beauty and instruction. It associates two ideas, those of the Church and of the Eucharist, which in him alone are almost correlative. And thus only is the problem solved, how wonderfully a parable spoken of the one can so beautifully apply to the other. ("Essays," i. 140.)

INSTITUTION OF THE COMMUNION

CHARITY and peace, the union of God with man, and of man with his God, the brotherhood of Jesus with us, the bond of love between God and His Spouse on earth—these are the gifts which the lips of our Divine Master drew forth unsparingly from the treasury of His Heart on that memorable night, and embodied in that matchless discourse, sealed by a prayer such as only God could utter to God, which has done more to raise man's dignity and ennoble his being and his thoughts than all the treatises of ancient philosophy or the efforts of modern civilisation.

And yet what was all this sublime teaching of love but merely the adornment of something more admirable still and more sublime, of something done as well as spoken? It was at the same time and at the same table that Jesus took bread and broke it, saying, "This is My Body;" took the cup and blessed it, saying, "This is My Blood." The Heart of Jesus has given us love, has given us peace, and in these words it gives us itself. It was that Heart's delight to be with the children of men, and thus it gained its object, to our infinite gain. What abundance of divine attributes were not required there to prompt and to pronounce efficaciously these words; unbounded wisdom to devise such a mode of uniting man to God, his Saviour; unfailing foresight to know that such an Institution, if made, would form the very life of the spiritual world in the midst of man's corruption; unerring prudence, to temper in it so perfectly the seen with the unseen as to fill the soul with the reality, and save to faith its merit; unlimited knowledge of man, his nature, his wants, his feelings, his frailties, his dangers, his powers, his wishes, such as only belongs to the Creator and the Searcher of the reins and heart, to adapt it exactly to every possible desire of his spirit and every imaginable craving of his weakness; almighty power to put nature in perpetual bondage to grace, so that to the end of time a marvellous combination of supernatural effects should take place, in obedience to a continuous law, without disturbing or ruffling the visible current of natural things; supreme dominion to communicate and delegate to man the exercise of this very act of omnipotence; and, above all, consummate and incomprehensible goodness and love, to set all the rest of these divine attributes in motion, and bind them in one harmonious action—such was the abundance of the Heart from which alone the mouth of Jesus could have spoken those words of life.

To them we owe the best and sweetest privilege of love, that of being able to draw grace and life from their very source, by receiving Him within us who contains it in Himself. There the heart of man reposes upon the Heart of his Redeemer—not outwardly, as John's did, but in closer and even holier union, when his frail and perishable body becomes the Temple of God, the

Tabernacle of his Lord, the abode, however humble, of his Saviour. Thence his very body sucks in immortality from that imperishable Body which could not see corruption; there his soul feasts spiritually upon the virtues and excellences which adorn the Soul of God made man; and there, more wonderful still, his whole being becomes invested with the dignity and glory of the Divinity, which dwells within him, and bestows on him rights and privileges that have their final fulfilment and possession in heaven. How truly, indeed, may it be said of man, that "God entertaineth his heart with delight!" ("Sermons," i. 355.)

BALANCE OF DANGER

BUT, my brethren, before concluding, there is one view of the doctrine under consideration more painful indeed, and fruitful in awful reflections—I mean the balance to be struck between the conflicting beliefs of Catholics and Protestants, and the stakes which we have respectively cast upon them.

On our side, I own that we have risked all our happiness and all our best possession here below. We have placed beside our doctrine the strongest effort of our faith, the utmost sacrifice of individual judgment, the completest renunciation of human pride and self-sufficiency, which are ever ready to rebel against the simple words of revelation. And not so content, we have cast into the scale the fastest anchor of our hope, considering this as the surest channel of God's mercy to us, as the means of individual sanctification, as the instrument of personal and local consecration, as the brightest comfort of our dying hour, the foretaste and harbinger of eternal glory. And as if these stakes were not of sufficient weight, we have thrown in the brightest links of golden charity, feeling that in this blessed Sacrament [the Eucharist] we are the most closely drawn to God, and the most intimately united in affection with our Saviour Christ Jesus.

All this have we placed on our belief; but if, to suppose an impossibility, we could be proved in error, it would at most be shown that we had believed too implicitly in the meaning of God's words; that we had flattered ourselves too easily that He possessed resources of power in manifesting His goodness towards man beyond the reach of our small intellects and paltry speculations; that, in truth, we had measured His love more lovingly than prudently, and had formed a sublimer, though a less accurate estimate of its power than others had done; in fine, that we had been too simple-hearted and childlike in abandoning our reason into His hands because He had "the words of eternal life."

But then, if our faith be right, ponder well what infinitely heavier stakes have been ventured on the other side; for on its supposed falsehood have been risked words of contumely and scorn, of railing and most awful blasphemy! The Holy Sacrament has been repeatedly profaned, and its adoration mocked at as idolatrous, and its priests reviled as seducers, and the very belief in it considered abundant ground for exclusion from political and social benefits. And if what I have advanced have been well proved, then are those who believe not with us living in the neglect of a sovereign command, a neglect to which is attached a fearful penalty. "Unless ye eat the Flesh of the Son of man, and drink His Blood, ye shall not have life in you."

And what conclusion can we draw from this balance of our respective dangers, but the necessity incumbent on all who are in the latter condition to try this important dogma to its foundation, and fully ascertain the ground on which they stand. ("Moorfields' Lectures," XVI.)

CARELESS COMMUNION

WHEN in this blessed Sacrament He comes into our breasts, alas! what does He find? A chamber, perhaps, but lately tenanted by His hateful enemy, sin, ejected thence a few hours before by a hasty repentance. Its paltry furniture is yet in the disorder and confusion which this foe had caused there, bearing on every side traces of the riot and havoc committed within it so long and so late. A few shreds and tattered scraps of virtuous protestations collected together in half-an-hour, out of the stores of our prayer-books, have been hung around it, to cover its habitual bareness. The remains of many a once precious gift, presents from God's bounty, the torn fragments of contracts of love and promises of service, lie scattered about, patched up for the moment by its passing fervour. And, perhaps, even in the corners of this den yet lurk, skulking from His sight, irregular attachments and dangerous affections, which we have not had courage to expel when we turned out His full-grown enemies, but still to His eyes monsters of hateful shape and nature. Into this cell, this dungeon, we invite Him, the King of Glory, and have the courage to introduce Him, the living God; and He remembers the first time He visited it, how clean and fair it was, how cheerful and pleasant a dwelling, and how He then decked it out for us with those gifts, and many others, long since broken, or lost, or flung away. And we—oh, do not we feel our cheeks burning with shame when we have thus received Him, to think what He has found within us, and to what a degradation we have dragged the Son of God! What was the hall of Herod, or the court of Pilate, or the house of Caiphas to this? ("Sermons," i. 94.)

COMMUNION OF JUDAS

JUDAS was the first unworthy communicant; for he received his Lord while in league with His enemies to betray Him into their hands, and notwithstanding the new pledge which he received of love, went on in his horrible purpose. All who, after him, receive the divine Sacrament of our Saviour's Body with similar dispositions, that is, with conscious guilt, are partakers of his treachery. But let me not be misunderstood.

You betray not your Lord if merely cold and faint you approach Him; if, conscious of daily and hourly imperfection, easily distracted in prayer, languid in God's service, subject to smaller transgressions, you seek for nourishment, and warmth, and support from the living Source of them all. You are as a child, or as one sick; you have a right to that which is milk to babes, as well as meat for the strong—to that medicine which strengthens and recovers, as well as confirms and perfects.

You betray not your Lord, if, struggling against the assaults of passion, you feel yourself staggering and miserably weak, nay, wounded and maimed; if, in spite of your determination, your frailty is surprised, and your good resolutions for a moment overthrown, and your virtue impaired; and you still nobly determine to repair immediately the fault, and to fight generously on, and not yield to the foe. You are as the Israelites in battle in the wilderness; you have a double claim to that bread from heaven, that manna which is at once a balm and a food, cure and strength.

You betray not your Lord, even if fallen into the very depths of sin, sunk into the lowest degradation of vice, dead in soul, you rise obedient to God's voice speaking to your troubled heart, and casting aside the garment of death, breaking through the winding bands of iniquity, you return to life. You are as the young woman whom Jesus raised from the dead in the house of Jairus, and to whom He bid her parents give food and refreshment, to recruit her exhausted state.

But you do betray Him, and that most cruelly, when you have entered into a previous compact with His enemy, when you have sold yourself to him for his slave, and are involved in his evil practices, and yet presume to approach the Holy Communion. It may be that you have only just fallen into a grievous sin, and feel all its remorse, but shame hath tied your tongue, and you have concealed your guilt from God's minister, and you suffer all the bitterness of repentance without its fruit, reconciliation, and do cruel penance without forgiveness. Or it may be that, by long habitual guilt, your heart hath become callous, your spirit hath sunk into cold apathy, and you neither take the trouble nor desire the effects of repentance, or you go through its conditions with hollow insincerity and without determination to amend. And so, when the usual periods for approaching the Lord's table come, you scruple not to save appearance by unworthily and wickedly approaching it. In either case what have you done? The blessed Jesus hath invited you as a disciple to His paschal feast, and you with others have come. At your right hand is one like Peter, full of ardour and zeal, burning for His honour, ready to share His sufferings, amazed at the condescension which can stoop so low for "a sinful man"; on your left is another, like to John, pure, virginal, in child-like innocence, who stretches forth to receive the pledge of love in simple confidence, in unassuming affection leaning upon the heaving bosom of his Master; others are around, scarcely less holy, repentant sinners like Matthew, or simple believers like Philip. And whose place do you occupy at the sacred board? Who is your type among the twelve? Look at that scowling wretch who, under a studied seriousness, masks a lurking disbelief; who, while he seems intent on the actions and words of his Lord, is absent in thought amidst very different scenes; who in all outward forms acts and speaks as a faithful follower, while he is in fact a base and scornful traitor. Can you trace no resemblance between yourself and him? You, too, have been lately dallying with the sworn foe of Jesus, sin; you have received its price, and you have given it a permanent lodging in your heart and body. Your mind is no less made up to go on with your transgressions after you shall have sat at His table. You speak with Him in your prayer of preparation, or you go over the mockery of an outward form of it, without sincerity, without serious meaning; you are like Judas, in truth a mocker, a scoffer at that sacred rite, a hypocrite in your prayer. And is not this false treachery?

Perhaps, as you proceed, a touching glance of reproach, a feeling word of expostulation, reaches your mind. In those forms of prayer which you recite, however coldly, there may be words whose force you cannot escape. Through them your sorrowing Lord seems to address you, and say, "Behold, one of you shall betray Me," yea, "he that dippeth his hand with Me in the dish;" or, in the words of the prophet, "Behold, the man of my peace, that eateth my bread, hath greatly supplanted me." Oh! when such words or such looks were addressed to Judas, the traitor's heart perhaps quailed for an instant beneath them; his hand perhaps faltered as it took the proffered morsel from his Master's, but he relented not; and dost thou? Dost thou abandon, unhappy wretch, thy villainous purpose; dost thou cast thyself down at thy Saviour's feet, and beg forgiveness, and desist? Or dost thou persevere in the fatal resolution of advancing still to the holy table and consummating the insult to divine love? And if thou dost, is not this a most unfeeling treachery?

But mark the traitor's purpose. He is, in that preparation for the first Christian Passover, arranging what must ensue. Yes, he has thought again and again what course will be best, in what way the treachery may be most securely accomplished. It shall be by a kiss of affection. He has hit upon this expedient as most likely to secure himself from suspicion, and to attain the quiet, undisturbed possession of his object. He is now resolved—he will betray the Son of man with a kiss! And soon—yes, in a few moments—that very Son of man will stand before thee; and hast thou resolved to meet Him in the semblance of one that loveth Him, with downcast eyes, and hands crossed upon thy bosom, and lips parted, as though chastely to salute thy welcome Lord? And *thus* He is to be delivered over to the enemies that lurk within. And is this other than a most fiendish treachery?

But, lo! the time is come; the awful words have been spoken; the mouth of unfailing truth hath declared His own Body to be there. All are reverently and silently awaiting their turn to partake of the tremendous gift: the first have tasted it, Peter is burning, John is melted into tears; the life-giving portion is proffered to Judas, and he stretches to receive it. Oh! in pity let us hope that he understands not, notwithstanding the words just spoken, what it is! O Son of God! exclaim, if Thou canst, "Father, forgive him, for he knoweth not what he doth!" Yet he seems to receive but as the rest; he does not turn pale, his throat is not scorched, his breast does not throb with anguish, and he makes way for a brother disciple, without his black deed of baseness being ever suspected. And how is it with thee? The same Lord of glory hath uttered the same words of power; and thou knowest it, the same effect hath ensued. It is not bread that hath been held up before thee: thou hast bowed down before it in real or seeming adoration as the sacred Body of Christ; and striking thy breast before Him, thou hast declared thyself unworthy that He should enter under thy roof. But He comes nevertheless; He comes as a friend, He comes as a brother, and thou takest advantage of His condescension and His love, of His eager desire to be united with thee. Thou hastenest forward to meet Him; thou openest the unclean gates of thy house to admit Him in; and thou closest them upon Him, to leave Him in the company of all that He hateth and abhorreth, while thou mockest Him by muttering some formal words of thanks and congratulation! And is not this a worse than Judas's treachery?

But this is not the worst. Judas, when he so cruelly betrayed his Lord, and outraged Him in His sacrament of love, could not know the extent of his crime. He lived not to see Him scourged and buffeted, and crowned with thorns. He saw not and heard not of Calvary. Three long hours of torture and anguish, endured for his sake, he knew nothing of nor foresaw not, as the consequence of his crime. The love of his Saviour he had experienced in life, but knew not of in death. The Eucharist with him preceded that which gave it efficacy: it was a commemoration of what was to be, rather than of what was. But to thee it is not thus. Thou hast seen Christ suffer and die for thee. Thou knowest that thy wickedness inflicted His cruel blows, and that through love for thee He was nailed and expired on a cross. All this He represents to thee in this living banquet; the fruit of all these sufferings He comes now to pour into thy breast; and yet thou dost not relent—thou heedest not all this love, but recklessly turnest this wonder of Almighty power and charity to the means and instrument of offending Him, of insulting and of outraging Him! And is not this—but no, this is a treachery which none upon earth, or in the abyss below, can commit, save a Christian; and God forbid that I should characterise it by that name!

Such is the infamous treason of an unworthy communicant. He takes advantage of the goodness of his Saviour, and of His most amiable institution, to sin against Him; he insults Him most grossly where He most specially wishes to be loved and honoured; and, to crown all, by his sacrilege he turns into poison His sweetest food, and into death His fountain of life. ("Sermons," ii. 150.)

FERVENT COMMUNION

WHEN, with a conscience cleansed by penance, of the lesser transgressions to which all are subject, and a heart at peace with itself, free from rancour, from anxiety, from disturbing fear, they approach their Saviour's feast, they feel their hearts so divided between eagerness and humility, love and a sense of unworthiness, as to tremble, they scarcely know if from hesitation or hope. But when they have drawn nigh unto the altar, and received the pledge of their salvation, He seems to come into their souls as rain upon the fleece, in calm and sweet serenity. Their hearts are too full for analysing their feelings; but there is a sense of silent, unutterable happiness—an absorbing overflow of tranquil joy which disdains the feeble expression of the tongue. The presence of their God is felt with sufficient awe to depress the soul into humble adoration—the presence of our loving Redeemer is experienced with an intensity of affection that burns in the heart, rather than breaks forth into a flame. But this deep paroxysm of heavenly feeling, this foretaste of future bliss, cannot last long, but that the outburst of contending affections must take place. It is as though so many different inmates of the heart, the children of the house, scarce restrained for a time from the presence of a brother they revere and love, at length broke open the door into his presence, and poured forth their tumultuous emotions upon him. There hope seems to seize upon his strengthening hand, and faith to gaze upon his inspiring eye, and love to bury its face in his bosom, and gratitude to crown his head with garlands, and humble sorrow to sit down at his feet and weep. And amidst this universal homage and joy of every affection and every power, the blessed Jesus sits enthroned, sole master of the heart and of the soul, commanding peace and imparting gladness, filling with sweetness, as with a heavenly fragrance, the entire being. True, the vision soon dies away, and leaves us to the drearier duties of the day, its burthen and its heat; but the dew of the morning will lie upon that Christian's soul long after the bright cloud that dropt it hath faded away. ("Sermons," i. 99.)

PROGRESS BY COMMUNIONS

AND in what terms shall I speak of that banquet of grace and of love, that daily food, simply to gaze on which in heaven, renovates each moment the immortality of the angels, to partake of which on earth, associates man with the Giver, and incorporates him with the exhaustless treasure, of redemption and grace? It is a paschal feast, which not only, by the sprinkling of its blood, secures us from the stroke of the destroying angel, merited by our transgressions, but if partaken of with girded loins, and feet shod in readiness to obey the call of heaven, gives us a sure pledge that the tumultuous waves of passion shall open before us, and that the pursuing array of our enemies shall be destroyed, to our salvation. It is a manna, the food of the strong, not only refreshing us after the toil of our preceding march, but giving vigour to undertake each day another stage towards our promised land. It is the bread of angels, not merely consoling us by the sweetness of its savour when escaped with Elias from the persecution of our foe, but renewing our youth as the eagle's, to push forward our journey to the mountain, where we shall see God. Oh! is it possible that we should periodically—perhaps daily—partake of food like this and yet make no sensible advance in grace; that receiving such additional means of sanctification, we should remain, from year to year, moving, as it were, round one point, receding, indeed, too often from it by transgression, then only anxious to regain it by amendment, but seemingly never able to advance our position a single step?

You will not, surely, screen yourself with the foolish apology, that all are not called to equal perfection; that the higher degrees of humility, mortification, meekness, or patience, are incompatible with your situation in the world; and that you have not in you the germs of that perfection to which others may aspire, but must be content merely to tread the beaten paths of obvious duty. Alas! alas! how do we deceive ourselves! Were your adversary to raise his voice and proclaim thus much to the world; were he to denounce you as one whom nature and grace have only destined to move in the lower spheres of virtue, as one whose barren heart was incapable of supporting the luxuriancy of full-grown excellence; if your friend were to whisper that he had observed in you no disposition to superior good, no prospect of your ever attaining distinguished virtue—oh! how would you rise in your indignation to strike down the one as a slanderer, and discard the other as a railing hypocrite! In fact, while we plead before God, with mock humility, our inability to reach perfection, our pride flatters us that it is perfectly within our grasp. We fancy that, if the days of persecution were to return, we should be able to display the courage of the martyrs, though at present our faith is cooled almost into indifference; that if the world were to turn upon us and unjustly condemn us, we could bear its unmerited scorn with fortitude and patience, while we now start into passion on the slightest provocation. Nay, even in the midst of our habitual lukewarmness, we imagine that a period will come when we shall be fervent indeed; and perhaps we picture to ourselves our last moments, as to be edifying to all around us by our resignation and calmness, by the tender and affecting piety in which we trust to breathe out our last. ("Sermons," ii. 137.)

MONUMENTAL WORSHIP

IF the Catholic Church, in all things essential of faith and worship, lays claim to apostolic antiquity, she no less holds a right to continuity of descent, and this, as well as the other, must be by monuments attested. When we cast our eyes over England and see in every part remains of ancient grandeur belonging to a very early age—raised lines of prætorian encampments and military roads, or sepulchral mounds with their lachrymals and brazen vessels; then in our search find nothing more till, many centuries after, noble edifices for worship, first somewhat ruder, then ever growing in beauty, begin to cover the land—we conclude, indeed, that it has long been peopled, but that the break of monumental continuities proves the later race to have had nought in common with the earlier, but that a dreary waste of some sort must have widely spread and lasted long between them. Not so, on the other hand, is it with this city [Rome], in which an unfailing series of public monuments from the earliest times shows that one people alone have ruled and been great within it, and guided its policy upon a constant plan. It is even thus with the Church which, in many and varied ways, has recorded its belief, its aspirations, and its feelings upon monuments of every age—in none more clearly than in her sacred offices. It would be unnatural to refer many of the rites now observed to the very earliest ages. What have joyful processions in common with the low and crooked labyrinths of the catacombs? How would the palm branch grate upon the feelings of men crushed under persecution, and praying in sackcloth and ashes for peace? These are the natural symbols of joy and triumph; they express the outburst of the heart when restored to light and liberty; they are forms of Christian lustration over scenes and places that have been defiled with previous abominations.

One striking difference between the Old and New Law seems to consist in this, that the latter was not content to form the spirit of the religious, but moulded its external appearance to an unalterable type. The Jewish nation might undergo any political modification, but the forms of its worship, its place and circumstances, its ceremonies and expressions, were ever to be the same. And yet with this stiff, unvarying character its worship was essentially monumental. The paschal solemnity was a ceremonial rite, acting dramatically, and so commemorating the liberation of Egypt; the Feast of Pentecost reminded every succeeding generation of the delivery of the law; that of Tabernacles celebrated the long sojourn in the desert. Later new festivals were added, to record the dedication of the Temple under Solomon, and its purification under the Macabees, and the salvation of the people from the cruel designs of Aman. Many of the Psalms, or canticles sung in the Temple, were likewise historical, or composed by David on particular passages of his life.

But in all this we see no power of development; no expressive force which allowed the feelings and powers of each age to imprint themselves on the worship, and characterise it in later times by the monumental remains of discipline and customs variable in every age. In the sense which I have spoken of the Jewish religion, the Christian worship is eminently monumental, as the very festivals of which we are treating do abundantly declare. And in addition to this, it has continued, from age to age, both to institute new festivities as memorials of its

Dramatic Worship

varied relations with outward things, and to mark its feelings at peculiar seasons, in every part of its offices and prayers. ("Lectures on Holy Week," p. 94.)

DRAMATIC WORSHIP

BUT the prevailing character of poetry throughout these services is the dramatic in its noblest sense. Before, however, exemplifying my observations, I have something to premise. I may be thought incautious in the selection of the term I have just used, as though it gave some countenance to the silly remark so often made upon the Catholic worship, as scenic, showy, or theatrical. Even if what I am going to say brought me in contact with such commonplace sneers, I should not shrink from it, because I do not think the poverty of words, which is felt in all languages, should be the basis of an argument. Nor, if pomp and magnificence, which formerly belonged to everything royal and noble, have in modern times been confined in our country to theatres, and have thence received a reproachful name, will any one conclude that the Church, which has preserved them, ought to abandon them in consequence ? Nay, I should think any one betrayed great want of sense who traduced as theatrical that which existed before theatres. The pomp of the Levitical worship was certainly great and imposing, and would bear that ignominious name as well as ours. Yet God commanded it; and it is but a poor speech that can find no better epithet to give it.

But when I speak of the dramatic form of our ceremonies, I make no reference whatever to outward display; and I choose that epithet for the reason already given, that the poverty of language affords me no other for my meaning. The object and power of dramatic poetry consists in its being not merely descriptive but representative, and that, not only when reduced to action, but even when only consisting of words. Its character is to bear away the imagination and soul to the view of what others witnessed, and excite in us, through their words, such impressions as we might have naturally felt on the occasion. The inspired poets of the Old Law, the prophets I mean, are full of this lofty and powerful poetry; nothing can be more truly dramatic, as Louth has observed, than the opening of the sixty-third chapter of Isaiah,[1] where the Messiah and a chorus are represented as holding a splendid colloquy together. The latter first asks, "Who is this that cometh from Edom with garments dyed in Bozra?" The other replies, "I am the proclaimer of justice, mighty in salvation." The chorus again demands, "Why then is thy raiment red, and thy garments as of one who hath trodden the wine-press?" And again he answers, "I have trodden the wine-press alone." This is dramatic in the noblest sense of the word, as are many other passages in the same sublime prophet. The Psalms are often constructed in the same manner, as I may have occasion to observe later; but the Canticle of Solomon and the Book of Job are examples of

[1] *De Sacra Poesi*, p. 318; Oxf. 1810.

Prayers against Evil Spirits

a dramatic composition of a much higher order, where scene succeeds to scene, and a growing beauty or majesty of dialogue respectively is exhibited, which will defy all rivalry from the fairest specimens of uninspired poetry. ("Lectures on Holy Week," p. 46.)

PRAYERS AGAINST EVIL SPIRITS

IT was manifestly the sense and conviction of those who composed the prayers of the ancient Church, that we are living in a perfect atmosphere of invisible and spiritual enemies, who disturb nature, thwart the providential direction of things, play foully on our imagination, trouble our peace, and try to pervert our reasons. They meddle with everything that is of use to man, and endeavour to mar its purposes. They infest every place in which they can tempt and seduce him—from his own dwelling to the house of God itself. Earth, and air, and water are equally their elements; the first is shaken and convulsed, the second is darkened by thunderclouds and tortured into whirlwinds, the third is lashed into foaming billows, by their permitted but most malicious agency. The doctrine on this head is clearly apostolical;[1] and that it was apprehended by the early Church, in a far more lively manner than by our duller faith, the writings of the Fathers clearly prove. Now, the Church, in all her prayers, considers herself appointed to be the antagonist and vanquisher of this hostile crew; and while she shows her deep and earnest

[1] Ephes. vi. 12.

conviction of the difficulties of the contest, she betrays no uneasiness about its results. She hath power to rule and to quell these spirits of darkness. Moreover, she is not alone in the conflict. Every part of her offices displays her assurance that a bright circle of heavenly spirits is arrayed around her for the protection of herself and her children; spirits who can wrestle upon equal terms with those unsubstantial foes, and whose swords are tempered for their subtle natures. There mingle, too, in all her religious actions, legions of blessed saints, who have loved and honoured her upon earth, and who now worship and pray, invisible, with her children. These strong impressions of the incessant conflict going on between the enemies and the friends of God are clearly and feelingly expressed by the Church in innumerable places. The whole rite of consecration of a church keeps before our eyes the efforts which will be made by our invisible tempters to spoil God's work. The cross is planted at the door, the walls are purified and blessed, prayers are repeatedly poured out, to shield the holy place and its worshippers against the fraud and violence of wicked spirits. The blessing of bells, of crosses, and of reliquaries have reference to the same idea. No substance is employed in any solemn rite (except the Eucharistic elements, which are deemed holy from their very destination) without a previous exorcism or adjuration of the enemy, that he quit all hold upon them, and presume not to misuse them. The water, the salt, and the oil, consecrated for sacramental unction, are all so prepared; and the blessing upon them, and upon other similar objects, is, that wherever they are presented, sprinkled, or used, evil spirits may be put to flight, and their malice and wiles be confounded. The solemn application of this feeling in the rite of baptism has been well enforced by Dr. Pusey in his "Tract on Baptism," where he regrets the loss, in the Anglican ritual, of that portion of the service so calculated to produce strong impressions on the faithful.

There is surely a mysterious sublimity in this idea, the effect of which is most striking and almost overpowering in these and other Church offices. The priest or bishop who attentively and devoutly performs them, feels himself necessarily as one acting with power and authority against a fearful enemy: in the name of the Church he is striving against him for mastery; he is wresting from his gripe, by a strong hand, one of God's creatures which he has enslaved; or he is beating off legions of dark, gloomy spirits, who flap their unclean wings, and with sullen flight retreat beyond the precincts from which they are driven, and hovering around them, as vultures kept from their prey, dare not violate the seal of Christ's holy Cross placed upon its anointed doors. Prayers composed to express and exercise this high authority must have a solemn and most elevated tone; the very idea must fill them with poetry of the highest order. It has often struck us that "the world of spirits" has been far too much forgotten amongst us; that we think more of the two visible powers in the triple confederacy of evil than of the far stronger and subtler of

P

the three—nay, the master of the other two. We seem literally to have renounced "the devil and all his works" by never troubling ourselves about them. With the exception of one or two prayers which we have borrowed from the Church office, an allusion to this state of conflict is seldom met with in our devotions. We fight our spiritual battles as if only with tangible foes, and, consequently, with material weapons; we arm ourselves with caution against danger, and with prudence against temptation; we study how we shall avoid sin by shunning men, how we shall escape passion by fleeing from conversation; but we forget that we have an enemy near and around us whom no foresight or prudence can elude or prevent, who will bring the dangers to us even in a desert, and surround us with temptations even in a cell. The only chance against him is in prayer, but in prayer such as the Church employs, full of deep conviction that what we pray against is a reality and no fiction, of earnestness proportioned to the perils to be averted, and of loving trustfulness in the protection of the God of heaven, who will make us walk on the asp and the basilisk, and in the guardianship of those blessed spirits who will bear us up in their hands through His commission. ("Essays," i. 414.)

DIABOLICAL SUGGESTIONS

THE soul of each is to its possessor the scene of conflicts which he cannot compose. He seems to find in himself a twofold being, a diversity of wills and desires, whereof one side ever seems opposed to his happiness, and hardly to belong to himself. He is conscious of evil suggestions, proposed with a suddenness and an inconsequence that make them seem to come from without—of envious or malicious whisperings which no inward reflections seem to have raised; of proud emotions which spring up with a startling newness, for which his familiar sentiments may in nowise account. And he feels that he loathes and fears these unsought ideas, and he turns him from them; yet they haunt him as phantasies which disappear not when the eyelids are closed, and he adjures them by every name that is most powerful, but they laugh at his spell as though raised not by him; and he grapples with them manfully, but they resist and wrestle with him as though having in them an energy and life distinct from his; and if he persevere and conquer, he seems to notice the sullenness of the retiring foe, who ever and anon looks round again and wishes to renew the skirmish, and keeps him for some space armed and upon his guard till once more he feels himself alone. In his solemn musings upon the holiest things, he experiences at whiles an impertinent intrusion on the part of discordant and uncalled-for recollections; in his secretest communion with his own spirit upon the surest truths, the voice no less secret of a scoffing adversary seems to be heard proposing ill-timed and jarring objections, which, even suppressed, cast a gloom over his consoling occupation, and spread a mysterious cloud over the blessed visions which his eye had caught. The purest soul seems to itself at times defiled by the presence of monstrous imaginings, before which it cowers down in shrinking horror; the aspirations of the most perfect after a union with God are checked and arrested by the interposition of a shifting adversary who seems ever to come before them; and the blessedness whereof man is capable, and which should be summed up in virtue, is alloyed and disturbed by the interference of another power, mischievous as unhappy, with every effort for its consummation.

This complication of moral phenomena forms that mystery of temptation which the revelation of God hath alone sufficiently explained, and which the gospel of this day has abundantly set forth.

For, in the first place, we here learn that, as in the first trial of man's fidelity, the evil spirit actively and perseverantly strives to bring us into the commission of sin, which at once explains that instigation to wickedness which, in spite of our desires and our repugnance, obstinately pursues us. Difficult as it is to account for this powerful energy opposed to our wishes and endeavours, though apparently springing from faculties under the mind's control, we should have attributed it simply to our now inborn corruption had not God's holy Word taught us to view the conflict in a more solemn light. "For our wrestling," says St. Paul, "is not against flesh and blood, but against principalities and powers; against the rulers of the world of this darkness, against the spirits of wickedness in high places" (Eph. vi. 12). Hence we see that the evil power is active indeed, though so only permissively and subordinately to a wisely counselling and well-directing power of good. We learn that the tempter is, in fact, a spirit that, having an existence distinct from ours, can yet communicate inscrutably with our minds; and thus without debasing, like them of old, the supreme Godhead into a contest with a rival power, or, still more, into a submission to a constraining destiny, the warfare is transferred to a lower stage, while man is elevated into the champion against an order originally higher than his own, but than his more fallen; and the justice and goodness of God in this permission to harass and annoy is amply vindicated in the triumphs of His might, through such feeble instruments as we, in the splendour of reward which crowns the victories of His conquerors, and in the unspeakable grandeur of redemption, which could not have been without the existence of this rampant energy of evil. ("Sermons," i. 255.)

THE ROSARY

WE have already observed that a great principle of Catholic devotion is the endeavouring to feel as we should have done amidst the scenes which excite it. The Church in her public offices suggests this idea; she takes us successively to all the great events in the history of our redemption, puts us vividly into them, presents us to the actors, and instils into us their feelings. . . .

We are told by Goethe that he trained himself to look at objects with the eye of the great artists, so that in a group he could discern what characteristics Raffaelle, or Guercino, or Michael Angelo would respectively have seized; and a landscape he would contemplate accordingly as Claude, or Salvator Rosa, or Poussin would have done, each drawing from it a different picture, though all true representations. And so surely, if one wish to contemplate the tender scene of our Lord's Nativity, one would gaze upon it through the eyes of those poor but happy shepherds who witnessed it, and try to feel and adore, humbly and lovingly, as they must have done; or one may approach it in the train of the Eastern kings, and, with more distant veneration, offer up such gifts as God has granted us. Again, if we go up, in devotion, to Calvary, we may place ourselves in many different positions and aspects: we may look upon the Cross from the gibbet of the penitent thief, and take comfort from words spoken towards it; or we may think of Magdalene, and gaze through her tearful eyes, and feel love, not unmixed with remorse, and perhaps with indignation, too, against the authors of all this woe (alas! ourselves); or we may stand with John, love predominating over every passion, noting diligently, with the evangelical eagle's ken, every minute detail of sorrow, and every marvellous mystery of charity. And after the glad third day, when He is risen again, we may find many ways of taking part in so joyful an event; it may be shame and sorrow stricken, like poor Peter, or with spouse-like eagerness, as Mary addressed the supposed gardener. But surely there is One, who had a share in these and all other such scenes, through whose eyes we should all be glad to view them, in whose heart we should long to feel them. If in the reflection upon another's soul we wish to view the occurrences—joyful, dolorous, or triumphant—through which mercy and glory were purchased for us, there is one "Mirror of Justice," bright, spotless, untarnished, which reflects them in their full clearness and truth. Shall we not strive to look upon it? If these events called up feelings in every spectator, in one breast alone they found depth, and breadth, and strength enough to do them full justice. Shall we not watch and study its heavings and powerful throes? The maternal heart alone could contain the ocean of bitterness, or the heaven of joy, which these various mysteries were fitted to create. And hence the natural desire of loving souls to be its associate, and to stand with its venerable possessor in sight of all that she saw, in hearing of all that she heard, in observance of all that she laid up in her heart. . . .

This is, then, the devotion which the Church of God proposes to us in the Rosary; the contemplation of the mysteries of this threefold portion of our Redeemer's life, in connection and sympathy with His loving Mother's feelings in each. It is essentially directed to Him; being, in fact, the noblest and perfectest mode of meditating on Him. There is still another view of it, which, it strikes us, will facilitate and endear its practice to many; and therefore we will venture to unfold it.

The Church realises to the utmost the communion of saints, by making the intercourse between earth and heaven as vivid as possible. The exclamations of the old Christians at the martyrs' tombs were as bold and direct as though they had been addressing the confessors in prison. And the Fathers represent them to their hearers as though present to them, defending their cities from visible enemies, and actively interesting themselves in their welfare. It is only doing in their regard what she wishes to make us do towards their Head and Lord—give the greatest possible reality to her belief concerning them. She existed in the small Apostolic College, and the handful of disciples who enjoyed our Lord's society on earth; the pious women from Galilee, and the few, like Joseph of Arimathea, formed her laity, as the others did her clergy. She increased in multitudes, but she strove to alter not in feeling. What the apostles felt towards their Master they continued, no doubt, to feel after He was ascended —the same veneration, the same love, the same trustfulness, the same desire to imitate Him. And these feelings they would leave as a legacy to their successors, who, in their turn, would continue to *them*, after they had sealed their testimony, similar attachment, similar respect. Could Polycarp fail, to the end of his days, communing spiritually with the beloved disciple John, by passing again and again in holy meditation over the many happy hours during which he had heard him recount every incident witnessed by him in his Saviour's life, and listened to the fervent accents of charity in

The Rosary

which they were related? The same kind of communion, only more exalted and more deeply respectful, we may easily suppose to have been kept up by those who enjoyed in life the familiarity of our Blessed Lady.

It has often struck us, that many who in latter times have not scrupled to use the coldest, and even disrespectful, language respecting her, would shrink from the idea of acting similarly towards her, had they lived in her day and had her near. When, particularly, we have heard the indignation of fancied zeal break from female lips against any respect being paid, or devotion expressed towards her who is the peerless glory, the matchless jewel of her sex, we have been led to think how differently the heart that gave the tongue such utterance would have felt, had its compassion been claimed by the venerable matron whose bereavement of the best of sons had been caused for its sake. Many who can speak unkindly of her in heaven would have melted into compassion over her on earth; would have kissed with deep reverential awe the hand that had lifted from the ground and received into a maternal embrace the same sacred Body, just born and just dead —the Infant and the Corpse; and would have deemed it a privilege inestimable, if granted them, to listen, low upon the ground, to her many tales of joy and sorrow— glowing in her delight, and softening in her grief, and exulting in her triumph. That some holy souls partook of such happiness no one can doubt. During the years that she survived her Son, she conversed with His and her friends, an object surely of affectionate regard and deep veneration. And of what would she discourse so willingly and so well as of Him of whom her breast was ever full? Or, how would they express their love better than by making Him their theme? How easily does the imagination depict the scene of some faithful follower, like Luke, anxious to have accurate knowledge of all things from the beginning, making inquiries concerning the earlier periods of our Lord's life, and then listening to the marvellous history most sweetly told; how fair and reverent the archangel came, and how her heart fluttered when she heard his salutation, and how her soul overflowed with consciousness of unheard-of grace, as she accepted his errand; how wonderfully Elizabeth greeted her, and how their infants mysteriously rejoiced in mutual recognition; how that cold December night was warmed and brightened by the first appearance of her godlike Child, and her breast enraptured with heavenly delights, as He thence drew His first earthly nourishment; how holy Simeon proclaimed His dignity, and showed Him honour in the Temple; and how her three days' tears were dried up, when she found her lost Son, sitting mild and radiant with celestial wisdom, amidst the old men of the Law. What looks, what emotions accompany the recital! With what breathless respect is it drunk in by the future Evangelist! Or, we may fancy John more privileged to tread upon that tenderer ground, on which both have walked together—the path of the Cross, on some sad anniversary, dwelling with her upon each afflicting event, recalling faithfully every sacred word, till she voluntarily felt over again the sword of grief which had pierced her soul; and then would she not change the theme, and pass over to the bright Sunday morning, which saw Him rise from the grave to comfort the sharers of His sufferings, and to how He mounted before them all to His proper seat, at the Father's right hand, and thence sent down His Holy Spirit on them? And who would now restrain her thoughts from following Him in spirit thither, and casting up a wistful glance towards the resting-place for which she longed, in which she saw Him, her sovereign Love, prepared to receive and crown her, when the fulness of her time shall be complete, and the perfection of her patience manifested?

Now, a contemplative mind, deeply, affectionately contemplative, not envying, but striving to copy those who had such singular happiness as we have described, will find in the holy Rosary the opportunity of most nearly approaching it. Looking at the Blessed Mother of God as only removed in place, not in affection—changed in situation, not in heart—he will love to entertain himself with her, as he would then have done; will fix his eye on her, as he discourses with her, in a devout salutation and prayer, upon each of those mysteries, successively, in which she had such an interest. Instead of the barren and distracting form of prayer, which some complain they find it, they will thus discover in it that mine of spiritual riches, and that sweetness of consolation which we know all those saints have found in it who have been particularly distinguished for their piety and devotion towards the life and death of the Son of God, as well as towards His loving Mother.

We may be asked—Is this what may be called the *popular* understanding of this devotion, and is it thus that the poor in Catholic countries practise it? We answer—It is, as far as their capacity goes. They know that each decade in the Rosary has reference to a particular mystery, and their catechism has taught them exactly to know them all; and whenever the Rosary is recited in common, the contemplation of each is expressly suggested. And this advertence is necessary to gain the indulgences granted to the devotion. They direct, therefore, their attention to the proper mystery, and say their prayers in its honour; this is sufficient. Ignorant persons cannot meditate as well as the more instructed, nor do they equally understand the words of prayers, or lessons from Scripture read to them. But their good-will and fervour do more than make up for this. Happy should we be if we could plead the same excuse! What we have wished to do is to recommend this devotion to those who fancy it insipid and unprofitable, by showing that the most spiritual-minded may find in it much food, wholesome and strengthening food, most sweet and delicious too. But we must likewise add that we have another ground for loving this devotion, and encouraging all to it—those even who find it difficult to realise in practice what we have said. It is because it is the devotion of the poor among Catholics, the devotion of the lowly, the ignorant, the afflicted, the humble beadsmen, the *pauperes Christi.* It is with theirs that we wish *our* prayers to be judged, not with the Pharisees'! We dread the thought of being one day interrogated concerning them, as men of education, men of information, book-men, that looked down upon the poor pilgrim at the church door, who could only repeat his Paters and Aves. We look with fear to being asked what we drew out of our silver-clasped, velvet-bound prayer-books, that the simple old peasant at the bottom of the church did not get out of her beads, which we despised. Whether we have thence become more earnest, more fervent, more humble, more devout. We like not that sentence of an ancient Father, " Surgunt indocti, et rapiunt regnum Dei ; et nos cum nostris literis mergimur in profundum." So will we be pleased to be reckoned among the poor, and asked to be held to have prayed with them. ("Essays," i. 497.)

" IMAGE-WORSHIP "

WE are there told of pictures which, carried in procession, stopped the plague and averted the cholera. That God *may* have made use of a pious representation for such a purpose seems no more impossible than that by a brazen serpent looked upon He should have stopped the plague of fiery serpents; whether He has done so in individual cases must depend upon historical evidence. Only let us not overlook the fervour of supplication, the uplifted hands and hearts of thousands who make up the procession in those cases, the strong cry and tears which issue from the crowds of suppliants (we speak experienced) that go before and behind, nay, the prayers of the Church and its ministers who attend it; and if, when these have been all set in action, whether by a representation of Christ or His Blessed Mother, or by the words of a living saint, violence is done to heaven, and the prayers of God's people are heard, let us not quarrel with names, and be astonished if men pay reverence to that which called forth the fervour of their prayers, by forming a rallying-point to their united supplications; nay, if they thus symbolise and express their feeling that her prayers whose image they accompanied, rather than their own, obtained for them what they asked. For, we suppose, no one ever imagined that when wonderful effects of this sort are attributed to any pictures of saints carried in procession, they are to be considered apart from the feelings which they excite and the prayers that accompany them. (*Dublin Review*, August 1841. "Essays," ii. 283.)

MEDITATION

IN the Catholic Church, besides public or private vocal prayer, every one is directed and urged to the practice of mental prayer or meditation. For this duty the Church furnishes simple rules and methods, varying somewhat, but all with one practical end. She has at hand almost countless models, forms, and even fully developed draughts, scarcely requiring to be filled in.

In carrying out this familiar practice, it will be obvious that very different degrees of success will be attained. To some it continues almost to the end irksome and trying, full of distraction and imperfection. This may easily arise from natural deficiencies in the mind, or from habitual negligence. But to a willing and persevering mind these difficulties will diminish, and the power of concentrating the thoughts and affections upon a given subject will increase and strengthen.

Thus far any one may aspire with every chance of success. Then comes a higher stage, when this power of fixing the mind is not only easy, but most pleasing; when, without formal guidance, the soul rests, like the bird poised upon its wings, motionless above the earth, plunged, as it were, in the calm atmosphere which surrounds and sustains it on every side. This is the state of contemplation when the placid action of a deeply inward thoughtfulness, undisturbed by other objects, is intent on gazing upon images and scenes fixed or passing as on a mirror before it, without exertion or fatigue, almost without note of time.

This condition, with its requisite power, is also attainable by those who regularly and seriously apply to meditation.[1] Yet, when we have reached it, we are

---

[1] Any one familiar with the Exercises of St. Ignatius will understand the difference between meditation and contemplation in the sense here used, and how from one he is led to the other. This is very different from the "prayer of contemplation," which belongs to mystical theology.

still standing on the ground, and have not set foot on the first step of the "mystical ladder" which St. John teaches how to mount.

Far above this earthly exercise of contemplation is one which belongs to a much higher and purer sphere, above the clouds and mists of the one in which we move. To reach it is given to few, and of those few fewer still have left us records of their experience. Yet —and this is sufficient for our present purpose—that the consummation of their desires and attainment of their scope was a closer union with God is acknowledged by all. The soul, thoroughly purified of all other affections, reaches a sublime and supernatural power of settling all its faculties in the contemplation of the Supreme Being with such clearness and intensity that its very existence seems lost in Him; the most perfect conformity and uniformity with all the emanations of His will are established as its guiding laws; and, as far as is yet compatible, union the most complete is obtained between the imperfect spirit of man and the infinite Spirit that created it to its own image and likeness. (Preface to "Works of St. John of the Cross.")

CONTEMPLATION

IT is well known that a mind naturally adapted to a pursuit, and thus led ardently to follow it, after having become thoroughly conversant and familiar with all its resources, becomes almost, or altogether, independent of its methods, and attains conclusions by compendious processes, or by intuitive foresight, which require in others long and often complicated deductions. Familiar illustrations may be found in our habitual speaking without thinking of our grammar, which a foreigner has constantly to do while learning our language; or the almost inexplicable accuracy of calculation in even children gifted with the power of instantaneous arithmetical solutions.

A mathematician acquires by study this faculty; and it is said that Laplace, in the decline of life, could not any longer fill up the gaps in the processes by which, at the age of greater mental vigour, he had reached, without effort, the most wonderful yet accurate conclusions.

What is to be found in these abstruser pursuits exists no less in those of a lighter character. The literary mind, whether in thinking, writing, or speaking, when well disposed by abilities and well tutored by application, takes in without effort the entire theme presented to it, even with its parts and its details. Sometimes it is like a landscape revealed, in a dark night, by one flash of lightning; oftener it resembles the calmer contemplation of it, in bright day, by an artist's eye, which is so filled with its various beauties that it enables him to transfer it at home to the enduring canvas, on which many may enjoy it.

The historian may see, in one glance, the exact plan of a work, with its specific aims and views; its sources, too, and its auxiliary elucidations. The finished orator, no less, when suddenly called upon, will hold from end to end the drift and purpose of his entire discourse, and deliver, without effort, what to others appears an elaborate composition. But, still more, the poet indulges in noblest flights up to the regions of sublime, or over the surface of beautiful thoughts, while he appears to be engaged in ordinary occupation, or momentarily musing in vague abstraction.

Indeed, even where manual action is required to give utterance to thought, the result is the same. The consummate musician sits down to a complicated instrument, silent and dumb, till his fingers communicate to it his improvised imaginings, bearing to its innermost organisation, by a sort of reflex action of the nerves of sensation on those of motion, the ready and inexhaustible workings of his brain, sweet melodies and rich harmonies, with tangled knots and delicious resolutions—effortless, as if the soul were in the hand, or the mechanical action in the head.

In the few examples which are here given, and which might easily be multiplied, the point illustrated is this, that where, with previous natural dispositions and persevering cultivation, perfection in any intellectual pursuit has been attained or approached, the faculty exercised in it becomes in a manner passive, dispenses with intermediate processes, and receives their ultimate conclusions like impressions stamped upon it. Labour almost ceases, and *spontaneity* of thought becomes its substitute.

In this condition of mind, familiar to any one possessing genius in any form, perceptions, ideas, reason-

Contemplation 243

ings, imagery, have not to be sought; they either dart at once complete into the thought, inborn, and perfect to their very arms, as Pallas was symbolically fabled to express this process; or they grow up, expanding from a small seed to a noble plant, but as if by an innate sap and vigour. There is a flow into the mind of unsought images, or reflections, or truths; whence they come one hardly knows. They were not there before; they have not been forged, or cast, or distilled within.

And when this spontaneous productiveness has been gained, the occupation of mind is not interrupted. St. Thomas is said to have concluded an argument against the Manichees alone at the royal table; Bishop Walmesley renounced his mathematical studies on finding them painfully distract him at the altar. Neither recreation, nor serious employment, nor noise, nor any condition of time or place, will suffice to dissipate or even to disturb the continuous, unlaborious, and unfatiguing absorption of thought in the mental region which has become its natural dwelling.

Let us now ask, Why may not a soul, that is the mind accompanied by the best feelings, be placed in a similar position with relation to the noblest and sublimest object which it can pursue—God? He and His attributes present more perfect claims, motives, and allurements, and more full gratifications, repletion, and reward to earnest and affectionate contemplation, than any other object or subject. How much soever the mathematician may strain his intellect in pursuit of the true, however the poet may luxuriate in the enjoyment of the beautiful, to whatsoever extent the moralist may delight in the apprehension of the good in its recondite quintessence, none of these can reach, in his special aim and longing, that elevation and consummation which can be attained in those of all the three by one whose contemplation is directed to the infinite in truth, in beauty, and in goodness.[1]

Why, then, should not this, so comprehensive and so grand a source of every mental enjoyment, become a supreme, all-exhausting, and sole object of contemplative fruition ? Why should not some, or rather many minds be found which have selected this as their occupation, their solace, their delight, and found it to be what none other can of its nature be, inexhaustible ? Everything else is measurable and fathomable, this alone unlimited.

Then, if there be no repugnance to such a choice being made in the aim of contemplation, it is natural for us to expect conditions and laws in its attainment analogous to what we find where the mental powers have selected for their exercise some inferior and more restricted object. There will be the same gradual and often slow course of assiduous training, the same difficulty of fixing and concentrating the thoughts, till by

---

[1] It is recorded of the celebrated, though perhaps eccentric scholar, Raymund Lully, that once he entered the school of Duns Scotus, to whom he was unknown. The lecturer addressed to him the question, "Quotuplex pars scientiæ est Deus?" ("What part of knowledge includes God?"). His reply overmastered the interrogator: "Deus non est pars, qui est Totum" ("God is in no part ; He is the Whole").

Contemplation

degrees forms and intermediate steps are dispensed with, when the mind becomes passive, and its trains of thought seem spontaneous and in-coming, rather than worked out by elaborating processes.

This state, when God is the sole occupier of thought, represents the highest condition of contemplation, the reaching of which mystical theology professes to direct. (Preface to " Works of St. John of the Cross.")

PART V
MISCELLANEOUS

DEVELOPMENT OF THE BIBLE CANON

WE have, then, two important facts before us: the giving of the Jewish religion was the work of a few hours; the formation of its Scriptures was the work of a thousand years. The first resembled the creation of man, the second the record of his civilisation. The first was life, the second culture. Whatever was necessary for life—that is, we repeat, salvation—was complete at once; the organisation for it could receive no addition. The later Jew could nourish his piety by the royal Psalmist's holy hymns; his children could learn wisdom from the Proverbs of Solomon; his descendants could pity former generations who had not enjoyed the sublime beauties and the consoling visions of the Prophets. These were like the growing riches of a prosperous, or rather a providential, system: but life was as entire before they were bestowed; its essential requirements grew not as they swelled. " Salvation was of the Jews," from Moses unto Christ, through the observance, in its spirit, of the Law delivered by God in the wilderness.

Now let us see how far the same course was observed in the bestowing of the second and better revelation.

As the Spirit of God came down, in the beginning, on the chaotic but inchoate elements of the material world, and fecundating them, predisposed them for organic existence, so did He, on the day of Pentecost (the festival of the previous law-giving), descend, with that same power of life, upon the component parts and latent germs of a new and spiritual and a divine creation. He touched them and they lived. In the apostles, timid and heartless, unwise and misunderstanding, there were laid up the rudiments of the future Church—its primacy, its episcopate, its priesthood, its sacraments, its powers. These had all been bestowed, but as yet appeared to be sealed up in fœtal life, within their unconscious bosoms. There too lay, locked up, commissions of boundless magnitude, to be teachers of the learned, the conquerors of the strong, the confounders of the proud, the salt of the earth, the light of the world. There slumbered in abeyance titles of highest dignity—apostles, martyrs, princes of God's kingdom, fathers of Christ's disciples, judges of His realm and of angels, foundation-stones and gates of the Heavenly Jerusalem. There dwelt as yet, powerless and useless, gifts destined to be of infinite profit to the world; the Keys of the Kingdom yet hung loose and untried from Peter's girdle; the rich vessel of love, borne away from His Master's bosom, yet remained unbroken, and with its odour undiffused in the heart of John; the evangelical pen was still undipped, in the hand of Matthew; miraculous powers invested in their very shadows, command of life and death, marvellous eloquence, prophecy, and discernment of spirits, lie dormant in the souls of all—like Samson's strength, awaiting the

The Bible Canon

Spirit that has to rouse it. It was like the preparation for sacrifice under Nehemias: the altar was built up, the wood was laid, the victim slain; but over all was poured what seemed to be but thick and miry water, a hindrance rather than an aid to fire. But soon as one ray of the sun darted upon the materials thus prepared, a brilliant blaze and a cry of joy proclaimed that the work of faith was crowned with success.[1] And so it was here. The appointed hour is come; a mighty wind announces the approach of God's Holy Spirit; His fire descends on each of them, with a kindling touch; their latent powers burst into life; their gifts rush into existence; the Church of God, in all its perfection and all its beauty, is born to all the world, and to all ages. Not to mention Mary and the others who were in their company, three thousand laymen are in a few hours joined to the clergy. As completely as the child of one day is the same as the man of twenty years, so is the Church of Whit-Sunday that of the third or the nineteenth century. There is the whole of its living machinery complete: its contains already whatever is necessary for salvation. He who joins it this day may die to-morrow in peace. The hierarchy which is to spread its co-ordinate and harmonious rule over the world is there; and Peter already leads its forces, and centres in himself its union. The body of docile and submissive faithful is gathered around them, not to dispute but to learn. Before evening the first sacrament baptism has been administered to multitudes, and the

[1] 2 Mac. i. 21.

next verse to that which so informs us tells us that they persevered "in the breaking of bread,"[1] that is, in the celebration of the Eucharistic Sacrifice and Sacrament. Soon many came to the apostles, confessing their sins, to obtain forgiveness; soon they placed their hands on the baptized, and gave them the Holy Ghost; soon they ordained new ministers, and soon the sick were anointed with oil, and were healed in soul and body.

Thus did the Church, the new means of salvation, come into being, in her hierarchical and sacramental organisation, as perfectly as did the Jewish system under Moses. From the beginning were in her all the gifts of life; and there was no want of a single instrument for attaining perfection in grace and the brightest crown of glory. Again we ask, By what were men then to be saved? By adhering to the pastors of the Church, by practising what they taught, by baptism, by the Eucharist, by the forgiveness of sins, by prayer. And that teaching included all that was necessary in faith, without a written record. Whatever might be done later could not invalidate this primitive institution, could not add to the system first established. There was no room for a further revelation. Whatever might be written by an inspired apostle could only be a record of what was already known and believed; a truly important, sacred, invaluable record, a treasure of wisdom, a gift of God, but still incapable of adding to the deposit of faith safely lodged in the Church's keeping.

Twelve years pass, and not a line is written intended

[1] Acts ii. 42.

The Bible Canon 253

to be permanent. The first Gospel then appears, but fifty more years elapse before the fourth is given to the world. St. John allowed more than sixty to intervene between the death of his Divine Master and his own record of His life. Who does not see, that if his Gospel, certainly the most beautiful and most instructive, had formed a part of a plan essential to salvation, St. John would not have risked such a lengthened space, would not have waited till he should become a very aged man, nor trusted to his being delivered alive from the boiling oil into which he was cast by Domitian, that is, to the not having to drink as fully as his brother James of the cup of martyrdom to which our Lord had equally pledged them both. It was, in fact, a new heresy that prompted him to write. Had it come a few years later, or had John's life only reached the apostolic average, we might have been deprived of his heavenly Gospel.

The Divine goodness, however, willed it otherwise, and gave us that, and the many other rich proofs of mercy, of which the New Testament are the archives. Looking at what we there possess—the knowledge of our Lord's life, character, actions, words, and sufferings; the history of the early Church, with its trials and triumphs; the wisdom of the Cross, and sublime instruction on abtruse points of doctrine, as well as the plain lessons for our homely duties, treasured in St. Paul's Epistles; the one flow of love which, like balm from its plant, continues inexhaustibly to exude, and diffuse itself, from every line in St. John's; the particular, but most precious, learning contained in the Catholic Epistles; and the dark but encouraging visions of the Apocalypse, bringing down the glories of the New Jerusalem to the level of our earthly imaginations—we cannot but consider it all not merely as a chance acquisition, but as a necessity for the Church. We are as much used to the enjoyment of all this as we are to that of sight. We cannot imagine what we should have done had we been created without it, nor what other organ, or instrument, for the apprehension of outward and distant objects, God could have substituted for it; yet we can perhaps no more conceive how the spiritual Jew lived before Psalm or Proverb or prophecy had enlightened him. Nor can we well imagine how multitudes of Christians grew to perfection, and died for the faith, before a line of the New Testament had been penned. They heard no doubt, still fresh from memory, the words and actions of their Lord, but they heard them from faithful witnesses only, not under the safeguard of inspiration. Might not those reminiscences, written down fresh, with all the diligence and conscientious verifications of a St. Luke, have satisfied the piety of future ages as well, and yet inspiration have been withheld? And as to faith, Jesus Christ had not promised inspiration to His apostles' writing, but He had secured to them infallibility in teaching; and this gift was to descend, through His own presence and assistance, to the end of the world. Still, with a gratitude which can never be too great, with a reverence which cannot be too deep, with a docility which can never be too simple, the Church of God, and each of her children, accepts, cherishes, and prizes the glorious gift of His words to man. It is the very charter of her authority, the storehouse of her evidences, the armoury of her defence. It is the inexhaustible repository of her lessons, whether of faith or of morals; the treasure from which she draws out things old, yet ever new, for our instruction. It is her counsellor, her wisdom, her glory. When she unfolds it, and solemnly reads from it to her children, the smallest passage of her Spouse's life, she orders the tapers of the sanctuary to burn around it, and the incense to perfume the very atmosphere in which its words shall resound; and when the priest, kissing the blessed text, whispers his prayer, "Per evangelica dicta deleantur nostra delicta," he expresses more confidence in the Gospel of Jesus than all the speeches in Exeter Hall can match. Nothing in fact can exceed the value which the Church has ever set, and must continue to set till the end of time, upon this inestimable inheritance which is exclusively hers, of which she alone holds at once the record and the key. (*Dublin Review*, Sept. 1852, p. 257.)

CHURCH AND WORLD

LET a mould be prepared, no matter by what hands; let it be a gem exquisitely engraved by an Athenian lapidary; be it composed but of rough gashes made on the face of a rock, by a carver of runes or an Indian warrior. Imagine it to be a die sunk in steel by the great Florentime medallist — be its instrument the diamond, flint, or iron — you will not see its form accurately, you will not judge its worth fairly, you will hardly understand it until you see the impression of it transferred upon some other substance, which will form its accurate counterpart. The seal, the cast, the medal, interpret to you the true intention of the artist, and represent to you his design or his record. If you press the pliant wax into the shape, it will not lose one line of its dimensions, or one grain of its weight, nor will the slightest change occur in its structure; yet it will bear impressed upon its surface the tenderest or the rudest lines, the finest angles or most rugged edges, the figure or the legend, or whatever else was meant to be admired or understood.

Something resembling this plastic faculty has God communicated to His Church, in its contact with the outward world. Without undergoing any organic or substantial modification, without being more or less at one time than another, she presents at every moment a surface to the great life of society, over which this rolls on, and imprints its features, its thoughts, its characteristic and specific qualities. The moral and social history of any age, or even portion of an age, can nowhere be so clearly deciphered as in the legislation, the discipline, the struggles, the literature, the arts, the biographies, nay, paradox as it may appear, in the very blank pages and lines of the Church. For what tells us more of the world's condition than where the annals of the Church seem to have had whole leaves, not torn out, but only here and there jotted over by a trembling hand, and its scanty records blurred by tears, or even blood?

We begin with the very first age of its infancy. It was too weak and too poor to raise commemorative monuments of its progress; it buried its memorials beneath the ground, and modern industry has sought and found them. At first sight of some chapels in the Catacombs the Christian antiquarian is startled, perplexed, almost scandalised. He can scarcely decide whether he has penetrated into a heathen tomb or into a Christian crypt. The freedom of design, the elegance of ornamentation, the vividness of colouring, and the arrangement of the parts in the general composition, recall perhaps to his mind the columbarium of the Augustan freedmen, or of the Nasones; and, moreover, he sees as leading figures, demigods of pagan fiction, engaged in scenes and actions of a hateful mythology. And yet the place, the disposition of its parts, its tombs, its inscriptions, and its emblems leave no doubt that we are in a most Christian cemetery, that bears, upon every panel and border, in its pictures and arabesques, on its vaults and walls, the forms of that early Roman art which had faded and vanished even before the later persecutions. The Church had taken up, and represented on its subterranean temples, the transitory art of the period, even with its uncongenial stories, which, by a happy symbolism, she robbed of their poison; and thus displayed her power of appropriating to herself one of the few good gifts which the most corrupt of worlds still possessed, and could communicate.

R

But, not to carry this illustration minutely through successive centuries, not especially to dwell on the marked influence, or rather impressions, manifested by the Church in her adoption of the basilica for her architectural model, and of the Roman law as the part-foundation of her canonical code and the precedent of her juridical proceedings, as evidences of her happier connection with the empire—recall to mind the later period, when Europe emerged from the grave of a departed civilisation, and struggled for one of its own, heaving up the accumulated ruins and soil of the past, like one of Michael Angelo's figures bursting from the tomb into the valley of judgment. What sort of times do you call those? You answer, "Of iron." And you are right: days of massive, close-grained, high-wrought iron. And that supposes strong-built frames and well-knit muscles to wield the double-handed sword or the knotted mace with unfailing prowess.

Well, even of this almost ferocious power the Church took the stamp—not in the feudal institutions merely, which she partly adopted, and which made barons of her bishops, and nobles of her abbots. No, if the age was iron-cased in its outward fashions, it was steel-tempered in its inward organs, the organs of intellectual life and power. If the Crusader could with ease often cleave to the shoulder, by one blow, the paynim's morion, it was no less the blow of a giant with which a Scotus could smash a sophism that protected error. If the fine-edged sword could cut through and through the truest-tempered mail on the infidel's breast, not because of the brute strength with which it was handled, but through the deftness and very delicacy of hand with which it was gracefully waved, no less easily were the intricacies of heresy or false theories ripped open, unravelled, and stripped off, by the intellectual keenness of a Thomas Aquinas, wielding the subtle weapons of the schools. Sturdy intellects rose side by side with stalwart frames, and robust brains shared the youth of noblest birth with sinewy arms. Both were offspring of the same conditions of life, of a fresh, unprejudiced, and original civilisation of barbarian blood, well combined from different races, under the engentling influences of Christian teaching, and the invigorating training of religious enthusiasm.

The Church took to herself the mighty mental development, and, with it yet clearly imprinted on her surface, retains the evidence of the wonderful vigour and strength of the epoch at once of knighthood and philosophy.

Nor was this all. The age of the troubadour, of the minstrel, of the romancer, and of high-minded chivalrous affection, was naturally that of hymnology and sacred song. The tenderest and most plaintive notes in which the Church sings her love or her sorrows breathe the spirit of those times. The tenderness of a Bonaventure, the sweetness of a Bernard, the flashing love that breaks out in the few lines left us by St. Francis (the troubadour, as he has been called, of love divine), by the softest heart that ever beat beneath the roughest of hair-shirts, were the natural productions of times when the rose and the lily as truly symbolised the noble dame, like Elizabeth of Hungary or of Portugal, as the helmet and sword did a Tancred or a Godfrey.

Then when this new social life created or adapted its own forms for recording its sensations, where do you look for them as representative of ideas, feelings, instincts, pulsations, and even involuntary action which all life must have? Of the royal palaces which every sovereign erected, from Scandinavia to Sicily, scarcely one remains inhabited; of the cathedrals which the Church contemporaneously built, scarcely one has fallen to decay. The few that *have* fallen have been victims of religious fury or of calculating avarice. As you sail along the Rhine, the feudal castles that crown its crags are but picturesque ruins; the parish churches of the same date that nestle at their feet are fresh and filled. Had not the Church preserved almost intact *her* share of the monuments of those ages, the beautiful architecture which is yet our model either would have been eternally lost or would have to be studied in fragments, scarcely less unintelligible than the history on Babylonian bricks.

The rough stem which, with a superhuman, or rather with an unearthly, effort, had broken into air and light, was soon covered with bright and beautiful blossoms and delicious fruit. New and different from whatever the world had heard or seen was this sudden and quickly matured produce. Since the creation of Paradise there had been no parallel. It began, as was natural, with poetry and art, and ended in the revival, too sadly soon abused, of all classical learning. And by whom was all that was beautiful adopted, nursed, cherished, and preserved? ("Essays on Religion and Literature," i. 7.)

CYCLES

BY dispensations which no physical research has yet mastered, cycles come and run a course, then give place to others: cycles of natural conditions, untraceable to any cause, unconnected with discoverable laws. Year after year the vineyards of continents are blighted and barren; the olives of provinces are withered and fruitless; the plant which feeds the poor population of a kingdom droops in its stem and rots at its root, and belies all the promises of the spring. We are told that these things have been before, and will come later again; that they follow a hidden law, like ague or neuralgia—like them have a periodicity. And so with the diseases that afflict humanity; for years their type is depressing and debilitating, and then return again the maladies of our forefathers, like sins visited on their children, with febrile energy and sanguine oppression. No study can modify these phenomena, no skill can retard or accelerate their appointed course. The simple-hearted will call them, when they come with violence and destruction in the field and in the body, *visitations*, and raise their arms in prayer; they are visitations of justice.

In like manner, unaccountably, gifts of some peculiar form seem to be poured out on mankind at a given time, and appear to be as visibly withdrawn. Thousands of artists rose simultaneously, and apparently spontaneously, in every part of Europe at a given period. Art was self-sown in Italy, in Spain, in Flanders, and in Germany at two distinct periods, just as now hundreds of men gifted with mechanical powers are to be found to answer to any demand for new and wonderful undertaking—men, any one of whom would have excited admiration and gained undying fame a century ago; just as some ages before every school of science or theology in Europe had its doctors, each surpassing in subtlety of intellect and accurate learning the most rarely gifted professor of our days. This periodical abundance of a peculiar gift wanted to help mankind forward another step has no connection with any law of progress. In no instance has the quality granted to society reached its perfectibility before it is withdrawn.

Is it not so even in the Church? Has she not, too, her periods of martyrdom, of asceticism, of mysticism, of learning, and of active charity? And is not this one more of those parallelisms between her nature and the social growth of man, which the more we find the more we are convinced, not by demonstration, but by intuition, that one Lord and Master rules and directs all, and that all which I have endeavoured to describe is nothing more than a common moulding impressed by Him who holds all in the hollow of His hand, and imprints the varied folds and lines of His ever-shifting mercies equally on every part of His creation?

Then, as I have said, there is another change: we

are come to a time, or rather a time has come to us, when a new spirit, to use the beautiful language of Him who gives it, is poured out upon the world—the spirit of scientific investigation. Humbly, gratefully, joyfully, I accept it from the treasury, and from the hand of the All-wise and the All-good. It is a new impulse to the intellect which He has bestowed on man; it is a new sharpening of the keenness of the wits which He has given him; it is a new sphere, a new world, which He has opened to his perception of the divine operations *ab extra*. Fool will man be if he misdirects these faculties, and makes not for himself a fresh and brilliant field, where to gather new tributes of admiration and love, and offers up his first and his later fruits in adoration of God, his Creator.

Be this as it may, I feel sure that this new phase of social pursuits will leave its well-marked forms impressed upon the Church, and that generations to come will trace that with admiration there which we see perhaps with some uneasiness. And has not this been always so? ("Essays on Religion and Literature," i. 16.)

LANGUAGES

BUT we are not, I think, to imagine that Divine Providence, in distributing to different human families this holy gift of speech, had no further purpose than the material dispersion of the human race, or the bestowing on them varied forms of utterance; there was doubtless therein a deeper and more important end—the sharing out among them of the intellectual powers. For language is so manifestly the embodying power, the incarnation, so to speak, of thought, that we can almost as easily imagine to ourselves a soul without a body as our thoughts unclothed by the forms of their outward expression. And hence these organs of the spirit's conceptions must, in their turn, mould, control, and modify its peculiar character, so that the mind of a nation must necessarily correspond to the language it possesses.

The Semitic family, destitute of particles and grammatical forms suited to express the relations of things, stiffened by an unyielding construction, and confined by the dependence of words upon verbal roots to ideas of outward action, could not lead the mind to abstract or abstruse ideas; and hence its dialects have been ever adapted for the simplest historical narratives and for the most exquisite poetry, where mere impressions or sensations are felt and described in the most rapid succession; while not a school of native philosophy has arisen within their pale, not an element of metaphysical thought occurs in their sublimest compositions. Hence are the deepest revelations of religion, the awfulest denunciations of prophecy, the wisest lessons of virtue, clothed in Hebrew, under imagery drawn from outward nature; and in this respect the author of the Koran necessarily followed the same course.

But to the Indo-European was given a wonderful suppleness in expressing the inward and outward rela-

Languages 265

tions of things by flexion in its nouns, by conditional and indefinite tenses in its verbs, by the tendency to make or adapt innumerable particles, but principally by the powerful and almost unlimited faculty of compounding words; joined whereunto is the facility of varying, inverting, and involving the construction, and the power of immediately and completely transferring the force of words from a material to a purely mental representation. Hence while it is a fit instrument for effecting the loftiest designs of genius, it is no less powerful in the hands of the philosopher, and in it and by it have arisen those varied systems which, in ancient India, and in later Greece, and in modern Germany, have attempted to fathom the human understanding, and analyse to their primitive elements the forms of our ideas.[1]

And do you not see in all this a subserviency to still nobler designs, when, in conjunction with these reflections, you look back at the order observed by God in the manifestation of His religion ? For so long as His revelations were rather to be preserved than propagated, while His truths regarded principally the history of man and his simplest duties towards God, when His law consisted of precepts rather of outward observance than of inward constraint, while the direction of men was

[1] As an illustration of these remarks, I may say that, in our times, the transcendental philosophy could hardly have risen in any country except Germany, whose language possesses the characteristics of the family more than any other, and could most easily permit or suggest the using of the first pronoun objectively, a violence too great, in other European languages, for them to have first devised it. In Latin, for instance, where there is no article, it is impossible to express it, nor could one using that language have conceived such an idea.

managed rather by the mysterious agency of seers into futurity than by the steady rule of unalterable law, the entire system of religion was deposited in the hands of that human family whose intellectual character and language were admirably framed for clinging with tenacity to simple traditions of early days, and for describing all that was on the outside of man, and lent themselves most effectually to the awful ministry of the prophet's mission.

But no sooner is a mighty change introduced into the groundwork of His revelation, and the faculties unto which it is addressed, than a corresponding transfer manifestly takes place in the family whereunto its ministration and principal direction are obviously committed. The religion now intended for the whole world, and for each individual of the human race, requiring in consequence a more varied evidence to meet the wants and satisfy the longings of every tribe, and every country, and every age, is handed over "to other husbandmen," whose deeper power of thought, whose over-eager impulse to investigate would more easily discover and bring to light its inexhaustible beauties; who would search out its connections with every other order of truth, every other system of God's dispensation, thus ever bringing forth new motives of conviction and new themes of praise. And in this manner Divine Wisdom, while it hath made the substance of religion one and immutable, hath yet in a manner tied its evidences to the restless wheel of man's endeavour, and mingled them with the other motives of his impelling desires, that so every step made in the prosecution of sound study and humble inquiry may give them also a new advance and a varied position, on which the reflecting mind may dwell with surpassing admiration. ("Science and Revealed Religion," Lect. 2.)

GEOLOGY AND POETRY

MANY, I know, entertain the idea that too minute an acquaintance with the material workings of nature greatly weakens that more enthusiastic and poetic feeling which the contemplation of her face excites, and thus produces a preponderance of a cold and scutinising over a warm and admiring disposition. Yet I know not how this can be, except from some defect in the method of communicating such knowledge. There can be no reason why the geologist should not stand enraptured on the mountain's brow and first range, with a poet's eye, over the splendid scene of an Alpine valley, before he descends to study and classify the various rocks which form its magnificent boundary. How should the comprehension of how nature works be at all opposed to the perception of beauty in the results of her labours? On the contrary, it should seem as though the one must form a natural counterpart to the other. The skilful musician will, by casting his eyes over the written score, unravel in a moment its mazy movements, give to each note its harmonic power, and so combine them in his mind together, as thence to drink more music through his eyes than the untutored listener will enjoy when he hears what has been written transformed into sound; and so may the learned in nature's laws measure her outward appearances by such just rule as must give him a truer perception of her charms than the mere observer can ever attain. To the unpractised eye the web which proceeds from the loom will appear exceedingly beautiful, and in design most orderly, while the machinery which produced it seems a pile of confusion through its complicated wheels and pulleys; yet is it necessarily the type of what it brings forth, and the experienced artisan will perchance read in it with equal admiration the beautiful pattern it is calculated to work. And in like manner may the learned naturalist construct, from his knowledge of nature's processes, all those beautiful objects and scenes which others cannot fancy, unless they have actually beheld them. The observation of how the rolled masses are disposed in the gorges and on the flanks of the southern Alps must have led the discoverer to form in his mind a newer and a truer picture than a poet's imagination could have conceived, of the course pursued by the huge inundation which burst through them, tore down their sides, and rode in rude triumph with their rough spoils into the plains of Italy. The contemplation of volcanic effects by a scientific eye which can distinguish the masses thrown up by explosion from the rolling scum of the fiery torrent, and can note, as at Glen Tilt, the strange and incomprehensible manner wherein the hardest granite, reduced into a vitreous fluid, has shot upwards into the superincumbent rock, and injected itself through its veins, and the accurate measurement of the causes proportioned to such mighty effects would convey, we may suppose, the sublimest idea possible of the terrible action of that powerful element under whose scourge this globe is yet in doom reserved. ("Science and Revealed Religion," Lect. 6.)

ALLIANCE OF CHURCH AND EMPIRE

THE Church, then, was completely constituted, when, after three hundred years, we find her coming publicly before the world. She needed to be taught by no one as to how she had to deal with those matters and those causes that related to herself. It is not to be supposed that it required the peace of the empire, and the favour of the emperors, to enable her to hold her councils or to promulgate her decrees. Long before that peace had come, long before her bishops assembled in universal synods, she had held in various parts of the world councils of her prelates, for the purpose of suppressing errors that had arisen; for, even in her very cradle, had this mighty Child been assailed by these ruthless serpents, and with her own hand, unaided, she had known how to strangle them and fling them aside. And so, in the second century, we have councils held at Rome, and in Gaul, and at Cesarea in Palestine. In the third century we have them again at Rome, at Alexandria, at Antioch, Iconium, and more than once at Carthage. In the fourth century, before the general Council of Nicæa had assembled, there had been held provincial synods at ten different places. The Church's system, then, of ruling and defining, in matters of faith, was antecedent to all connection with imperial or with royal power. Her connection, in fact, with that power was purely accidental. She had been sufficient for herself, and for all her wants for three hundred years, without it. She would have persevered to the end, had it so pleased Divine Providence, in the same condition. When that power became favourable to her, she took advantage of it, and naturally enlisted it in the good cause. She accepted it in the same way as she took the basilicas which had been heathen temples, and converted them into churches. She took it as she took the limits of provinces, according to the imperial or civil division, as the most simple and most natural mode of dividing her own spiritual territories. She took it, in fine, as she took the measures of Horace's lascivious Odes, and attuned to them the sweetest hymns of her worship. It was part of her destiny, or rather it was part of her gift, to be able to seize on all that earth might place within her reach, and to sanctify it, and to turn it to holiest purposes. Had she found a republic instead of an empire, she would have known as well how to demean herself, and how at once to assert her own rightful independence, and yet to show the deference ever due to every rightly constituted authority in what regards its own sphere of jurisdiction. Then she could not fail but revere and honour that power which made Christianity

Church and Empire 271

a very part of the civil and social order over which it ruled; she could not but even, in some respects, bow before that crown of which that iron nail which pierced our Saviour's sacred flesh in His Passion was considered the most precious gem. She used, therefore, gladly the power and wealth of the emperors for the many purposes whereby she was connected with this world. Their decrees added force to her canons; their protection enabled bishops to travel from distant regions, and safely to meet together.

But, as if to show how purely accidental, how totally unessential to her existence and to her laws was this state of union and alliance with this power, it was permitted that shortly the imperial power should declare itself the protector of the Arians; it became heretical, and the Church remained orthodox and Catholic. . . . Such was the position of the Church after peace: in a state even still, with regard to faith, of incessant conflict with the civil power, and never for one moment admitting its authority to pronounce upon any matter of doctrine or of faith.

And thus it continued in subsequent ages. . . . It may be said that in some sort they were like the powers which are to be found in most kingdoms, the civil and the military. When they go together in good accord, when that which ought to have the disposition and rule can command the energies and vigour of the other, then all is peace, all is tranquil and happy; but so soon as that which should act in dependence on the principles of the other takes upon itself to command—when the sword pretends to give law to the nation—then comes misery and havoc and ruin. And yet the two powers are necessary for one another, and will seek for reconciliation, and endeavour, if possible, to adjust their claims. ("The Final Appeal in Matters of Faith," p. 8.—Sermon, 1850.)

VILLAGE WORSHIP IN ITALY

TRAVELLERS go forth with a standard formed in their mind upon models at home. The religion of England is the religion of one day in the week. The church is but a useless building on the other six; its bells are silent, and its portals closed; and the religious spirit, whether pent up, or suffered to evaporate during that period, is concentrated upon this one; the thoughtlessness of the week changes, by a convulsive reaction, into a melancholy gravity, and the want of all worship on those days is thought to be compensated by the denial of every recreation and occupation, however innocent, on that day. Well, be it so. But go into a country where every day summons the people to do public service to God, where religion necessarily mingles with the daily duties of life, where its institutions so surround them as habitually to bring it into their thoughts, and, at the same time, provide wholesome checks for total forgetfulness; where the hand of God has planted in their bosoms a heart as cheerful and smiling as their skies, and where education has taught them to feel that hilarity and joy are the best manifestations of a peaceful conscience—and will you not be unreasonable if you expect that one day should repress such innocent feelings, and make men violate all truth of character, or imagine that God is to be honoured on it with a different soul and spirit from those wherewith they have served Him on the other six? Go any morning into the villages of Italy, and see, before the sun has risen, the entire population crowded in the church, and kneeling during the same liturgy as forms the Sunday service, and hear them raise their clear and cheering voices in a choral litany; then watch them as they depart, from calling down the blessing of Heaven on their daily labour, dispersing in merry groups down the hill, to dress the vine, joining with the lark in their shrill ritornello; the little ones tripping in joyous haste before the sober elders, in their picturesque costumes, till they vanish through the side-scenes of mingled vines and olives, to toil through the sultry day. Then when the evening bell tolls, an hour before sunset, and the labour ceases, see them return, fatigued yet cheerful, to enjoy —perhaps some rest at home? No, not till they have once more met before God's altar, to praise Him for His daily blessing! And when you have every day witnessed this scene, tell them who have daily stood before God, and therefore have been joyful, while the sun played fiercely upon them, and the blight nipped their crops, and poverty and want afflicted their bodies —tell them that to-day they must look sad, and freeze all innocent joy in their souls, and repress all mirthful expression, because forsooth it is the day of the Lord's rest! They, whom prayer has made cheerful in toil and fatigue, must look, and be gloomy when it brings them exemption from their yoke!

Or visit one of those beautiful villages on its special festival. In the morning you are aroused from your slumber by the loud peal of the church bells, and the discharge of a hundred small mortars, to which the surrounding hills reply by their successive echoes, as if to accept, on behalf of their inhabitants, the joyful invitation which the summons conveys. With no fear that any interruption will come from the weather in that delicious climate, you wander forth, through a pure and fragrant air, and admire the preparation of days, on which all the resources of natural taste and practised ingenuity have been expended. The triumphal arch, erected at the gate, in proportions that gratify an artist's eye, covered and festooned with evergreens, so well selected as to imitate the architectural members and ornaments of a more solid building; the draperied inscription, which tells, in a Latinity that would shame that of English cathedrals, of the glories of the saint and the piety of his votaries; the neatly printed sonnets, warm from the pen of village poets, which are affixed to the doorposts of the church; the band, probably composed of inhabitants, parading in their rich uniform; the little knot of peasants who arrive from the neighbourhood, or issue from their houses, in all the bravery of their elegant and rich costumes; the constant stream which flows from every side into the open doors of the church — all this, seen under the cloudless canopy of a summer sky, with a background of chestnut-woods, and a horizon of bold mountains just catching the rising sun, will make you feel that the religion of these simple rustics is where it ever should be, deep in the heart, yet overflowing, from its full capacity, into their looks and actions, mingled inseparably with the best and purest of natural feelings; that it must manifest itself towards God as filial love does towards man, and express itself towards the All-powerful and All-wise, even as their own little ones' affections do to them, whom they deem able to help and to direct them. And these feelings will go on increasing with the day: as you witness the church tapestried and lighted at their willing cost, the most solemn music which the nearest towns can afford, the procession with the several confraternities arrayed in flowing robes, with their banners and crosses, the evening litany, in which the organ is powerless amidst the choral shout of thousands ringing against the lofty vault—in short, the arrangement, conduct, and feeling of the entire scene will satisfy you that religion humanises, refines, and, to use a stronger word, ennobles the minds of that peasantry down to a rank which, in other countries, is rude, churlish, and nearly brutal. The municipal character of the Italian villages, the right of local administration which they all possess, seems to localise the attachments of their inhabitants; and they know not how better to announce these feelings than by displaying their superior taste in all the concerns of their little commonweal; and religion, in a Catholic country, is necessarily the channel through

which such a disposition will best be manifested.
Those who have witnessed the dignity with which the
notables of the place take lead in all church ceremonies
and processions, the good order and respectable de-
meanour of the poorer peasantry who swell them with
their numbers, and the edifying deportment of the poor
but pious clergy who officiate; those who have witnessed
the one harmonious feeling of brotherhood which binds
together the entire population on such occasions, and
through their influence at all times; they who have
heard with what true discrimination the harmonies of
the Church-chant are caught up by the old and young
without dissonance or timidity, will acknowledge that
they have felt themselves drawn, like ourselves, into
the swell of feeling which heaved around them; yea,
and thought that they were raised above the dull level
of daily emotions, by finding themselves associated in
voice and heart with the vine-dresser and the moun-
taineer. And when thus overpowered for a season
by the might of virtuous sympathy, and feeling the
practical effects of the great Catholic principle, which
causes the individual to be absorbed in the harmonious
unison of the multitude, had any traveller of the Rae
Wilson cast whispered to us about "the buffoonery"
of such religious exhibitions, and "despised us in his
heart," as Michol did David, when he allowed the joy
of his soul to break forth in signs of extravagant gladness before the people, we should have been satisfied
to give that monarch's reply, "Before the Lord . . . I
will both play and make myself meaner than I have

done, and will be little in mine own eyes;" and to stand by the award of that authority which adds, that "*therefore* Michol, the daughter of Saul, had no child to the day of her death." (*Dublin Review*, July 1836. "Essays," iii. 507.)

IRISH CHARACTER

AND now, if I may use my own experience, I will say that nothing struck me more in Ireland than the characteristic resemblance which I found everywhere among the people. You can find in different parts of Ireland what you may call different national families. In some parts you will find more robust growth, a greater physical development; while in other parts you may observe a "race," as it is called, not so strong, nor possessing such powerful physical characteristics. Now, these varieties are to be traced in every part of England, and in every country of the world. But in the character of the people it seemed to me that everywhere there was a resemblance which was the stamp of the most strict complete nationality; and that nationality seemed all to be one in its great principles, as well as in all that it was doing, or trying to do. The manners of the people, their looks, the countenances may be different, but one expression pervades them; there is in every man of them, wherever you go, a warmth and expansion of heart which is totally different from what you find— from what I have found—in any other country. There is a spontaneity of expression; there is a facility of giving utterance to their thoughts; there is a brilliancy, even a poetry about them which animates the whole of the peasantry. They have a smile upon their countenance which is bright and cheering; the light of their eye is not only brilliant, but most tender; and I was surprised, in the multitude of persons, whom I saw congregated, to the amount of thousands, to observe the sort of natural gentleness of bearing which belongs most markedly to a moral people. I never in the whole of my tour, and I have said my observation extends to tens of thousands of people, saw a rude act by one man or youth to another. When a crowd of persons came together, one group of them who had gratified their feelings would give way and say, "Now let others come forward," with a considerate and courteous manner which would do honour to any assembly of the wealthy, and what we call the educated classes. Gentlemen, I believe a moral peasant is more of a gentleman than one who is merely born or bred so. The manner too in which they make known their gratification or their joy is the same throughout. I have seen for miles along the road houses shut up, the windows and doors closed, but all adorned with flowers and boughs, when they who had left behind them their emblems of their good feelings could not receive a word or a look of commendation in return. It was their way of showing the spontaneousness of their feelings, and this was the case all over the country; the same form of demonstration seemed to prevail everywhere. (Lecture in Hanover Square Rooms, 1858. "Irish Tour," 391.)

THE IRISH FAMINE

Now, my dear brethren, I have dwelt long upon the past trials of our faith in this country. I have spoken of things which belong rather to generations now gathered to their fathers than to you; for you live in an age of promise, in an age of hope, and yet you, almost every one who listens to me, have witnessed perhaps the most severe and terrible of all the trials to which that Church has ever been exposed in this country. I have described two trials. One consisted in the destruction of worldly prosperity and the reduction of the great bulk of those who professed the Catholic faith to a state of abject misery; the other in that overwhelming persecution which threatened to destroy, and which, as far as its influence went, tried to annihilate the Church itself, by depriving her children of spiritual succour. The one reminds me of those messengers who rushed to Job to tell him that the Sabeans had come from one side and the Chaldeans from another, and destroyed his fields, swept away his herds, killed the herdsmen, and left him a poor and wretched man. The second brings before me that still more terrible trial which went sorely to his heart, when the children of his house were gathered together in the home of their elder brother. Oh, what was that home to all of us, the sons and daughters of the Church, but the home of our elder brother, Christ Jesus, in which, like the children of Job, your forefathers were gathered to partake of His own banquet, when in a moment the four winds of heaven came contending, rival powers—religions of opposite and conflicting creeds — that blew from every side against that house, and it was cast down and made a heap of ruins, underneath which a certain number perished.

Neither of these trials shook for a moment the faith, or seemed, I may say, to disturb that deep-rooted religion which existed in the hearts of the people; but the Evil One knew that he could inflict another trial still. "Skin for skin," he said, "and all that a man hath he will give for his life. But stretch forth Thy hand, and touch their bone and their flesh, strike them with famine—strike them with pestilence—and see if they will not bless God and die" (Job ii. 4). And the blight came and the pestilence came, and the children of the land were laid low; and fathers and mothers wept over whole families whom the hand of death struck down before their eyes, and they mingled their tears with those of their pastors, who were themselves despoiled by their own charity, and by the prevailing want of what was necessary to sustain their lives. Yet, blessed be God, under this awful, this unparalleled affliction, this great and truly patient people spoke not a foolish thing against their Maker, and sinned not with their lips. In unmurmuring, in patient suffering, they recognised in this affliction the hand of God. They saw in their deep misery but the chastising of children by their Father. They bowed their heads, and died as if they had been an army struck by the Angel of

The Irish Famine

Death passing over them. They were buried in silence and in sorrow; and those who survived went again to the holy work, blessing and praising God, without a murmur or complaint.

And was not this final trial enough almost to have shaken in the hearts of the people that continued confidence in God, and to have made them think that they were hardly treated by their heavenly Father? No, like Job, they bore all, meek and unrepining: but yet the hardest trial was to come. For then it was, when the people were thus stricken almost with what looked to the world a leprosy—when nothing but sorrow and suffering seemed to be the inevitable lot of this country—then it was that the comforters came—then it was that men appointed from various religions in the three kingdoms met together, and came with food in their wallets to tempt, and with money in their purses to bribe, with light in their hands, like the cunning fowler, only to mislead, and they sat on the ground around their victim; for their comfort was reproach, and their consolation but rebuke. They pretended to have come in charity, to lighten the hand of God upon the people; but in truth their mission was to lay it as heavy as possible upon them, and make them believe, if it could be done, that their Almighty Father had abandoned them, or rather that they were—for these were almost the very words used—given up in their hunger and misery into their hands to relieve them, but only on condition of a sacrilegious apostasy.

Oh! sad alternative, to betray the faith which for

ages no trial had shaken, or to see their children starve to death before themselves! This was the trial of trials—and by it was accomplished in the history of this people what was symbolised in the holy patriarch of old. Surely the patience and long-suffering of this country will be rewarded, and there will come, like the friends of Job, those who will give their "sheep or their earrings" (Job xlii. 11) to restore something of what belonged to the poor sufferers of days gone by. (Sermon at Ballinasloe, 1858. "Irish Tour," 34.)

ENGLISH MISSIONARY PRIESTS

THE MARTYRS

(From a Sermon preached in the English College, Rome, in 1826, when Wiseman was not quite twenty-four.)

LOOK back on that line of illustrious martyrs who, within these very walls, prepared themselves for their missionary labours. They had to arm their minds, not against the cant of the sectary, but against the terrors of the judge; they had to steel their souls, not against the reproach of religious opponents, but against the weight of public ignominy and disgrace; they had to harden their bodies and their feelings, not only against the rigours of missionary duties, but against the knife of the executioner. Then, indeed, might the mind of our young seminarists have stood appalled at the prospect before them, and felt cold on entering their career. But no, they rejoiced like a giant to run their course;

English Priests 283

they boldly advanced to grapple with the united powers of earth and hell—they wrestled and they conquered. Oh! these men, indeed, *sowed* in tears; and what they thus sowed, what they even watered with their blood, we are now called only to reap, and to reap in exultation. ("Sermons," ii. 358.)

THE RETURNED EXILES

(*Written at age of thirty-seven.*)

THAT noble race of clergy is fast disappearing from the midst of us, who in worse days abandoned home and country to study the science of religion under learned foreigners—then returned to minister its comforts to scattered congregations, or to small timid flocks assembling together in some back alley of a populous town. They were men of the solid learning of a former age, of the school of the Gothers, the Mannings, the Hawardens, the Challoners and the Dodds: concealing under a homely garb hearts worthy of the ancient confessors; ripening often within a rough exterior the rich mellow fruits of a charity tender and heroic; men whose virtues were those of the olden Church—a zeal indefatigable, a spirit unconquerable, a trust in Providence unlimited, a disinterestedness impregnable, a character unsullied, a life unstained. Their memory is in benediction among the aged; and their names and sayings are handed down to the children in their congregations. They lie many of them without a record or a stone, but their monuments are all over the land, in the altars they raised and the flocks they founded. The few that yet remain have further claims upon our gratitude and reverence. They belong, for the most part, to the last generation of that glorious line which the French Revolution found in possession of its ancient seats, and on which it vented its irreligious fury. They were cast into bonds, and, after long sufferings, endured with the spirit of the martyrs, never relaxing even in prison from the discipline, or departing from the organisation of their former life, they were by the blessing of Providence, banished, so to speak, into their own country.

But before they quitted their ancient homes they caught up and then bore with them no small spark but a burning brand from their domestic hearth; nor rested till they had transferred it to many altars—first, humble and unsettled, but which soon grew up into others more magnificent and stable. No record has been kept—at least on earth—of the privations endured, of the sacrifices made, of the perseverance held by these our fathers in that intermediate state, that time of dwelling in tents and tabernacles between their expulsion from their foreign seminaries and the establishment of our present splendid colleges. Crowded into some small farm-house or country priest's residence, generally in some secluded situation, where sympathy could hardly reach them; straitened on every side by want, not merely of the comforts of ordinary life, but of those conveniences which almost the poorest can command; with hardly any of the accommodations which a place of education requires; often reduced to pinching want, always constrained to practise the most self-denying parsimony; feeling strangers in their own country; participating not in that charitable generosity which first stretched out and then opened so wide the hands of their countrymen towards the Catholic clergy of France, their fellow-sufferers—these virtuous, self-devoted men, carried on the work of ecclesiastical education, and occupied themselves in literary pursuits with unconquerable endurance. (*Dublin Review*, February 1840, p. 254.)

ISOLATION OF THE ANGLICAN CHURCH

THIS Church, which is ever glorying through those who speak as her particular admirers and defenders—this Church, which calls itself a branch of the Catholic Church, which considers herself as forming one of the many Churches united together under the name of the Universal and Catholic Church—is she then so completely alone in her insular existence, as that she can awake no cry, not even a feeling of sympathy and of sisterly affection? Oh, this country can do much to arouse the thoughts and the actions of the whole world. She can send forth her fleets to the very extremities of earth, and her behests are obeyed, and her very name is respected, and kings tremble at the thought of her power. She can send forth a peaceful message over the whole of the world and it is immediately responded to. You have called together the whole of the nations to come and bring here together the produce of their skill, and that cry has thrilled through the entire world.[1] You have excited to activity the sluggish inhabitants of the banks of the Ganges—you have aroused the weakly inhabitants of Thibet, in the luxurious valleys—and you have inspired new energy and power into men of every caste and of every race. You have put activity into their brain, and industry into their hands; and the furnaces, and the workshops, and the looms of the world are at work to bring to your feet, as a tribute to the queen of the nations, the works of their hands, elaborated with their utmost skill, as if you were the judges and the supreme in all that is great, and noble, and beautiful on earth. And is there in this country all this wonderful power of commanding the sympathies, and even the activity of men, in regard to what is of this earth; and its Church, which speaks even as if it were the purest branch, the most apostolical of all the Churches of the earth, can she be in distress, can she be, as men speak for her, trampled under foot, can she be on the point of being extinguished, can the most solemn doctrines of which she has been the depositary, be, as it were, slipping from her hand, torn thence by the cruel grasp of her enemies, and does she cry out—and not one response? The Vatican remains in its solemn silence. That word, which formerly spoken, was echoed in the hearts of the faithful throughout the world, which called for their prayers, and their lively interests in the struggle of a depressed or afflicted Church—that voice is silent and will not be raised, even

[1] The great Exhibition of 1851 was in preparation.

though desolation should take place, and this whole fabric of men's hands (for no more is it in our estimation) should crumble to pieces. And even from the neighbouring coasts, to which the very cry of distress may be supposed to reach, there will be sent back no sympathetic or loving reply; but all will be dead in her regard, save this, that all and every part of the great and glorious Church of Christ stands, as in awe, to see what will become of that Establishment which has been raised up to great worldly excellence and magnificence, till it has towered on high amidst the nations as a mighty and splendid fabric, which learning and genius, and great individual worth, as well as the loftiest social position, have conspired to embellish and enrich with every human and earthly advantage. Yes, they are watching to see how this structure is able to resist the shocks, not of the power of man, but of that interior element of dissolution which seems to have begun its work within her, and to be agitating her to and fro to her destruction. They are looking upon all this as men look upon a great judgment that has come down in mighty power from on high. They are looking at it with that interest which a great crisis naturally excites in things of earth, and only subject to human laws, but the end, the destiny of which is as yet concealed. These various parts of the living Church of Christ can in fact only look on the agitated Establishment of this country as men can do from a firm and lofty shore, upon a frail and shattered bark tossed upon the billows. To save it, and guide it into port, is totally beyond their power; they can only pray for those who are on board, that when it shall break to pieces on the rock, they may be borne on its fragments towards the only safe shore, and stand ready to stretch forth a helping hand to them in that hour. But, as a Church, as a religious body, one which has any claim upon them, they heed it not, they leave it to itself. And thus it is shown how truly indeed the great principle of unity has been here lost, and once lost, cannot be recovered, save by total change, and return again to the ways that have been departed from. Surely, my brethren, this ought to make some impression on those who believe, or affect to believe, that the English Church is a living member of the great and holy Body of Christ's Church. For if it be true doctrine that one member cannot be afflicted or injured but the others must hasten to comfort and assist it, how is it that the present distress of this religious community does not thrill as a pang through the entire Catholic frame? It needs must be that the present sore is but as a gangrene, on a palsied and withered limb, which can convey no message of the affliction to the centre of life, and all that beats in unison with it. ("The Final Appeal"—Sermon, 1850, p. 31.)

ANGLICAN WORSHIP

Do we not all know a Church possessed of every material engine of power, that hath in its hands most glorious temples, marvellously designed to be the theatres of boundless influence over countless multitudes?—and such were they once; while now they are all day so empty and waste, as to seem rather the mighty tombs of a departed, than the temples of a living worship. And how else hath this sad change been wrought? The religion which built them in ages past was one of many sisters, obedient and subject to a common mother. For centuries she had ruled by authority, spiritual and ecclesiastical, and her reign had been peaceful and splendid. But a forward spirit arose within her, and in the pride of her heart she exclaimed, "I need not, that men may honour, and court, and obey me, these badges of authority and rule, which at the same time mark my dependence too. For my own comeliness will I be worshipped. I will none of those touching memorials around me, the tombs of martyrs or the rival beauty of saintly images; for what are they to me? or what have I to do with the memory of past days? I scorn the bravery of sumptuous raiment, and the dazzling procession of ministers, and the clouding of their incense, and the brightness of their tapers; I will sit me down alone in the midst of my naked dwelling-place, as a white-robed virgin, and men shall love, and serve, and worship me for my own sake." And for a season it was done—so long as those lived who remembered the days of her glory, and loved her as a remnant and memorial of what once she was.

But after these came a generation that knew not those days, men with arms upfolded on their bosoms, and brows bent in perpetual frownings; and when they came before her, she found that they had learnt rebellion from her example, and from her lips had caught up the words of scorn and infamy wherewith she had disgraced her mother; and they cast her down, and trampled her in the dust, and did make her eat her very heart for sorrow. Then, indeed, by the arm of power she was once more set up, but only to undergo a crueller and more lingering doom; to see, year after year, her worshippers slinking away, and her temples less frequented, and her many rivals' power exalted, as well as their numbers ever more increased. And even now, are not men dicing over her spoils, and quarrelling how they had best be divided? Do they not speak irreverently of her, and weigh her utility in iron scales, and value in silver pieces the souls whom she serves? Is she not treated with contumely by those that call themselves her children? Is not her very existence reduced by them to a question of worldly and temporal expediency?

And, when we see the cathedral service shrunk into the choir originally destined for the private daily worship of God's special ministers, or when we find the entire congregation scattered over a small portion of the repaired chancel, while the rest of the edifice is a majestic ruin, as I but lately witnessed, surely any one must be more prone to weep than to exult at the change which has taken place since these stately fabrics were erected. Who can visit that beautiful church beyond the river, so lately restored,[1] and dwell on the exquisite

---

[1] St. Mary's Overbury, or St. Saviour's.

screen which overshadows the altar, with its numerous niches and delicate traceries, and not feel that the great object to which all these were accessories hath been removed; that men would not have laboured so, and given their time and ability, only to prepare a standing-place for that ordinary table, on which all turn their backs who worship there, but that *there* was once an altar which men loved and revered, and which it was deemed most honourable to honour. Who can witness the worship as performed in a cathedral, and see so many points yet recalling ancient practices, so much effect curtailed of its power by the destruction of the feeling and motive which gave it rise, such a wish, but so manifestly baffled, to fill with religious majesty the mighty edifice, more by the organ's voice than by the emblems of God's presence, or by any accord of feeling thrilling through the hearts of a multitude, and not weep to think how a nation can have been cheated out of the most beautiful and moving parts of its religion, and glory in retaining but its shreds and fragments?

Assuredly, when I see these things, and still more, when I hear men admiring the English liturgy as a matchless and sublime composition, and not reflecting how it is all taken from ours, which they abolished—only that what they have retained, and what forms the essential part of their service, is with us but a part inferior and preparatory to a more solemn rite; that their sublime collects, with the Epistle and Gospel, are amongst us but as an introduction and preface to a sublimer action; when I see this Church thus treasuring up and preserving from destruction the accessories of our worship, so highly prizing the very frame in which *our* liturgy is but enclosed, I cannot but look upon her as I would on one whom God's hand hath touched, in whom the light of reason is darkened, though the feelings of the heart have not been seared—who presses to her bosom, and cherishes there, the empty locket which once contained the image of all she loved on earth, and continues to rock the cradle of her departed child! ("Moorfields' Lectures," v.)

WORK OF THE LAITY

AND, first, my dear and respected friends, the laity of the London district, a generous, a zealous, and devout flock, allow me, as charged with the care of your salvation and of your religion, to warn you against one of the great dangers of our time, the influx into ecclesiastical and spiritual affairs of principles belonging to temporal and social interests. For the sake of peace, of charity, and of good understanding, let us keep a well-drawn boundary-line between our respective spheres of action. To you we give up the world and its great concerns—the wide field of political ambition—the ruling of nations, the framing of laws, the public offices of the state. To you we willingly yield the earth and its rulers, its commerce, its lands, its rich mines and their produce; the sea and its trade, and its fleets of richly laden ships. To you we give up the sphere of human ambition, the army, and its brilliant honours, its statues, its medals, and its stars; the navy and its gallant deeds, and national trophies and public monuments. To you we readily make over every profession which enriches or ennobles, every pursuit which gives fame and honour, by research in science, or genius in art, or popularity in literature. To you we gladly resign the courts of princes, and the palaces of the great, the public resort, and the busy haunts of men; and we envy you not the rule of your little domestic commonwealth, and the happiness and comfort of your peaceful homes.

All this is surely enough—enough for care, enough for variety, enough for ambition, enough, too, for responsibility, and for an account to be rendered. One only thing we reserve for ourselves, on only one thing we make a jealous claim—THE CHURCH OF GOD. Leave this, I entreat you, to us alone. Leave it to those whom the Church has trained, and God has anointed for this purpose; to those who from infancy have walked in cloisters, or lived in the sanctuary, like Samuel, chosen to govern God's people; to those who have studied to obtain knowledge, have meditated to acquire wisdom, have prayed to obtain grace for this purpose; to those who meddle not with the things of the world, that they may have undivided hearts, unparcelled affections for their only love on earth—the Bride of the Lamb; to those who live by her law, are familiar with her desires, are attempered in mind and soul to her tone and her spirit; throb, breathe, live only in her. The Ark of God's New Covenant belongs to the sons of

Aaron and the seed of Levi. Its tables of the Law, its vessel of heavenly manna, its dry and hard but blooming rod of authority, are our only inheritance. On us it is incumbent not only to carry and to adorn this sacred Ark, but to support, to protect, and to defend it. We have our weapons for this purpose, and we will ever rally round it in the day of need. Say not that zeal urges you forward, when you think you see it in danger, and God's priests slow to come to its aid. Oza thought and reasoned thus, no doubt: he saw the Ark of God, a poor emblem though of ours, drawn along by dull and heavy oxen, and the roads were rough, and they seemed restive, and the Ark was in danger of falling. In his zeal, he stretched out his unanointed hand to support it, and—I shudder to write the rest. The Church does indeed often want your zealous co-operation, your social influence, your learned or ready pen, your skilful pencil, your brilliant talents, your weighty name, your abundant means. But the direction, the rule, belongs to us. Think not that these will prosper, while unsubordinate to those whom God has placed to direct them. We will call you forth when the Church of God wants your aid; we will always gladly see you working with us, but we cannot permit you to lead, where religious interests are concerned; and where there is danger, it would be base in us to do so.

I have spoken to you freely, because it becomes my office so to speak, and I well know you will consider it, in me, but a proof of love.

And you, most revered, sincerely esteemed, and beloved fellow-labourers in the Gospel, clergy of a city which, more than any other on earth, requires united energies and well-combined efforts to discharge effectually the duties of our ministry, to you I will only make one request. Let no one succeed in raising discord or dissension amongst us. Rely on me, as I rely on you, with singleness of purpose and oneness of heart, that we may carry out the great work by God committed to our charge. Fear not that the interests of religion will be jeopardised in my hands; least of all where the cause of the Holy See is particularly concerned. "Would to God you could bear with some of my folly! but do bear with me: for I am jealous of you with the jealousy of God."[1] But need I remind you or others of where or how I have been nourished in the faith; how from early youth I have grown up under the very shadow of the Apostolic Chair; how week after week I have knelt at the shrine of Peter and there sworn him fealty; how I have served, as good masters, successive pontiffs, in their very households, and have been admitted to confidence, and if I dare say it, friendship by them? And is it likely that I shall be behind any other, be he neophyte or Catholic of ancient stock, in defending the rights of my holy Lord and Master under Christ; or that I can require the summoning to watch, with jealous eye, any attempts to infringe them? The *second* altar at which I knelt in the Holy City was that which marks the spot whereon St. Peter cemented the foundations of his unfailing throne with his blood. The *first* was that of our

[1] 2 Cor. xi. 1.

own glorious St. Thomas. There I returned thanks for the great blessing of being admitted among his children. For two-and-twenty years I daily knelt before the lively representation of his martyrdom; at that altar I partook ever of the bread of life; there for the first time I celebrated the Divine Mysteries; at it I received the episcopal consecration. He was my patron, he my father, he my model. Daily have I prayed and do pray to him to give me his spirit of fortitude, to fight the battles of the Church, if necessary unto the shedding of blood. And when withdrawn from the symbols of his patronage, by the supreme will of the late pontiff, I sought the treasury of his relics at Sens, and with fervent importunity asked and obtained the mitre which had crowned his martyred head; and I took, myself, from the shrine of the great confessor-defender of religious rights, St. Edmund, a part of that right arm which so often was stretched forth to bless your forefathers.

It is in the presence of these two sacred memorials that I have written to you. It is not the name of St. Thomas of Canterbury which can justify what is done by men, as they may think, for the Church—it is his spirit, his virtues, that we must cultivate: but one thing we have, which others want—his mission from God for this purpose. His crosier cannot pass to secular hands, his office cannot be made over. It is ours, my reverend brethren, and let it not be usurped. Let us, bishop and clergy, fast bound in charity and mutual dutifulness, in zeal and in fervour, direct the course and guide the actions of the flock. Let us form them in peaceful and meek habits, in gentleness towards all, in docility and obedience to the teaching of their pastors, in simplicity and earnestness of devotion, " ut ex profectu sanctarum ovium fiant æterna gaudia pastorum." (From a Pastoral Letter, dated 4th April 1848, called " Words of Peace and Justice.")

HOPEFULNESS

WE certainly must plead guilty to belonging to the class of the Hopeful. This Review was founded upon a *couleur de rose* principle. It was started simply in hopefulness, in buoyant, bounding confidence, that there was "a good time coming." Nay, its complexion at birth was deeper than the paly rose-bud—it was sanguine. There were croakers then as much as now; men who liked the cineraria better than roses, preferred cypress to myrtle, the raven to the nightingale. What was prospect then is retrospect now. Were the croakers right then, in prophesying that not a single conversion would emerge from the "Oxford Tracts," that the eloquent voice in St. Mary's would never resound in a Catholic pulpit, and that there was no more vitality in the "movement" than there was in the time of Laud, or of the Nonconformists? All was to them a sham. It is plain, then, that carrying back the two parties twenty years, the roseate people were safer than the sooty. What reason have we to believe the order to be reversed, and the future of to-day to be different from that of years ago? There was indeed a moment, when the dark foreboders seemed to have it all their own way, when the atrocious onslaught on the hierarchy began. Then indeed there were more than ugly omens, something worse than mares' tails in the clouds, and Mother Carey's chickens on the curling waves; there were breakers ahead, there was a scowling lee-shore, there was a hissing trough of sea, there was a murky sky above head, and there was roaring blast around the frail-looking bark of England's catholicity. Well, she drove straight on, neither ported her helm nor put it hard a-lee; she unshipped not her top-gallants, nor close-reefed her mainsail, but trusted to the heavenly steersman, who sometimes appears to slumber in the boat, but always awakes in time. This was a glorious time for the prophets of evil; their predictions were coming most satisfactorily true: all the consolations of past years had been delusive; we had been going much too fast, and the whole was going to end in what is denominated "universal smash."

Now, if it had pleased God to give us a much harder trial, and subject us to a harsh, and searching, and long persecution, had we been pushed back civilly (in one sense of the word) into the last century, we should have remained still *couleur de rose*. Never did sweeter rose of resignation blow than Job upon his dunghill. We should have seen the hand of God in our humiliation and depression, and should have made every effort to suppress the croak that rose into our throat. Was Job wrong in looking at his own future brightly from that vilest seat, with earthquakes, pillagers, pestilence all round him; and what was worse, with three good hearty croakers seated before him for seven days and seven nights, then, with his gentle wife to back them, bidding him take as gloomy a prospect as possible of everything, past, present, and to come? The worldly hero may boast that reverses have plundered him of all but his honour; the Christian will admit that, bereft of all else, his enemy cannot pluck hope from his bosom. So thought Job; and he was right.

But it pleased God that we should not endure so severe a tribulation. The storm subsided, we found ourselves again in smooth water, to be troubled again only if it pleases God. Is not this liberation an encouragement to our hope? Did not the trial prove that the trustful had been right, and the despondent mistaken?

If then among Catholics there must be two parties designated by colours, we will hold to the *Bianchi*, be who choose of the *Neri*. And the paragraph before us proposes good motive for our preference. "Openings of new missions, churches, schools, functions, devotions, sermons, conversions" are things, or facts, solid and palpable, on which hope may stand and rest; they are unmistakable realities which may be entered into account. The sanguine man as he is called reckons them up, and finds they come to something at the end of the year, to carry forward into the next; for they are durable and not evanescent, perennial, not annual. But the dark-eyed man who sees a "black spot" everywhere (physically this would indicate a diseased organ) sees in reality nothing, but only absence of something, the "blot" is merely a screen interposed between the object and the vision. In plain language, the croaker sees the defects on everything, its imperfections, its shortcomings; he cannot deny the existence of the thing. "We have new churches," he says, "it is true; but thousands never go into them; schools, but with inferior education; devotions, but they are merely passing excitement; conversions, but they are more than counterbalanced by perversion." Now let all this be true. If thousands neglect going to the new churches, hundreds do go to them who did not go at all; schools with imperfect education are better than no schools at all, and the education may be improved in them; devotions may excite, but a single good communion more, and some scores of acts of faith and love additional have their fruit; and as to conversions, suppose the fact to be true that for every Puseyite gained two poor Irish are lost, as one is not effect of the other, one may surely rejoice at that which is good, and rather have it than not, while we deplore the loss. It is plain that every one of those things which are enumerated as forming the hopeful man's joy, is a diminution of every reason which the desponding one has for his dark views. Every new church, mission, or school must remove a blot or dark spot from the system.

But this is a deeper and graver subject than it looks at first sight. That men who overlook all defects are wrong, and that in their calculations they will be as mistaken as an astronomer would be who should overlook the mutual perturbations of the planets, there can be no doubt. But that they who can never see anything but faults, repine and grumble ever, and will not look about them with a cheerful eye, are at least equally wrong, is no less certain. A middle course is therefore to be chosen, and what is this? To say "I will be neither one nor the other" is almost equivalent to proclaiming indifference. This will not do. The true medium seems to us very clear, and we hope has its rule highly sanctioned. Does the croaker and grumbler look at the work before him as that of God or of man? Surely not as the first, or it would be blasphemy to murmur. He looks then at the whole as man's work, as the fruit of his industry, skill, and ability. Openings of missions, churches, schools, &c., are all in his eyes only results and evidences of activity, good management, human powers. He picks holes in them, and criticises them as he would the opening of new worldly institutions. He has no confidence in their solidity or duration, because they come from a perishable workman.

The sanguine man may be easily understood to reason contrariwise. The progress of religion is God's care, and can be granted by Him alone. Every step gained, every advantage secured, is a new blessing from Him; and surely any manifestation of His blessing, any evidence of His love, is "enchanting, hopeful, and glorious." And what is every new "opening of mission, church, or school," every solemn "function" performed with the requirements of the liturgy, every "devotion" such as that of the Forty Hours, every "conversion," but an outward sign of that superintending watchfulness, which makes the rising up of a new church or school in a desolate district as true a mark of itself as is the springing up of the snowdrop or the crocus an evidence of care over the earth? Each may be humble, but each is God's work.

But while in this, which is of God, we rejoice and exult, and feel sanguine of success, we will go all the way with the murmurers and discoverers of black spots and flaws, the moment we turn from the beautiful work to its clumsy instruments. That he is a useless servant, that he is only in others' way who would do better, that he is blundering, feeble, obstructive, and doing all as badly as possible, is a conviction quite as consistent with the full belief in a man, that, not by or through him, but in spite of him, God's work will go on prosperously, blessedly, and gloriously. (*Dublin Review*, Dec. 1856, p. 465.)

WORKS BY CARDINAL WISEMAN.

MEDITATIONS ON THE SACRED PASSION OF OUR LORD.

With a Preface by H. E. CARDINAL VAUGHAN.

Crown 8vo, cloth, 4s.

"These Meditations take a high line always, yet they are very human. They do not weary, and they never offend. They seem to be throughout the sincere expression of a heart that has felt all that it sets forth, and that has seen whatever it describes. It is a book for any and for all days, if ever there was one. The Meditations have nothing technical or limited about them. They are for all people who love to dwell upon the Redemption, and they are of daily and of hourly application throughout the whole year."—*Weekly Register.*

FABIOLA : A Tale of the Catacombs.

New Cheap Edition. Crown 8vo, cloth, xii.-324 pp. 2s.

Also an Edition on better paper, bound in cloth, richly gilt, gilt edges. 3s. 6d.

And an *Edition de Luxe*, printed on large 4to paper, embellished with Thirty-one Full-page Illustrations and a Coloured Portrait of St. Agnes. Handsomely bound. £1, 1s.

"This story of the persecutions of the early Christians contains as graphic and minute a description of the Catacombs as has ever been written.

"'Fabiola' has well maintained the high place in fiction which it obtained at the very outset, and to-day it may be said to be one of our English classics. . . . The present editions are brought out in most excellent style."—*Catholic Times.*

A FEW FLOWERS FROM THE ROMAN CAMPAGNA.

Small 4to, cloth gilt, printed in red and black. 1s. net (postage 2d.).

NEW VISITS TO THE BLESSED SACRAMENT.

Edited by CARDINAL WISEMAN.

Containing Devotions for the Quarant' Ore and other Occasions of Exposition and Benediction. Cloth, red edges. 2s.

BURNS & OATES, LIMITED,
28 ORCHARD STREET, LONDON, W.

No. 1.   1898.

Selection
FROM
Burns & Oates'
Catalogue of Publications.

Latest Publications.

Characteristics from the Writings of Cardinal Wiseman.
Edited and with a Preface by the Rev. T. E. BRIDGETT, C.SS.R. Crown 8vo, cloth. 6/-.

Cardinal Wiseman's Meditations on the Sacred Passion of our Lord. With a Preface by H. E. CARDINAL VAUGHAN. Crown 8vo, cloth. 4/-.

THE FOURTH VOLUME OF THE POPULAR EDITION OF
The Formation of Christendom as seen in Church and State.
By T. W. ALLIES, K.C.S.G. Crown 8vo, cloth. 5/-.

Genesis and Science. Inspiration of the Mosaic Ideas of Creative Work. By JOHN SMYTH. Crown 8vo, cloth, with Illustrations. 3/6.

Jewels of Prayer and Meditation from Unfamiliar Sources.
By PERCY FITZGERALD, M.A., F.S.A. Fancy cloth, gilt. 2/6.

St. Francis de Sales as a Preacher. By the Very Rev. H. B. CANON MACKEY, O.S.B. Wrapper. 1/-.

India: A Sketch of the Madura Mission. By the Rev. H. WHITEHEAD, S.J. Crown 8vo, cloth, with Map and Illustrations. 3/6.

NEW AND POPULAR EDITION.
Life of Don Bosco, Founder of the Salesian Society.
Translated from the French of J. M. VILLEFRANCHE by Lady MARTIN. Crown 8vo, 302 pp. Wrapper, 1/- net (postage 3d.).

BURNS & OATES, LIMITED,
Granville Mansions, 28, Orchard Street, London, W.

ALEXIS-LOUIS, PÈRE (O.C.D.).
Five Thrones of Divine Love upon the Earth, The. The Womb of Mary, the Crib, the Cross, the Eucharist, and the Faithful Soul. From the French. Crown 8vo, cloth. 3/6.

"A book of devotion, consisting of a series of short readings or meditations, chiefly on the Incarnation, the Blessed Eucharist, the Crucifixion and the principles which underlie and govern the spiritual life, whether among the Priesthood, the cloistered Religious, or the laity. The sum of the experimental knowledge of a Carmelite priest, it breathes the very inner spirit of St. John of the Cross, and contains the essence of affective theology."—*Monitor.*

ALLIES, T. W. (K.C.S.G.).
A Life's Decision. Second and Cheaper Edition. Crown 8vo, cloth. 5/-.

"Interesting, not only in the way in which all genuine personal narratives are interesting, but also for the many letters from well-known persons that it contains. It is a valuable contribution to the history of the Anglican Church in the eventful years which followed Newman's secession."—*Guardian.*

THE FORMATION OF CHRISTENDOM SERIES.

Vol. I. The Christian Faith and the Individual. Popular Edition. Crown 8vo, cloth. 5/-.

Vol. II. The Christian Faith and Society. Popular Edition. Crown 8vo, cloth. 5/-.

Vol. III. The Christian Faith and Philosophy. Popular Edition. Crown 8vo, cloth. 5/-.

Vol. IV. Church and State. Popular Edition. Crown 8vo, cloth. 5/-.

H. E. CARDINAL VAUGHAN says:—"It is one of the noblest historical works I have ever read. Now that its price has placed it within the reach of all, I earnestly pray that it may become widely known and appreciatively studied. We have nothing like it in the English language."

The Throne of the Fisherman, built by the Carpenter's Son. The Root, the Bond, and the Crown of Christendom. Demy 8vo, cloth. 10/6.

"The most important contribution to ecclesiastical history which has been given to the world for many a long day."—*Tablet.*

The Holy See and the Wandering of the Nations. Demy 8vo, cloth. 10/6.

Peter's Rock in Mohammed's Flood. Being the Seventh Volume of Mr. Allies' great work on the "Formation of Christendom." Demy 8vo, cloth. 10/6.

ALLIES, MARY.
Pius the Seventh, 1800-1823. Crown 8vo, cloth gilt. 5/-.

"Miss Allies has narrated the history of the long and memorable Pontificate of the first Pope of this century with a thoroughness of research and a dignity of style worthy of her illustrious father."—*Irish Monthly.*

Leaves from St. John Chrysostom. With Introduction by T. W. Allies, K.C.S.G. Crown 8vo, cloth. 6/-.

"The selections are well chosen, and Miss Allies' rendering is smooth, idiomatic, and faithful to the original. There is no existing book which is better adapted to make the English reader acquainted with the most eloquent of the Fathers of the Church."—*Dublin Review.*

ALLIES, MARY—*(continued)*.

History of the Church in England, from the Beginning of the Christian Era to the Death of Queen Elizabeth. In Two Vols. Crown 8vo, cloth. Vol. I. From the Beginning of the Christian Era to the Accession of Henry VIII. 6 -. Vol. II. From the Accession of Henry VIII. to the Death of Queen Elizabeth. 3/6.

"Miss Allies has admirably compressed the substance, or such as was necessary to her purpose, of a number of authorities, judiciously selected. . . . . As a narrative the volume is capitally written, as a summary it is skilful, and not its least excellence is its value as an index of the best available sources which deal with the period it covers."—*Birmingham Daily Gazette*.

ARNOLD, THOMAS (M.A., Fellow of the Royal University of Ireland).

Notes on the Sacrifice of the Altar. Crown 12mo, cloth gilt. 1/6.

"A very useful treatise on the Mass. The end of the Holy Sacrifice is first explained. Then the author takes occasion to point out the essential difference between the Anglican service and the Mass. Lastly, Mr. Arnold, following the course of the ritual, brings out clearly the meaning and object of each part of the sacred function. In his illustrative remarks he imparts a good deal of interesting information."—*Catholic Times*.

BAKER, VEN. FATHER AUGUSTIN (O.S.B.).

Holy Wisdom *(Sancta Sophia)*. Directions for the Prayer of Contemplation, &c. Edited by Abbot Sweeney, D.D. New and Cheaper Edition. Crown 8vo. Handsomely bound in half leather, xx.-667 pp. 6/-.

"The thanks of the Catholic public are due to Dr. Sweeney for re-editing this famous work. It does not belong to the catalogue of ephemeral publications. It is of a totally different standard. . . . To lovers of prayer and meditation it will be a most acceptable guide and friend."—*Tablet*.

BIBLES, &c.

N.B.—For full particulars of Bindings, &c., see Illustrated Prayer Book Catalogue, sent post free on application.

Holy Bible. POCKET EDITION (size, 5¼ by 3¼ inches). Embossed cloth, red edges, 2/6; and in leather bindings, from 4/6 to 7/6. MEDIUM EDITION (size, 7¼ by 4¾ inches). Cloth, 3/6; and in leather bindings, from 6/- net to 10/6 net (postage 6d.). OCTAVO EDITION (size, 9 by 6 inches). Cloth, 6/-; and in a great variety of leather bindings, from 8/- to 35/- net. Family Editions in quarto and folio. Prices upon application.

New Testament, The. POCKET EDITION. Limp cloth, 6d. (postage 2d.). Cloth, red edges, 1/-. Roan, 1/6. Paste grain, round corners, 3/-. Best calf or morocco, 4/6 each. ROYAL 8vo EDITION (size, 9 by 6 inches). Cloth, 1/- net (postage 3d.). NEW MEDIUM EDITION. LARGE TYPE. Crown 8vo (size, 7½ by 5 inches). 500 pp. Cloth, boards, gilt lettered, 2/-. Paste grain, limp, round corners, red or gold edges, 4/6. German calf, limp, round corners, red under gold edges, 8/6. Morocco, limp, round corners, red under gold edges, 8/6. Also in better bindings for presentation.

BLESSED SACRAMENT, OUR GOD; or, Practical Thoughts on the Mystery of Love, The. By a Child of St. Teresa. Cloth gilt. 1/-.

"It is written in the spirit of reverence and earnestness in simple and forcible language. This little work is calculated to do much good, and we heartily commend it."—*Dublin Review.*

BOWDEN, REV. H. S. (of the Oratory), Edited by.

Dante's Divina Commedia: Its scope and value. From the German of Francis Hettinger, D.D. With an engraving of Dante. Second Edition. 10/6.

Natural Religion. Being Vol. I. of Dr. Hettinger's "Evidences of Christianity." With an Introduction on "Certainty." Third Edition. Crown 8vo, cloth. 7/6.

Revealed Religion. Vol. II. of Dr. Hettinger's "Evidences of Christianity." With an Introduction on the "Assent of Faith." Crown 8vo, cloth. 5/-.

"The two together ('Natural Religion' and 'Revealed Religion') supply a real want in our Catholic literature. Nothing is more common nowadays than for a priest to be asked to recommend a book, written from a Catholic point of view, on the evidence for the Christian religion. And in future he will be able to recommend Father Bowden's 'Hettinger'. . . . It may be confidently affirmed that all who have taken interest in the war against religion raised by its modern adversaries will find in Father Bowden's pages many of their chief difficulties helpfully dealt with."—*Month.*

BRIDGETT, REV. T. E. (C.SS.R.).

Lyra Hieratica: Poems on the Priesthood. Collected from many sources by the Rev. T. E. Bridgett, C.SS.R. Fcap. 8vo, cloth. 2/6 net (postage 3d.).

"The idea of gathering an anthology of Poems on the Priesthood was a happy one, and has been happily carried out. Priests and laity alike owe a debt of gratitude to Father Bridgett for the many beautiful things he has brought together."—*Tablet.*

The True Story of the Catholic Hierarchy deposed by Queen Elizabeth, with fuller Memoirs of its last Two Survivors. By the Rev. T. E. Bridgett, C.SS.R., and the late Rev. T. F. Knox, D.D., of the London Oratory. Crown 8vo, cloth. 7/6.

Wisdom and Wit of Sir Thomas More, The. Crown 8vo, cloth. 6/-.

"Every page in this delightful volume bespeaks the master hand, the clear head, the deep and tender heart. It is lively, eloquent, impressive, genial; without stiffness of parade of learning, but as full as good things as it can hold."—*Catholic Times.*

BROWNLOW, BISHOP.

Memoir of Mother Rose Columba Adams, O.P., first Prioress of St. Dominic's Convent, and Foundress of the Perpetual Adoration at North Adelaide. With Portrait and Plates. Crown 8vo, cloth, 384 pp. 6/6.

"It is a work of the deepest interest and edification. In a handsomely printed and beautifully illustrated volume, Bishop Brownlow tells us the story of a remarkable woman's life and work, drawing on his own recollections of her career, and with the help of her own letters and reminiscences of many friends, giving us a life-like picture of a singularly earnest, devoted, and saintly soul."—*Tablet.*

BUTLER, REV. ALBAN.
People's Edition of the Lives of the Saints. Twelve Pocket Volumes, each Volume containing the Saints of the Month. Superfine paper, neat cloth binding, gilt lettered. 1/6 each; or the complete set (comprising over 6,000 pages), in handsome cloth case to match, 18/-.

DALE, REV. J. D. HILARIUS.
Ceremonial according to the Roman Rite. Translated from the Italian of Joseph Baldeschi. New and Revised Edition. Crown 8vo, cloth. 6/6.

"This work is our standard English directory on the subject. Few functions of any importance are carried on without a glance at it. It is a familiar guide and friend—in short, a classic."—*Catholic Times.*

The Sacristan's Manual; or, Handbook of Church Furniture, Ornament, &c. Fourth and Enlarged Edition. Crown 8vo, cloth. 2/6.

DIGNAM, FATHER (S.J.).
Conferences given by Father Dignam, S.J., with Retreats, Sermons, and Notes of Spiritual Direction. With a Preface by His Eminence Cardinal Mazzella, S.J. Crown 8vo, cloth gilt. 6/- net (postage 4d.).

FABER, FATHER.
All for Jesus; or, The Easy Ways of Divine Love. New Edition. Crown 8vo, cloth, 407 pp. 5/-.

Bethlehem. New Edition. Crown 8vo, cloth, 500 pp. 7/-.

Ethel's Book; or, Tales of the Angels. A New and Cheaper Edition. Beautifully bound in cloth, extra gilt, gilt edges. 2/6.

Growth in Holiness; or, The Progress of the Spiritual Life. New Edition. Crown 8vo, cloth, 464 pp. 6/-.

Hymns. Complete Edition. Crown 8vo, cloth, 427 pp. 6/-.

Notes on Doctrinal and Spiritual Subjects. Fourth Edition. Two Vols. Crown 8vo, cloth, 759 pp. 10/-.

Poems. Complete Edition. Crown 8vo, cloth, 582 pp. 5/-.

Sir Lancelot. A Legend of the Middle Ages. Crown 8vo, cloth, 347 pp. 5/-.

Spiritual Conferences. Eighth Edition. Crown 8vo, cloth, 403 pp. 6/-.

The Blessed Sacrament; or, The Works and Ways of God. New Edition. Crown 8vo, cloth, 548 pp. 7/6.

The Creator and the Creature; or, The Wonders of Divine Love. New Edition. Crown 8vo, cloth, 416 pp. 6/-.

The Easiness of Salvation. Cloth gilt. 1/-.

The Foot of the Cross; or, The Sorrows of Mary. Crown 8vo, cloth, 432 pp. 6/-.

The Precious Blood; or, The Price of our Salvation. Fifth Edition. Crown 8vo, cloth, 308 pp. 5/-.

FABER, FATHER—*(continued).*
  The Life and Letters of Frederick William Faber, D.D.
  By Rev. John E. Bowden, of the Oratory. Third Edition. Crown 8vo, cloth, 447 pp. 6/-.
  Father Faber's May Book. Compiled by an Oblate of Mary Immaculate. A New Month of May, arranged for Daily Reading, from the writings of Father Faber. 18mo, cloth, gilt edges, with Steel Frontispiece. 2/-.
  A Brief Sketch of the Early Life of Frederick William Faber, D.D. By his Brother. Limp cloth. 1/-.

FITZGERALD, PERCY.
  Jewels of Prayer and Meditation from Unfamiliar Sources. Fancy cloth, gilt. 2/6.
  Jewels of the Imitation. A Selection of Passages with a Little Commentary. Cloth, extra gilt. 2/-.
  "It is an excellent book for spiritual reading in itself, and it will help its readers to read that holiest of books with more relish and fruit. Mr. Fitzgerald's pithy, up-to-date comments throw a new light on many a wise saying of Thomas à Kempis."—*Irish Monthly.*
  Eucharistic Jewels. Second Edition. Fancy cloth, gilt. 2/6.
  "Every page is bright with some exquisite passage, and Mr. Fitzgerald's little commentaries, as he carries us along, are not unworthy of the glorious companionship in which he has placed them."—*Freeman's Journal.*
  Jewels of the Mass. A Short Account of the Rites and Prayers used in the Holy Sacrifice. Sixth Edition. Fancy cloth gilt. 2/-.
  "A treatise on the Mass, in which the author proves himself a sound theologian, an accomplished master of ecclesiastical history bearing on the question, a cultured scholar, and the possessor of a very charming style."—*Nation.*
  The Layman's Day ; or, Jewels of Practical Piety. Second Edition. Cloth, extra gilt. 2/-.
  "An effort to induce people to consider their every-day life from the point of view of practical common-sense. . . . Admirably done."—*Catholic News.*

FULLERTON, LADY GEORGIANA.
  Grantley Manor. An Interesting Story of Catholic Life and Society. New Edition. Cloth gilt, gilt edges, 349 pp. 3/6.
  Life of St. Frances of Rome. New Edition. Cloth gilt. 2/-.
  Life of Mère Marie de la Providence, Foundress of the Helpers of the Holy Souls. Third Edition. With Preface and Appendix by the Rev. Sydney F. Smith, S.J. Cloth. 1/6 net (postage 3d.).

GIBSON, REV. HENRY.
  Catechism made Easy: being a Familiar Explanation of the Catechism of Christian Doctrine. Tenth Edition. Two Vols. Fcap. 8vo, cloth, 800 pp. 7/6.
  "Contains a course of fifty-eight instructions on Catholic doctrines, each accompanied by from one to eleven stories, legends, anecdotes, &c., expressly designed to illustrate their meanings and to fix them in the minds of children.
  "This work must be of priceless worth to any who are engaged in any form of catechetical instruction. The best book of the kind that we have seen in English."—*Irish Monthly.*

GILLOW, JOSEPH.
Biographical History, and Bibliographical Dictionary of the English Catholics. From the Breach with Rome in 1534 to the Present Time. Vol. I., A-C, 612 pp. Vol. II., D-Grad, 557 pp. Vol. III., Grah-Kem, 688 pp. Vol. IV., Kem-Met, 572 pp. Demy 8vo, cloth. 15/- each.

"The patient research of Mr. Gillow, his conscientious record of minute particulars, and especially his exhaustive bibliographical information in connection with each name are beyond praise."—*British Quarterly Review.*

HAMMERSTEIN, REV. L. VON (S.J.).
Foundations of Faith: The Existence of God Demonstrated. From the German of Fr. Ludwig von Hammerstein, S.J. With an Introduction by the Rev. W. L. Gildea, D.D. Crown 8vo, cloth. 6/-.

"Popular, interesting, forcible, and sound. It is well to have a book like Father von Hammerstein's to put into the hands of serious inquirers; it forms a valuable addition to our apologetic literature."—*Tablet.*

HEDLEY, BISHOP.
The Christian Inheritance. Second Edition. Crown 8vo, cloth gilt, 430 pp. 6/-.

"We do not know any book we could more confidently recommend to intelligent inquirers after truth, perplexed by the prevailing unbelief, than this new volume, in which the Bishop of Newport prints some twenty discourses preached by him on various occasions."—*Tablet.*

Our Divine Saviour, and other Discourses. Second Edition. Crown 8vo, cloth gilt. 6/-.

A Retreat: Consisting of Thirty-three Discourses, with Meditations: for the use of the Clergy, Religious, and Others. Fourth Edition. In handsome half-leather binding. Crown 8vo, 428 pp. 6/-.

"The book is one which, beyond the purpose for which it is directly intended, may be strongly recommended for spiritual reading."—*Month.*

LIGUORI, ST. ALPHONSUS.
A Translation of the Works of St. Alphonsus, edited by the late Bishop Coffin:—

Christian Virtues, and the Means for obtaining them, The. Cloth gilt. 3/-. Or separately, cloth flush—1. The Love of Our Lord Jesus Christ. 1/-. 2. Treatise on Prayer (in many Editions a great part of this work is omitted). 1/-. 3. A Christian's Rule of Life. 1/-.

Eternal Truths. Preparation for Death. 2/6.

The Redemption. Meditations on the Passion. 2/6.

Glories of Mary. New Edition. 3/6.

Reflections on Spiritual Subjects and on the Passion of Jesus Christ. 2/6.

LIVIUS, REV. T. (M.A., C.SS.R.).
St. Peter, Bishop of Rome; or, the Roman Episcopate of the Prince of the Apostles. Demy 8vo, cloth. 12/-.

LIVIUS, REV. T. (M.A., C.SS.R.)—*(continued).*
Explanation of the Psalms and Canticles in the Divine Office. By St. Alphonsus Liguori. Translated from the Italian by Thomas Livius, C.SS.R. With a Preface by his Eminence Cardinal Manning. Crown 8vo, cloth, xxx.-512 pp. 7/6.

Mary in the Epistles; or, The Implicit Teaching of the Apostles concerning the Blessed Virgin. Crown 8vo, cloth. 5/-.

The Blessed Virgin in the Fathers of the First Six Centuries. Demy 8vo, cloth. 12/-.

McDONALD, REV. WALTER (D.D.).
Motion: Its Origin and Conservation. An Essay by the Rev. Walter McDonald, D.D., Prefect of the Dunboyne Establishment, St. Patrick's College, Maynooth. Demy 8vo, xii.-458 pp. 7/6 net (postage 4d.).

MADDEN, REV. W. J.
Disunion and Reunion. Crown 8vo, cloth. 3/-.
"The volume contains a good deal of practical information in a plain and popular style."—*Catholic Times.*

MANNING, CARDINAL.
Confidence in God. 32mo, neat cloth gilt. 1/-.

Lost Sheep Found. A Sermon. Wrapper. 6d. Being an Appeal for the Convents of the Good Shepherd.

Miscellanies. First Series. Crown 8vo, cloth, 387 pp. 6/-.

Miscellanies. Second Series. Crown 8vo, cloth, 391 pp. 6/-.

Religio Viatoris. Crown 8vo, cloth. 1/6.

Sermons on Ecclesiastical Subjects. Crown 8vo, cloth, 456 pp. 6/-.

Sin and its Consequences. Crown 8vo, cloth. 4/-.

The Blessed Sacrament the Centre of Immutable Truth. 32mo, neat cloth gilt. 1/-.

The Eternal Priesthood. Crown 8vo, cloth. 2/6.

The Four Great Evils of the Day. Crown 8vo, cloth. 2/6.

The Fourfold Sovereignty of God. Crown 8vo, cloth. 2/6.

The Glories of the Sacred Heart. Crown 8vo, cloth. 4/-.

The Grounds of Faith. Crown 8vo, cloth. 1/6.

The Holy Ghost the Sanctifier. 32mo, neat cloth gilt. 2/-.

The Independence of the Holy See. Crown 8vo, cloth. 2/6.

The Internal Mission of the Holy Ghost. Crown 8vo, cloth, 494 pp. 5/-.

The Love of Jesus to Penitents. 32mo, neat cloth gilt. 1/-.

The Office of the Church in Higher Catholic Education. 6d.

MANNING, CARDINAL—(continued).
The Temporal Mission of the Holy Ghost; or, Reason and Revelation. Crown 8vo, cloth. 5/-.
The True Story of the Vatican Council. Crown 8vo, cloth. 2/6.
The Workings of the Holy Spirit in the Church of England. New Edition. Crown 8vo, cloth. 1/6.

MARTIN, LADY.
Life of Don Bosco, Founder of the Salesian Society. Translated from the French of J. M. Villefranche. New Popular Edition. Crown 8vo, 302 pp. Wrapper. 1/- net (postage 3d.).
"We possess in this volume a popular life of a saintly man whose good works are bearing abundant fruit, and the glory of whose life will continue to stimulate zeal in many lands. Lady Martin's translation is admirable, and the book is extremely cheap at a shilling."—*Catholic Times.*

Life of Princess Borghese (née Gwendalin Talbot). Translated from the French. Crown 8vo, tastefully bound in cloth gilt. 4/-.
"The life of the charming and saint-like young Englishwoman will come as a welcome surprise to the readers of a later generation, who will find how completely the spirit of Catholic faith and charity was combined in the person of Lady Gwendalin Talbot with the rarest beauty and the most accomplished talents."—*Tablet.*

MEMORIES OF THE CRIMEA. By Sister Mary Aloysius. With Preface by the Very Rev. J. Fahey, D.D., V.G. Crown 8vo, cloth gilt. 2/6.
"The venerable Sister, upon whom Her Majesty the Queen bestowed the decoration of the Royal Red Cross a few months ago, tells her touching story of heroic self-abnegation with a modest simplicity that is far more impressive than the most elaborate and picturesque style of descriptive writing."—*Daily Telegraph.*

NEWMAN, CARDINAL.
The Church of the Fathers. Fcap. 8vo, cloth, 361 pp. 4/-.
An attempt to illustrate the tone and modes of thought, the habits and manners of the early times of the Church.
Detailed List of Cardinal Newman's Works on application.

NORTHCOTE, VERY REV. PROVOST (D.D.).
Mary in the Gospels; or, Lectures on the History of our Blessed Lady as recorded by the Evangelists. Second Edition. Cloth gilt, 344 pp. 3/6.

PERRY, REV. JOHN.
Practical Sermons, for all the Sundays of the Year. First and Second Series. Sixth Edition. Fcap. 8vo, cloth. 3/6 each.

POPE, REV. T. A. (of the Oratory).
Life of St. Philip Neri. Translated from the Italian of Cardinal Capecelatro. Second and Revised Edition. Two Volumes. Crown 8vo, cloth. 12/6.
"Altogether this is a most fascinating work, full of spiritual lore and historic erudition, and with all the intense interest of a remarkable biography. Take it up where you will, it is hard to lay it down. We think it one of the most completely satisfactory lives of a Saint that has been written in modern times."—*Tablet.*

PORTER, ARCHBISHOP (S.J.).

The Banquet of the Angels: Preparation and Thanksgiving for Holy Communion. New Edition. 18mo, blue cloth, gilt. 2/-. Also bound in a variety of handsome leather bindings suitable for First Communion memorial gifts. From 6/6 to 12/6 net.

PRACTICAL MEDITATIONS FOR EVERY DAY IN THE

Year, on the Life of our Lord Jesus Christ. Chiefly for the use of Religious. By a Father of the Society of Jesus. With Imprimatur of Cardinal Manning. New Edition, Revised. In two Volumes. Cloth, red edges. 9/-.

These volumes give three different daily points for consideration and application. "A work of great practical utility, and we give it our earnest recommendation."—*Weekly Register.*

PRAYER BOOKS, &c.

N.B.—For full particulars of Prayer Books, see *Illustrated Prayer Book Catalogue*, sent post free on application.

Catholic's Daily Companion. With Epistles and Gospels. Roan, 1/-; and in various leather bindings, 1/6 to 5/-.

Catholic Piety. Containing a Selection of Prayers, Reflections, Meditations, and Instructions adapted to every state in life. By the late Rev. Wm. Gahan, O.S.A. 32mo Edition, with Ordinary of the Mass. Cloth, 6d.; post free, 8d.; roan, 1/-. With Epistles and Gospels, 1/6, 2/-, 2/6, 4/6, &c. Messrs. BURNS & OATES also publish two other Editions of this book.

Catholic's Vade Mecum. A Select Manual of Prayers for Daily Use. Compiled from approved sources. 34th Thousand. With Epistles and Gospels. Calf, 5/6, and also in better bindings.

Children's Pictorial Mass Book. (Abridged.) New Edition. Forty-three Illustrations. 2d.; cloth, 6d.

Daily Exercise. Cloth limp. 6d.

Flowers of Devotion. Being a Collection of Favourite Devotions, for Public and Private use. Compiled from approved sources, and with the Imprimatur of His Eminence Cardinal Vaughan. New Edition. Leather bindings. 1/6 to 5/-.

Spirit of the Sacred Heart, The. A new large-type Prayer Book. Cloth, 3/6; leather, 5/6; German calf or morocco, 8/6.

Garden of the Soul. 700th Thousand. Approved by the Cardinal Archbishop of Westminster, and revised by a Priest of the Archdiocese. New Edition. In which many devotions will be found which now form a necessary part of every Catholic Prayer Book. Cloth, 6d.; post free, 8d.; roan, 1/-. With Epistles and Gospels, cloth, 1/-; and in leather bindings, at 1/6, 2/-, 2/6, 3/-, 3/6, 4/-, 5/-, and upwards.

Messrs. BURNS & OATES have just issued a new Pocket Edition of the "Garden of the Soul," size 3¾ by 2½ inches, with red line borders, and Devotions for Mass in large type. This Edition can now be had in various bindings, from 1/- to 5/-. They also publish three other Editions.

CATALOGUE OF PUBLICATIONS. 11

PRAYER BOOKS, &c.—(continued).

Golden Manual. A Guide to Catholic Devotion, Public and Private, Compiled from approved sources. Fine Paper. Leather, 6/-. With Epistles and Gospels, 7/- and upwards.

Imitation of Christ, Of the. By Thomas à Kempis. NEW POPULAR EDITION FOR DISTRIBUTION. Cloth, red edges, 6d. (postage, 2d.). Leather, red edges, 1/-. SUPERFINE POCKET EDITION. Fancy cloth extra, with red borders, 1/6. And in leather bindings, from 2/6 to 10/-. PRESENTATION EDITION (size, 6¼ by 4¼ inches). With red border on each page. Cloth extra, 3/6. And in leather bindings, from 7/- to 15/-.

Key of Heaven. A Manual of Devout Prayers. 32mo Edition. Cloth, 6d. ; post free, 8d. ; roan, 1/-. With Epistles and Gospels, 1/6, 2/-, 2/6, 3/-, 4/6, &c. They also publish two Smaller Editions.

Manual of Prayers for Congregational Use. As authorized by the Bishops of England and Wales. With an Appendix containing Prayers for Mass, Confession, and Communion. Cloth, 1/- ; leather, 2/6, 5/-, and upwards.

Manual of the Sacred Heart. Compiled and Translated from approved sources. New Edition. Cloth. 2/- upwards.

Missal. New and Complete Pocket Missal, with the Imprimatur of H. E. Cardinal Vaughan, in Latin and English, with all the New Offices, and the propers for Ireland, Scotland, and the Jesuits. (Size, 5¼ by 3¼ inches). Roan or French morocco, 5/- ; Rutland roan, limp, 7/- ; best calf or morocco, four styles, 8/6 each. Also in better bindings, from 11/- to 30/- net.

Missal for the Laity. Cheap Edition. 6d. ; post free, 8d. ; and in leather bindings, at 1/6, 2/6, 4/6, and 5/-.

Path to Heaven. Containing Epistles, Gospels, and Hymns, &c. Cloth, 2/- and 2/6 ; leather, 3/-, 4/-, 4/6, 6/-, and upwards.

Prayers for the People. By the Rev. F. D. Byrne. Imperial 32mo, cloth, extra gilt. 2/-.

QUARTERLY SERIES. Edited by the Jesuit Fathers. 98 Volumes published to date.

SELECTION.

The Life and Letters of St. Francis Xavier. By the Rev. H. J. Coleridge, S.J. Second Edition. Two Volumes. 10/6.

The Life and Letters of St. Teresa. By the Rev. H. J. Coleridge, S.J. Three Volumes. 7/6 each.

Pious Affections towards God and the Saints. Meditations for every Day in the Year, and for the principal Festivals, From the Latin of the Ven. Nicholas Lancicius, S.J. 7/6.

The Life and Teaching of Jesus Christ in Meditations for every Day in the Year. By Fr. Nicholas Avancino, S.J. Two Volumes. 10/6.

QUARTERLY SERIES—*(continued)*.

The Life of St. Alonso Rodriguez. By Francis Goldie, of the Society of Jesus. 7/6.

Letters of St. Augustine. Selected and Arranged by Mary H. Allies. 6/6.

Acts of the English Martyrs, hitherto unpublished. By the Rev. John H. Pollen, S.J. 7/6.

The Life of St. Francis di Geronimo, S.J. By A. M. Clarke. 7/6.

Aquinas Ethicus; or, The Moral Teaching of St. Thomas. By the Rev. Joseph Rickaby, S.J. Second Edition. Two Volumes. 12/-.

The Spirit of St. Ignatius. From the French of the Rev. Fr. Xavier de Franciosi, S.J. 6/-.

Jesus, the All-Beautiful. A Devotional Treatise on the Character and Actions of our Lord. Edited by the Rev. J. G. Macleod, S.J. Second Edition. 6/6.

The Manna of the Soul. By Fr. Paul Segneri. New Edition. In Two Volumes. 12/-.

Life of Ven. Joseph Benedict Cottolengo. From the Italian of Don P. Gastaldi. 4/6.

Life of St. Francis Borgia. By A. M. Clarke. 6/6.

Life of Blessed Antony Baldinucci. By the Rev. F. Goldie, S.J. 6/-.

Distinguished Irishmen of the Sixteenth Century. By Rev. E. Hogan, S.J. 6/-.

Journals kept during Times of Retreat. By the late Fr. John Morris, S.J. Edited by Rev. J. Pollen, S.J. 6/-.

Life of the Rev. Mother Mary of St. Euphrasia Pelletier. By A. M. Clarke. 6/-.

Jesus: His Life, in the very Words of the Four Gospels. A Diatessaron by Henry Beauclerk, S.J. Cloth. 5/-.

First Communion. A Book of Preparation for First Communion. Edited by Fr. Thurston, S.J. Third and Cheaper Edition. With nineteen Illustrations. 3/6.

The Life and Letters of Fr. John Morris, S.J. By Fr. J. H. Pollen, S.J. Cloth. 6/-.

The Story of Mary Aikenhead, Foundress of the Irish Sisters of Charity. By Maria Nethercott. Crown 8vo, cloth. 3/-.

Life of the Blessed Master John of Avila. Secular Priest, called the Apostle of Andalusia. By Father Longaro Degli Oddi, S.J. Edited by J. G. Macleod, S.J. Cloth. 4/-.

Notes on St. Paul; Corinthians, Galatians, Romans. By Joseph Rickaby, S.J. 7/6.

RENDU, A. (LL.D.).
The Jewish Race in Ancient and Roman History.
Translated from the Eleventh Corrected Edition by S. T. Crook. Crown 8vo, 440 pp. 6/-.
" This should prove a very useful book."—*Dublin Review.*
" The story is well and lucidly told."—*Schoolmaster.*

RICKABY, REV. JOSEPH (S.J.).
Oxford Conferences. Lent and Summer Terms, 1897. Crown 8vo. Wrapper, 1/- net (postage 2d.).

RIVINGTON, REV. LUKE (D.D.).
Rome and England; or, Ecclesiastical Continuity. Crown 8vo, cloth. 3/6.
"Fr. Rivington's method of exposition is admirable—brief and lucid without meagreness, pointed and telling without harshness. . . . . A book to be grateful for; useful alike to the controversialist, the historical student, and the general reader."—*Tablet.*

RUSHE, VERY REV. JAMES P. (O.D.C.) (Father Patrick of St. Joseph).
Carmel in Ireland. A Narrative of the Irish Province of Teresian or Discalced Carmelites. A.D. 1625-1896. Crown 8vo, cloth. 3/6 net (postage 4d.).
" . . . . Written in an easy, historical style. The history of the Carmelite Abbeys in Ireland is here told with much graphic power in a series of interesting chapters, which will be valued by very many readers. . . . . The author is most painstaking, and has consulted all available books of reference to make his record complete."—*Irish Times.*

ST. BENEDICT'S SERIES.
The Life and the Rule of our Holy Father, St. Benedict.
Being the Second Book of the Dialogues of St. Gregory the Great, with the Rule of the same Holy Patriarch. In Latin and English. Cloth gilt. 5/-.

St. Benedict and Grottaferrata. Limp cloth, gilt. 1/-.

A Visit to Subiaco, the Cradle of the Benedictine Order. 47 pp., 8vo, wrapper. 6d.

Life of Helen Lucretia Cornaro Piscopia, Benedictine Oblate, and Doctor of the University of Padua. Cloth gilt. 4/6.

Life of the Blessed Joanna Mary Bonomo. With Portrait. Cloth gilt. 3/6.

ST. FRANCIS DE SALES, The Works of.
Translated into the English Language by the Very Rev. Canon Mackey, O.S.B., under the Direction of the Right Rev. Bishop Hedley, O.S.B.

Vol. I. Letters to Persons in the World. Third Edition. Crown 8vo, cloth. 6/-.

Vol. II. The Treatise on the Love of God. Fr. Carr's Translation of 1630 has been taken as a basis, but it has been Modernised and thoroughly Revised and Corrected. Second Edition. 6/-.

ST. FRANCIS DE SALES —(continued).

Vol. III. The Catholic Controversy. Crown 8vo, cloth. 6/-.

Vol. IV. Letters to Persons in Religion, with Introduction by Bishop Hedley on "St. Francis de Sales and the Religious State." Second Edition. Crown 8vo, cloth. 6/-.

"We earnestly commend these volumes to all readers, and we desire their widest diffusion, as we desire also that the doctrine and spirit of St. Francis may reign in all our hearts, both of pastors and of people."— Cardinal Manning in the *Dublin Review*.

St. Francis de Sales as a Preacher. Wrapper. 1/-.

SALVATORI'S PRACTICAL INSTRUCTIONS FOR NEW
Confessors. Edited by Fr. Anthony Ballerini, S.J., and Translated by Very Rev. William Hutch, D.D. Third Edition. 18mo, cloth gilt, 314 pp. 4/-.

SCHOUPPE, REV. F. X. (S.J.).

Purgatory: Illustrated by the Lives and Legends of the Saints. Second Edition. Crown 8vo, cloth. 6/-.

"Solid, instructive, practical, and interesting as a romance, this book will go far to dispel the vague and erroneous ideas entertained among the faithful on the subject of Purgatory. Its careful perusal will repay the thoughtless Christian, the devout Catholic, and the zealous priest."—*Irish Ecclesiastical Record*.

SMYTH, JOHN.

Genesis and Science. Inspiration of the Mosaic Ideas of Creative Work. Crown 8vo, cloth, with Illustrations. 3/6.

"In the following pages abundant proof is given that the several phenomena recorded in the first chapter of Genesis are scientifically certain. And as the Mosaic days can be shown to embrace, and include, the æons of the geologist, all apparent contradictions vanish. With the Mosaic ideas of creative work thus unfolded in their true light, the inspiration of the first chapter of Genesis becomes manifest."—PREFACE.

SWEENEY, RIGHT REV. ABBOT (O.S.B.).

Sermons for all Sundays and Festivals of the Year. Fourth Edition. Crown 8vo, handsomely bound in half-leather. 10/6.

"For such priests as are in search of matter to aid them in their round of Sunday discourses, and have not read this volume, we can assure them that they will find in these 600 pages a mine of solid and simple Catholic teaching."—*Tablet*.

THOMPSON, EDWARD HEALY (M.A.).

Letters and Writings of Marie Lataste, with Critical and Expository Notes. By two Fathers of the Society of Jesus. Translated from the French. Three Volumes. 8vo, cloth. 5/- each.

Life of Jean-Jacques Olier, Founder of the Seminary of St. Sulpice. New and Enlarged Edition. Post 8vo, xxxvi.-628 pp. 15/-.

The Hidden Life of Jesus. A Lesson and Model to Christians. By Henri-Marie Boudon. Translated from the French by E. Healy Thompson, M.A. Third Edition. Cloth gilt. 3/-.

The Life and Glories of St. Joseph. Grounded on the Dissertations of Canon Vitali, Fr. José Moreno, and other Writers. Second Edition. Crown 8vo, cloth. 6/-.

The Unity of the Episcopate. Crown 8vo, cloth. 4/6.

THOMPSON, EDWARD HEALY (M.A.), Edited by.
LIBRARY OF RELIGIOUS BIOGRAPHY.

Life of St. Aloysius Gonzaga (S.J.). Eleventh Edition. Globe 8vo, cloth, xxiv.-373 pp. 5/-.

Life of Marie Eustelle Harpain; or, The Angel of the Eucharist. Fifth Edition. Cloth, xxi.-388 pp. 5/-.

Life of St. Stanislaus Kostka. Fifth Edition. Cloth. 5/-.

Life of Marie Lataste, Lay Sister of the Congregation of the Sacred Heart. With a Brief Notice of her Sister Quitterie. Second Edition. Cloth. 5/-.

Life of Leon Papin-Dupont, The Holy Man of Tours. Fourth Edition. Cloth. 5/-.

Life of Jean Baptiste Muard, Founder of the Congregation of St. Edme and of the Monastery of La Pierre-qui-Vire. 8vo, cloth, xix.-540 pp. 6/-.

Life of St. Charles Borromeo, Cardinal Archbishop of Milan. Second Edition. Cloth gilt. 3/-.

ULLATHORNE, ARCHBISHOP.

Christian Patience: The Strength and Discipline of the Soul. Sixth and Cheaper Edition. Demy 8vo, cloth, 256 pp. 7/-.

The Endowments of Man considered in their Relations with his Final End. Fifth and Cheaper Edition. Demy 8vo, cloth, 404 pp. 7/-.

The Groundwork of the Christian Virtues. Fifth and Cheaper Edition. Demy 8vo, cloth, 411 pp. 7/-.

Memoir of Bishop Willson, first Bishop of Hobart, Tasmania. With Portrait. Crown 8vo, cloth. 2/6.

The Autobiography of Archbishop Ullathorne. Edited by Augusta Theodosia Drane. Second Edition. Demy 8vo, cloth. 7/6.

"As a plucky Yorkshireman, as a sailor, as a missionary, as a great traveller, as a ravenous reader, and as a great prelate, Dr. Ullathorne was able to write down most fascinating accounts of his experiences. The book is full of shrewd glimpses from a Roman point of view of the man himself, of the position of Roman Catholics in this country, of the condition of the country, of the Colonies, and of the Anglican Church in various parts of the world, in the earlier half of this century."—*Guardian.*

The Letters of Archbishop Ullathorne. Arranged by A. T. Drane. (Sequel to the "Autobiography.") Demy 8vo, cloth, 550 pp. 9/-.

"Compiled with admirable judgment for the purpose of displaying in a thousand various ways the real man who was Archbishop Ullathorne. . . . . This book is very cordially recommended, not only for the intrinsic interest, but also for the sage and prudent counsel which characterizes the intimate correspondence of Archbishop Ullathorne."—*Tablet.*

ULLATHORNE, ARCHBISHOP—*(continued)*.

Characteristics from the Writings of Archbishop Ullathorne, together with a Bibliographical Account of the Archbishop's Works. By the Rev. M. F. Glancey, Crown 8vo, cloth. 6/-.

WALPOLE, F. GOULBURN.

A Short History of the Catholic Church. Crown 8vo, cloth. 3/-.

This work may be described as a Skeleton History of the Church. It is been compiled from notes made by the author for his own instruction, and he hopes that it may prove useful to those who may not have leisure or inclination to study the voluminous standard works upon which it is based.

WHITEHEAD, REV. H. (S.J.).

India: A Sketch of the Madura Mission. Crown 8vo, cloth, with Map and Illustrations. 3/6.

"There are few books of missionary experiences which equal this in interest. This sketch will be deeply appreciated by all who read it."—*Catholic Times.*

WISEMAN, CARDINAL.

Meditations on the Sacred Passion of our Lord. Crown 8vo, cloth. 4/-.

In the Preface H. E. CARDINAL VAUGHAN says:—"The characteristic of these Meditations, as indeed of most of Cardinal Wiseman's writings, is that you will nearly always find in them a 'Hidden Gem.' The beauty and richness of his mind seemed to illustrate and justify every topic he treated by suddenly striking some vein of thought or some point of feeling which, if not new, is at least presented in a new light or reference."

Fabiola. A Tale of the Catacombs. New Cheap Edition. Crown 8vo, cloth, xii.-324 pp. 2/-. Also an Edition on better paper, bound in cloth, richly gilt, gilt edges. 3/6. And an *Edition de luxe* printed on large 4to paper, embellished with thirty-one Full-page Illustrations and a Coloured Portrait of St. Agnes. Handsomely bound. £1 1/-.

A Few Flowers from the Roman Campagna. Small 4to, cloth gilt, printed in red and black. 1/- net (postage 2d.).

New Visits to the Blessed Sacrament. Edited by Cardinal Wiseman. Containing Devotions to the Quarant' Ore and other Occasions of Exposition and Benediction. Cloth, red edges. 2/-.

Characteristics from the Writings of Cardinal Wiseman. Edited, and with a Preface by the Rev. T. E. Bridgett, C.SS.R. Crown 8vo, cloth. 6/-.

New Classified Catalogue of Standard Books (84 pages), comprising every class of book in demand among Catholic Readers, post free on application.

BURNS & OATES, LIMITED,
Granville Mansions, 28, Orchard Street, London, W.